W9-BMQ-274

HITLER AND NAZI GERMANY

Hitler and Nazi Germany provides a concise introduction to Hitler's rise to power and Nazi domestic and foreign policies through to the end of the Second World War. Combining narrative, the views of different historians, interpretation and a selection of sources, this book provides a concise introduction and study aid for students.

This second edition has been extensively revised and expanded and includes new chapters on the Nazi regime, the SS and Gestapo, and the Second World War. Expanded background narratives provide a solid understanding of the period, and the analyses and sources have been updated throughout to help students engage with recent historiography and form their own interpretation of events. This should be invaluable for coursework and examination preparation.

Stephen J. Lee is the former Head of History at Bromsgrove School. He has published over twenty books, including *European Dictatorships* (3rd edition, 2008) and, in this series, *The Weimar Republic* (2nd edition, 2009) and *Imperial Germany, 1871–1918* (1998).

QUESTIONS AND ANALYSIS IN HISTORY SERIES

Edited by Stephen J. Lee, Bromsgrove School, Sean Lang, Hills Road Sixth Form College, Cambridge, and Jocelyn Hunt, Education Officer, Cabinet War Rooms. *Questions and Analysis in History* provides short texts on central historical issues. Each book is structured to provide:

- Clear and concise background information
- A discussion of key issues
- Examples of documentary material with related questions
- Sample worked answers
- Guidance on using sources and on further reading.

Questions and Analysis in History

Edited by Stephen J. Lee, Sean Lang and Jocelyn Hunt

Other titles in the series:

Modern History

Imperial Germany, 1871–1918
Stephen J. Lee

The Weimar Republic (2nd Edition)
Stephen J. Lee

The Spanish Civil War
Andrew Forrest

The Cold War
Bradley Lightbody

Stalin and the Soviet Union
Stephen J. Lee

Parliamentary Reform, 1785–1928
Sean Lang

British Foreign and Imperial Policy, 1865–1919
Graham D. Goodlad

The French Revolution
Jocelyn Hunt

The First World War
Ian C. Cawood and David McKinnon-Bell

Anglo-Irish Relations, 1798–1922
Nick Pelling

Churchill
Samantha Heywood

Mussolini and Fascism
Patricia Knight

Lenin and Revolutionary Russia
Stephen J. Lee

Gladstone and Disraeli
Stephen J. Lee

Russia and the USSR, 1855–1991
Stephen J. Lee

Early Modern History

The English Wars and Republic, 1636–1660
Graham E. Seel

The Renaissance
Jocelyn Hunt

Tudor Government
T. A. Morris

Spain, 1474–1598
Jocelyn Hunt

The Early Stuart Kings, 1603–1642
Graham E. Seel and David L. Smith

The Mid Tudors: Edward VI and Mary, 1547–1558
Stephen J. Lee

The Reign of Elizabeth I, 1558–1603
Stephen J. Lee

HITLER AND NAZI GERMANY

Second Edition

STEPHEN J. LEE

LONDON AND NEW YORK

First published 1998
by Routledge
2 Park Square, Milton Park, Abingdon, Oxon OX14 4RN

Simultaneously published in the USA and Canada
by Routledge
270 Madison Ave, New York, NY 10016

Routledge is an imprint of the Taylor & Francis Group, an informa business

Second edition published 2010

Typeset in Akzidenz Grotesk, Perpetua and Scala Sans by
Book Now Ltd, London

Printed and bound in Great Britain by
TJ International Ltd, Padstow, Cornwall

British Library Cataloguing in Publication Data
A catalogue record for this book is available from the British Library

Library of Congress Cataloging in Publication Data
A catalog record for this book has been requested

ISBN10: 0–415–47324–1 (hbk)
ISBN10: 0–415–47325–X (pbk)

ISBN13: 978–0–415–47324–8 (hbk)
ISBN13: 978–0–415–47325–5 (pbk)

CONTENTS

LIST OF ILLUSTRATIONS

OUTLINE CHRONOLOGY

1918		
November	9	Proclamation of Weimar Republic by Scheidemann
	11	Armistice with the Allies
1919		
January	9	Formation of *Deutsche Arbeiterpartei* DAP in Munich
February	11	National Assembly convened in Weimar; Ebert elected President
June	28	Signing of Treaty of Versailles
October		Hitler joined DAP
1920		
February	24	DAP became NSDAP; Twenty-Five Point programme
June	6	**Reichstag elections**
1921		
April	27	Reparations fixed at 132,000 million gold marks
July	29	Hitler leader of NSDAP
November	4	Formation of SA
1923		
January	11	French occupation of the Ruhr
August	13	Stresemann appointed as Chancellor
September	26	Kahr State Commissioner of Bavaria
November	8	Hitler's Munich Putsch

1924		
February	26	Beginning of Hitler's trial
April	1	Hitler sentenced to imprisonment
May	4	**Reichstag elections:** NSDAP: 32 seats (6.5 per cent of the vote)
December	7	**Reichstag elections:** NSDAP: 14 seats (3.0 per cent off the vote)
	20	Hitler's release from prison
1925		
February	27	NSDAP refounded
	28	Death of President Ebert
April	25	Hindenburg elected President
December	8	Publication of *Mein Kampf*
1926		
February		Bamberg Conference
1928		
January	6	Himmler appointed *Reichsführer SS*
May	20	**Reichstag elections:** NSDAP: 12 seats (2.8 per cent of the vote)
1929		
October	3	Death of Stresemann
	24–9	Wall Street Crash
1930		
March	30	Brüning succeeded Müller as Chancellor
September	14	**Reichstag elections:** NSDAP: 107 seats (18.3 per cent of the vote)
1931		
May	11	Collapse of Kreditanstalt
October	11	Formation of Harzburg Front
1932		
April	10	Hindenburg re-elected President
	13	Brüning banned SA and SS
June	1	Papen succeeded Brüning as Chancellor
June	14	Ban on SA and SS revoked
July	20	*Preussenstreich*: von Papen's assumption of control over Prussia
	31	**Reichstag elections:** NSDAP: 230 seats (37.3 per cent of the vote)

November	6	**Reichstag elections:** NSDAP: 196 seats (33.1 per cent of the vote)
December	4	Schleicher succeeded Papen as Chancellor

1933

January	4	Meeting between von Papen and Hitler
	30	Hitler succeeded Schleicher as Chancellor, with Papen as Vice-Chancellor
February	1	Reichstag dissolved for elections
	27	Reichstag fire
	28	Presidential Decree for the Protection of People and State
March	3	Arrest of members of KPD
	5	**Reichstag elections:** NSDAP: 288 seats (43.9 per cent of the vote)
	5–7	'Coordination' of state governments
	8	Establishment of concentration camps
	13	Ministry of People's Enlightenment and Propaganda under Goebbels
	21	Potsdam ceremony; KPD members prevented from taking up Reichstag seats
	23	Enabling Act
	31	Law for Coordination of the Federal States
April	1	National boycott of Jewish shops
	7	Law for the Restoration of a Professional Civil Service; introduction of office of Reich Governor (*Reichsstatthalter*)
	22–5	Measures against Jewish doctors, teachers and students
May	2	Abolition of free trade unions
	6	Formation of DAF
June	28	Ministry of the Interior introduced Committee of Experts for Population and Racial Policy
July	5	Dissolution of Centre Party (Z)
	8	Concordat with Pope Pius XI
	14	NSDAP declared only legal party in Germany; Law for the Prevention of the Hereditarily Diseased Progeny
September	22	Establishment of Reich Chamber of Culture
	29	Reich Entailed Farm Law
October	14	German withdrawal from Disarmament Conference and League of Nations

November	24	Law Against Dangerous Habitual Criminals
	27	Creation of SdA and KdF
	30	Establishment of Gestapo

1934

January	26	Nazi–Polish Non-Aggression Pact
June	30	Night of the Long Knives
July	20	Independence of SS from SA
	25	Assassination of Austrian Chancellor Dollfuss
August	1–2	Law concerning the Head of State of the German Reich; death of Hindenburg; army's oath of allegiance to Hitler
September		Schacht's New Plan
October	24	Formation of DAF

1935

January	13	Saar plebiscite
March	16	Introduction of conscription; repudiation of military clauses of Treaty of Versailles
April	11–14	Stresa Conference setting the Stresa Front (Britain, France and Italy)
May		Military Service Law
June	18	Anglo-German Naval Agreement
October	2	Italian invasion of Abyssinia
	18	Law for the protection of the Hereditary Health of the German People
November	14	Law for the Protection of German Blood and Honour; Reich Citizenship Law

1936

March	7–28	Remilitarisation of Rhineland; plebiscite on remilitarisation
August	1	Opening of Berlin Olympics
October	19	Four Year Plan announced
November	1	Rome–Berlin Axis
	25	Anti-Comintern Pact with Japan (Italy joined 6 November 1937)

1937

January	22	Law on the Punishment of Juvenile Offenders
March	14	Papal Encyclical *Mit brennender Sorge*
April	27	German bombing of Guernica

June	23	German withdrawal from Non-Intervention Committee
November	5	Hossbach Memorandum
1938		
January	25	Resignation of General von Blomberg
February	4	Fritsch dismissed as Commander-in-Chief; abolition of War Ministry; establishment of OKW under Hitler
March	11	Invasion of Austria
	13	Annexation of Austria to the Reich (*Anschluss*)
April	10	Plebiscite on the *Anschluss*
September	15	Chamberlain's visit to Hitler at Berchtesgaden
	22	Chamberlain's visit to Hitler at Bad Godesberg
	29	Munich Conference on the Sudetenland
	30	Munich Agreement ceding Sudetenland to Germany
November	9–10	*Kristallnacht*
	12	Decree for the Exclusion of Jews from German Economic Life
	26	Resignation of Schacht as Economics Minister
1939		
March	15	Occupation of rest of Bohemia
	16	Protectorate of Bohemia and Moravia
	21	Hitler's demands for Danzig and Polish Corridor
	23	Occupation of Memel
	31	Anglo-French guarantee to Poland
May	22	Pact of Steel with Italy
August	23	Nazi–Soviet Non-Aggression Pact
September	1	Invasion of Poland
	3	British and French declarations of war on Germany
	27	Formation of RSHA
October	8	Western Poland incorporated into Reich
1940		
April	9	Invasion of Norway and Denmark
May	14	Surrender of Netherlands
	28	Capitulation of Belgium
	29	(to 3 June) Evacuation at Dunkirk
June	22	Armistice between Germany and France

1941		
April	6	Invasion of Yugoslavia
May	1	Occupation government in Greece
June	22	Invasion of Soviet Union
August	11	Atlantic Charter (Churchill and Roosevelt)
October	2	Beginning of Battle for Moscow
December	7	Japanese attack on Pearl Harbor
	11	German declaration of war on USA
1942		
January	20	Wannsee Conference
February	8	Speer succeeded Todt as Armaments Minister
1943		
January	31	Surrender of von Paulus at Stalingrad
February	8	Soviet capture of Kursk
	18	'Total War' speech by Goebbels
1944		
July	20	Stauffenberg attempt to assassinate Hitler
1945		
February	4–11	Yalta Conference (Churchill, Stalin, Roosevelt)
April	30	Hitler committed suicide
May	1	Goebbels committed suicide; Doenitz head of state
	7	German surrender
July	17	(to 2 August) Potsdam Conference (Truman, Attlee, Stalin)

SERIES PREFACE

The Questions and Analysis series has two main aims.

The first is to separate narrative from interpretation so that the latter is no longer diluted by the former. Each chapter starts with a background narrative containing essential information. This material provides the basis for a section focusing on analysis through specific questions. The main purpose of this is to tighten up essay technique.

The second aim is to provide a comprehensive range of sources for each of the issues covered. The questions are of the type which appear on examination papers and some have worked answers to demonstrate the techniques required.

The chapters may be approached in different ways. The background narratives can be read first to provide an overall perspective, followed by the analyses and then the sources. The alternative method is to work through all the components of each chapter before going on to the next.

For Charlotte

INTRODUCTION

Hitler and Nazi Germany, was first published in 1998 as the second contribution to the Questions and Analysis series. Since then, numerous changes have taken place in the structure of examination questions and it is no longer possible to replicate these precisely: the focus in this volume is therefore more on the *style* of question rather than on the precise wording or mark allocation. Also, later volumes in the series have included a significant increase in the study of historiography, intended for students both at A2 and in higher education: this I have tried to reflect through a more extensive inclusion of historical debates covering all aspects of the Nazi period. Further, I have updated a number of specific interpretations and have allowed more space for the treatment of nearly every issue. These additions explain why this Second Edition is substantially longer than the First, expanding from seven to ten chapters.

Finally, when dealing with historiography, I have kept to my usual habit of referring to particular historians in the present tense – unless there is a clear chronological reason for doing otherwise. Even when they are no longer with us, their ideas continue to engage us.

ACKNOWLEDGEMENTS

Author and publisher are grateful to the following: K.D. Bracher, *The German Dictatorship* (trans. J. Steinberg) (Penguin, 1973); C.R. Browning, *The Origins of the Final Solution: The Evolution of Nazi Jewish Policy, September 1939–March 1942* (Heinemann, 2004); M. Burleigh, *The Third Reich: A New History* (Macmillan, 2000); M. Burleigh and W. Wippermann, *The Racial State: Germany 1933–1945* (CUP, 1991); D. Cesarini (ed.), *The Final Solution: Origins and Implementation* (Routledge, 1994); E. Crankshaw, *Gestapo: Instrument of Tyranny* (Putnam, 1956); D. Crew (ed.), *Nazism and German Society 1933–1945* (Routledge, 1994); J. Dülffer, *Nazi Germany 1933–1945: Faith and Annihilation* (trans.) (Arnold, 1966); Documents on German Foreign Policy, Series D, Vol. I (Government Printing Office, Washington, DC, 1949); R.J. Evans, *The Third Reich in Power 1933–1939* (Allen Lane/Penguin, 2005); J. Fest, *Plotting Hitler's Death: The German Resistance to Hitler 1933–1945* (trans.) (Weidenfeld and Nicholson, 1996); C. Fischer, *The Rise of the Nazis* (Manchester University Press, 1995); G. Fleming, *Hitler and the Final Solution* (University of California Press, 1984); R. Gellately, *The Gestapo and German Society: Enforcing Racial Policy 1933–1945* (OUP, 1990); D.J. Goldhagen, *Hitler's Willing Executioners: Ordinary Germans and the Holocaust* (Little Brown & Co., 1996); P. Hayes (ed.), *Themes in Modern European History 1890–1945* (Routledge, 1992); K. Hildebrand, *The Third Reich* (George Allen & Unwin, 1984); G. Hirschfield (ed.), *The Policies of Genocide* (Unwin Hyman, HarperCollins, 1986); H. Holborn (ed.), *Republic to Reich: The Making of the Nazi Revolution* (Pantheon Books, Random House, 1972); M. Housden, *Resistance and Conformity in the Third Reich*

(Routledge, 1997); T.L. Jarman, *The Rise and Fall of Nazi Germany* (Signet Books, 1961); Thomas Jones, *Lloyd George* (Cambridge, MA, 1951); I. Kershaw, *The Nazi Dictatorship: Problems and Perspective of Interpretation* (Arnold, 4th edn, 2000); I. Kershaw and M. Lewin (eds), *Stalinism and Nazism: Dictatorships in Comparison* (CUP, 1997); T. Kirk, *Nazi Germany* (Palgrave Macmillan, 2007); M. Kitchen, *Nazi Germany at War* (Longman, 1995); H.W. Koch (ed.), *Aspects of the Third Reich* (Macmillan, 1985); W. Laqueur (ed.), *Fascism: A Reader's Guide* (Scolar Press, 1991); D.C. Large (ed.), *Contending with Hitler: Varieties of German Resistance in the Third Reich* (CUP, 1991); J. Laver, *Nazi Germany 1933–1945* (Hodder & Stoughton, 1991); C. Leitz (ed.), *The Third Reich: The Essential Readings* (Blackwell, 1983; 1999 edn); Louis P. Lochner (ed.), *The Goebbels Diaries 1942–3* (Washington, DC, 1948); G. Martel (ed.), *Modern Germany Reconsidered 1870–1945* (Routledge, 1992); H. Mommsen (ed.), *The Third Reich Between Vision and Reality: New Perspectives on German History 1918–1945* (Berg, 2001); J. Noakes and G. Pridham (eds), *Documents on Nazism* (Jonathan Cape, 1974); J. Noakes and G. Pridham (eds), *Nazism 1919–1945, Volume 1, The Rise to Power 1919–1934: A Documentary Reader*, new edition (University of Exeter Press, 1998); J. Noakes and G. Pridham (eds), *Nazism 1919–1945, Volume 2, State, Economy and Society 1933–39: A Documentary Reader*, new edition (University of Exeter Press, 2000); J. Noakes and G. Pridham (eds), *Nazism 1919–1945, Volume 3, Foreign Policy, War and Racial Extermination: A Documentary Reader*, new edition (University of Exeter Press, 2001). Please note that the extracts used have been taken from the earlier editions of these three volumes: J. Noakes and G. Pridham (eds), *Nazism 1919–1945* (University of Exeter Press, 1983–8). D. Orlow, *The History of the Nazi Party*, Vol. 2 (David and Charles, 1971); D.J.K. Peukert, *Inside Nazi Germany: Conformity, Opposition and Racism in Everyday Life* (trans.) (Penguin, 1989); J. Remak, *The Nazi Years* (Prentice-Hall, 1969); G. Rempel, *Hitler's Children: The Hitler Youth and the SS* (University of North Carolina Press, 1989); H. Schacht, *Account Settled* (Weidenfeld & Nicholson, 1949); L.L. Snyder, *The Weimar Republic* (Anvil Books, 1966); P.D. Stachura (ed.), *The Nazi* Machtergreifung (Allen & Unwin, 1983); M. Stibbe, *Women in the Third Reich* (Arnold, 2003); Otto Strasser, *Hitler and I* (London, 1940); A.J.P. Taylor, *The Origins of the Second World War* (Hamish Hamilton, 1961; Penguin edn, 1964).

Every effort has been made to obtain permission to reproduce copyright material. If any proper acknowledgment has not been made, copyright holders are invited to inform the publisher of the oversight.

1

THE RISE OF NAZISM

BACKGROUND

The Nazi movement originated in Munich as the German Workers' Party (DAP), established immediately after the end of the First World War. Hitler, previously an impoverished Austrian artist who had served in the German army, joined in November 1919. He was placed in charge of the Party's propaganda and was largely responsible for drafting the *25 Point Programme* in 1920 and for renaming the movement the National Socialist German Workers' Party (NSDAP). The following year he supplanted Anton Drexler as party leader and extended National Socialist (Nazi) activities into the media, with the acquisition of the *Munich Observer* (*Münchener Beobachter*), and into paramilitary activism with the formation of the *Sturmabteilung* (SA).

The early conception of Nazism was revolutionary. In 1923 Hitler made a bid for power in Munich, clearly encouraged by the success of Mussolini's March on Rome the previous year. The attempt ended in failure; Hitler was tried for treason and sentenced to a term of imprisonment in Landsberg Castle. While he was out of circulation the NSDAP fell into disarray and had to be refounded on his release. Hitler now proceeded to revitalise the party and to alter his whole strategy for achieving power. Instead of coming to power by revolution, he now proposed to achieve his objective by legal means and then to introduce the revolution from above. Between 1925 and 1929 he succeeded in winning over the northern contingents of the

NSDAP under Gregor Strasser and Goebbels, and in establishing his authority through a series of local party officials known as *Gauleiter*.

The actual results of these developments are contentious. On the one hand, the NSDAP performed very badly in the Reichstag (or elected chamber) elections, dropping seats between 1924 and 1928. On the other hand, there is evidence of a major upheaval below the surface within the middle classes which made them more receptive to the appeal of Nazism from 1928 onwards, a process which was accelerated by the Great Depression. The working class, too, became more fragmented and a substantial portion was detached from its normal political allegiance. The electoral impact of such changes was startling. The NSDAP won 107 seats in 1930 and were easily the largest party in the elections of July and November 1932.

This chapter focuses on the meaning of Nazism – in terms of its ideas and what it came to mean to those who joined the NSDAP or came eventually to vote for it. Analysis 1 considers the origins and growth of Nazism as an ideology, the influences upon it and where it fits into the modern world. It also considers whether it was part of a more generic phenomenon – the crisis of modernism – or whether it grew in the unique environment of Germany's own past. Above all, was Nazism entirely the creation of Hitler?

Analysis 2 deals with the growing support in Germany for Nazism. It starts with the changes made after the Munich Putsch within the NSDAP in terms of strategy, organisation and propaganda; it then looks at the way in which these changes attracted support within every sector in German society to make the NSDAP the largest and most diverse of the parties in the Reichstag.

The increase in popular support for the Nazis did not inevitably mean their rise to power: after all, Hitler never held a majority in the Reichstag and he lost the Presidential election to Hindenburg in 1932. Nevertheless, the way in which others viewed the surge of Nazism after 1931 meant that Hitler was eventually appointed Chancellor as the result of political intrigue. This element of his rise is covered separately in Chapter 2.

ANALYSIS 1: WHAT WAS 'NATIONAL SOCIALISM' AND WHY DID IT BECOME ESTABLISHED IN GERMANY?

The main components of National Socialism can be found in three main sources: the *25 Point Programme*, *Mein Kampf* and the *Zweites Buch*. Further policies and ideas were contained in Hitler's Speeches and the *Tischgespräche*, the latter based on records of his table conversations.

The *Programme*, formulated in 1920, contained principles which could be seen as both nationalist and socialist. The former predominated, demanding 'the union of all Germans in a Greater Germany' (Article 1); the 'revocation of the peace treaties of Versailles and Saint-Germain' (Article 2); the acquisition of 'land and territory to feed our people and settle our surplus population' (Article 3); the replacement of Roman Law by German Law (Article 19); the formation of a people's army (Article 22); and the establishment of 'a strong central state power' (Article 25). The nationalist component was given further emphasis by a strong racial slant. Hence, Jews were to be excluded from German nationhood (Article 4); all 'non-German immigration must be prevented' (Article 8); and non-Germans should be excluded from any influence within the national media (Article 23). The socialist element was apparent mainly in the emphasis on 'physical or mental work' (Article 10); the 'abolition of incomes unearned by work' (Article 11); the 'confiscation of war profits' (Article 12); extensive nationalisation of businesses (Article 13); 'profit-sharing in large industrial enterprises' (Article 14); the extension of old-age insurance (Article 15); and land reform (Article 17).[1] These clauses, however, reflect the radicalism of Hitler's ideas less than *Mein Kampf*. Written between 1924 and 1926, this focused more on racial rather than economic explanations for major historical trends. Here he argued that 'The adulteration of the blood and racial deterioration conditioned thereby are the only causes that account for the decline of ancient civilizations; for it is never by war that nations are ruined, but by the loss of their powers of resistance, which are exclusively a characteristic of pure racial blood'.[2] Anti-Semitism was conjoined with anti-Marxism which, in turn, made Soviet Russia Germany's main external enemy. This meant that 'the end of Jewish rule in Russia will also be the end of Russia as a state'.[3] Through future expansion, Germany would achieve its rightful *Lebensraum* at the expense of the 'inferior' races of the east, a theme he revisited in 1928 in his *Zweites Buch*, largely concerned with foreign policy, and more randomly in his *Tischgespräche*.

The consensus among historians is that National Socialism was irrational and disordered as an ideology. It was certainly looser and more eclectic than Communism, which was based on the tighter format of dialectical materialism. The *25-Point Programme* was the closest the movement ever came to a list of objectives – but the name at the bottom of this document was that of Drexler, not Hitler. The latter felt no fundamental commitment to all of its provisions, preferring to articulate his ill-defined aims separately and with a much heavier emphasis on race. According to Kershaw, 'Hitler's ideology has been seen less as a "programme" consistently implemented than as a loose framework for action which only gradually stumbled into the shape of realistic objectives'.[4]

Where did these ideas come from? Hitler was certainly affected in his early years in Vienna by the far-right and anti-Semitic influences of Karl Lueger, leader of the Christian Social Party and Georg von Schönerer, a prominent member of the Pan-German movement in Austria: Hitler was particularly influenced by the latter's propaganda for the union of all Germans within a Greater Germany. *Mein Kampf also* reveals a partially digested and incompletely understood version of a range of nineteenth-century philosophers including Hegel and Nietzsche. Reflecting a general consensus on this, Bullock argues that 'Every one of the elements in his world-view is easily identified in nineteenth-century and turn-of-the-century writers, but no-one had previously put them together in quite the same way'.[5] There is, however, disagreement as to why Hitler's own synthesis should have led so readily to the conquest of Germany by National Socialism. Three broad routes of transmission have been suggested. The first is that Germany's own past made it particularly susceptible, the second that the spread of National Socialism was the most extreme manifestation of a general European phenomenon, and the third that Hitler himself exerted a unique impact unequalled by anyone else.

Some historians have emphasised that Germany was especially receptive to National Socialism because of its own unique history or 'special path' (*Sonderweg*). Three separate strands can be identified. One is the failure of Germany's middle classes to capture the political initiative in 1848 and 1849; this 'lost revolution' meant that Germany was eventually united by force and came under the authoritarian rule of the Kaiserreich (1871–1918). The fracturing of German liberalism remained apparent even during the era of the Weimar Republic (1919–33), as National Socialism was able to slip through the defences of parliamentary democracy and establish at least a degree of continuity between the Third Reich and the Second. A.J.P. Taylor took the argument further. The whole process, he maintained, involved the surrender of Germany to authority. 'During the preceding eighty years the Germans had sacrificed to the Reich all their liberties; they demanded as reward the enslavement of others. No German recognized the Czechs and Poles as equals. Therefore every German desired the achievement that only total war could give.'[6] Other historians have seen in this more than a simple abandonment of collective judgement. Shirer, for example, argued the case for an underlying continuity between National Socialism and Germany's cultural past, which produced a 'spiritual break with the west'.[7] In this sense, *Mein Kampf* offered 'a continuation of German history'.[8]

But the *Sonderweg* approach is seen by many as too restrictive as an explanation for the emergence of National Socialism. An alternative interpretation is that Nazism was the most radical part of a process which was not confined to Germany, but which affected other parts of Europe. It is, for example, a long-established Marxist view that Nazism was one manifestation of a general crisis of capitalism; East German historians, in particular, maintained that Hitler was above all the tool of big business. As a variant of fascism, Nazism represented a late phase in the development of capitalism, in which a declining political structure has to be replaced by something more robust if monopoly capitalism itself is to survive. According to the East German historian, Eichholtz, 'Fascism represents no separate socioeconomic formation, no new phase within the capitalist social order; its economic foundations and trends are monopoly-capitalistic, imperialistic'.[9] Hence Hitler had little independent input: he was merely part of a larger process. This analysis is, however, deeply flawed. It is based on a preconceived formula for historical change which was used to provide ideological justification for the political system that replaced Nazism in East Germany. As such, it fails to explain why some countries remained democracies in spite of experiencing similar problems. Capitalism, in other words, was equally capable of assuming democratic forms.

Non-Marxist historians also acknowledge an economic influence but place this within a broader context of national and international influences. Particular sections of the German population were vulnerable for economic reasons which had their roots in the nineteenth century: the middle classes experienced a crisis of industrialisation which made them susceptible to radical ideas. These, too, had a long history, in the form of pan-Germanism and anti-Semitism, and in the quest for *Lebensraum* ('living space'). During the Second Reich (1871–1918) these ideas had been confined to the fringe but, within the crisis of Germany's experience between the Wars, they became the focal point. None of them were new, but Nazism was particularly effective – in an eclectic sense – in combining 'snippets of ideas and dogmas of salvation', which could be used as 'a deliberate simplification of political world views'.[10] Many – although not all – non-Marxists also believe that Nazism was part of the fascist mainstream. The roots were a widespread disillusionment with modernism and rationalism and the emphasis on a curiously-twisted form of romanticism. Fascism also emphasised the profound threat of communist and socialist parties, while, at the same time, drawing upon a number of socialist ideas which had been modified to appeal to the middle classes. Fascism everywhere was militaristic and expansionist, focusing upon the revival of centralism within the state and future conquest outside it. All fascist parties depended upon the cult of a father-figure and developed mass movements to energise the masses with enthusiasm and commitment. According to Broszat, therefore, National Socialism was rooted in a combination of 'the general European crisis' and 'Germany's national history and its peculiar divergence from the West'.[11]

For many historians nothing comes close to rivalling the personal influence of Hitler himself in the development of Nazism. Some even suggest that Nazism had become crystallised in his mind even before he came to power in Germany. Trevor-Roper, for example, believes that the formative period for this was the First World War, and that by 1923 it had taken the 'systematic form' which was later 'deducible from his Table Talk'.[12] In all this, Hitler's 'personal power was in fact so undisputed that he rode to the end above the chaos he had created, and concealed its true nature'.[13] Bullock, too, accentuates the personal influence of the Führer:

> More important is the fact that, having created his own version, the essential elements of which were set out in *Mein Kampf* and completed by the time he wrote his *Zweites Buch* in 1928, Hitler never altered it. There is a recognizable continuity between the ideas he expressed in the 1920s, his table talk in the 1940s, and the political testament which he dictated in the bunker just before he committed suicide in April 1945.[14]

All three approaches have to be used to explain the rise of Nazism in Germany, although their exact proportion will always be controversial. There are, however, certain leads. Fascism without Mussolini is just about imaginable, and historians have even drawn a distinction between 'Mussolinianism' and fascism. But no one has seriously suggested separating 'Hitlerism' from Nazism: an integral component of Nazism was the 'Führer principle' (*Führerprinzip*). It is true that the cult of leadership is to be found in all fascist movements, but it was of particular importance in the Nazi context since Hitler's ideas were crucial in defining the eclectic nature of Nazism. Above all, Hitler provided Nazism with a unique vision of racial purity and anti-Semitism which were initially absent in Fascist Italy. In this respect, as in others, the generic label of German fascism hardly seems appropriate. On the other hand, we should not write out longer-term approaches. The popularity of Hitler is impossible to explain without the existence of a strong degree of receptivity within Germany – and this could well be set in a wider European context. There was much in Hitler which was ludicrous: it was converted into a compelling form of radicalism because it worked upon the needs of the population at the time.

	1919 Assembly	1920	1924 May	1924 Dec	1928	1930	1932 July	1932 Nov	1933
NSDAP	- -	- -	32 6.5	14 3.0%	12 2.6%	107 18.3%	230 37.3%	196 33.1%	288 43.9%
DNVP	44 10.3%	71 15.1%	95 19.5%	103 20.5%	73 14.2%	41 7.0%	37 5.9%	52 8.3%	52 8.0%
DVP	19 4.4%	65 13.9%	45 9.2%	51 10.1%	45 8.7%	30 4.5%	7 1.2%	11 1.9%	2 1.1%
Zentrum	91 19.7%	64 13.6%	65 13.4%	69 13.6%	62 12.1%	68 11.8%	75 12.5%	70 11.9%	74 11.2%
BVP	- -	21 4.4%	16 3.2%	19 3.7%	16 3.1%	19 3.0%	22 3.2%	20 3.1%	18 2.7%
DDP	75 18.6%	39 8.3%	28 5.7%	32 6.3%	25 4.9%	20 3.8%	4 1.0%	2 1.0%	5 0.9%
SPD	165 37.9%	102 21.7%	100 20.5%	131 26.0%	153 29.8%	143 24.5%	133 21.6%	121 20.4%	120 18.3%
USPD	22 7.6%	84 17.9%	- 0.8%	- 0.3%	- 0.1%	- -	- -	- -	- -
KPD	- -	4 2.1%	62 12.6%	45 9.0%	54 10.6%	77 13.1%	89 14.3%	100 16.9%	81 12.3%
Others	7 1.6%	9 3.0%	29 8.6%	29 7.8%	51 14.7%	82 13.9%	11 3.1%	12 3.3%	7 1.6%

Figure 1 Reichstag election results 1919–33

Questions

1. Was 'National Socialism' the right name for Hitler's movement?
2. Were the Nazis 'fascist'?

ANALYSIS 2: HOW AND WHY DID THE NAZIS ATTRACT INCREASED SUPPORT BETWEEN THE EARLY 1920S AND 1932?

Between 1920 and 1932 the National Socialist German Workers' Party (NSDAP) was transformed from a fringe *völkisch* group with a very limited appeal to the largest political party in Germany. The process was slow at first, the Nazis winning only 12 seats in the Reichstag in 1928. Within two years, however, it had become the second largest party in the Reichstag, with 107 seats. This was followed in 1932 by a further increase to 230 in

July, before a drop to 196 seats in November. The latter was not, however sufficient to prevent Hitler from being appointed Chancellor in January 1933. This was partly because of the special circumstances in which the government of the Weimar Republic found itself at the end of 1932 (see Chapter 2, Analysis 1) and partly because the NSDAP had held its position as the most widely-supported of all the Reichstag parties.

This sudden acceleration between 1928 and 1932 was based partly on the attraction of new and first-time voters, but more substantially on the transfer of allegiances from other parties. Key to this process was the declining fortune of the Weimar Republic, faced after 1929 with the impact of the Wall Street Crash and the Great Depression. But the NSDAP benefited from these developments because a series of fundamental changes made to its internal structure and policies during the 1920s had optimised its chances of attracting mass support from the victims of harder times. Most of these changes were introduced as a result of lessons learned from the failure of the Munich Putsch of November 1923.

Changes in strategy to extend the range of Nazi support

Hitler's early emphasis for the NSDAP had been revolutionary. Initially he had hoped to come to power by direct action, influenced, no doubt, by Mussolini's success in seizing the initiative in Italian politics. His activism was a combination of nationalist propaganda in his new paper, now renamed the *Völkischer Beobachter*, paramilitary violence from the *Sturmabteilung* (SA), and attempts to coerce the political leadership of Bavaria under Kahr. He hoped to intimidate a vulnerable national regime into making major concessions, as Mussolini had done in Italy in 1922. But the situation in Germany differed to that in Italy. Despite the range of its problems in 1923, the central government proved more stable and resilient, while Kahr proved that entrenched local conservatism was more than a match for fringe radicalism. In the absence of a German equivalent of the March on Rome, Hitler had to introduce major changes to his whole political approach.

The most fundamental of these was his route to power. The failure of the Munich Putsch had demonstrated that direct action through revolution was no longer possible; instead, the Nazis would have to settle for a 'legal' path. At the same time, he was still wedded to the concept of a future 'seizure of power' (*Machtergreifung*), which meant that there was an underlying contradiction. This, however, was rationalised by Hitler: 'legality' was nothing more than a strategy to achieve the *Machtergreifung*. There would be no real conversion to the principles of constitutional democracy: parliamentary politics would be the means, not the end. For the time being it would be necessary, in Hitler's words, 'to hold our noses and enter the Reichstag alongside Marxist and Catholic deputies'. Revolution would be the ultimate aim of this strategy, but would now be the result of having achieved power rather than the means by which power would be achieved. It was, in the meantime, necessary to secure mass support at two levels. On the surface were the NSDAP as a parliamentary party, aiming at gaining electoral support at the expense of their rivals. At the same time, the Nazi movement would be intensified in the form of the SA and other paramilitary influences, with street action against Communists, Social Democrats and other mass rivals. Both the NSDAP and the Nazi movement would have to extend their appeal. How would this be done?

First, the Nazis had to move away from their initial narrow working-class base. They could not hope to compete effectively for the working-class vote with its two larger rivals – the moderate Social Democrats and the revolutionary Communists. This was shown in the 1928 Reichstag election, in which the NSDAP won only 2.6 per cent of the vote, compared with 29.8 per cent for the SPD and 10.6 per cent for the KPD. Hitler's disillusionment was apparent even before then. In 1927 he told his economic adviser, Keppler, that the economic goals of the original 1920 Programme were now 'unusable'. He therefore reformulated the basic policy by moving away from socialism, even though this antagonised the 'left' wing of the Party under Gregor and Otto Strasser. By attacking socialism and the left, Hitler began to exercise more of an appeal to the middle classes and the conservative–traditionalist right. He sought to make the Nazis more widely acceptable in two ways. He appealed directly to the interests of each class and sector within the electorate by making specific pledges calculated to meet its individual needs. This was in addition to the more general policies based on nationalism and race. This duality would ensure that the NSDAP became the only party in the Weimar Republic able to project a sustainable appeal to all sectors of the population.

All this required effective propaganda and disciplined party structure. Hitler's main ideas on this were clearly stated in *Mein Kampf*. 'Propaganda works on the general public from the standpoint of an idea and makes them ripe for the victory of this idea.' To work on the collective emotions of crowds, his message to them had to be kept simple, striking and memorable. 'The receptivity of the great masses is very limited, their intelligence is small, but their power of forgetting is enormous.' Therefore, propaganda 'must be limited to a very few points', which must be constantly repeated to establish them as incontrovertible facts. It was vital to make the individual feel important only in the context of the crowd and to establish stereotyped enemies and targets by means, if necessary, of 'the big lie'. Organisation, of course, was essential for the maintenance of mass commitment, hence the vast number of marches and rallies, the uniforms and paramilitary drill, and the street fights with Communists and Social Democrats. Again, the essentials were set out in *Mein Kampf*. 'The function of propaganda', he argued, 'is to attract supporters, the function of organization is to win members.' After its collapse between 1924 and 1925, the party structure was recentralised under the 'leadership principle' (*Führerprinzip*) and subdivided into regional units, each under a *Gauleiter*.

Although the integration of party and mass movement proved possible with such a system, it all took time. There was little immediate sign of success, especially since the Nazis won only 12 seats in the Reichstag elections of 1928. Clearly they were disadvantaged by the years of 'relative stability' experienced by the Weimar Republic between 1924 and 1929. During this period the Nazi movement developed more rapidly than the NSDAP itself, the latter making only a few inroads into established electoral patterns. Then came a change in the Republic's fortunes with the financial crises of 1929 and 1931, the onset of depression and the collapse of coalition politics upon which democracy had depended. In these circumstances, parts of the electorate became radicalised and more receptive to the restructured Nazi policy and appeal. How did this manifest itself?

Origins of increased Nazi support

A considerable amount of research has seen carried out on the defection to the NSDAP during the late 1920s and early 1930s. The initial tendency was to see Nazism as having an appeal primarily to the middle classes, with minority additions from the working class and from the upper levels of society – neither of whom were as volatile in transferring their political allegiance. The overall emphasis of this has now been modified in favour of a more widespread support for Hitler.

In 1960 Lipset argued that the moderate section of German politics, mainly from the middle class, became radicalised by Nazism and became the primary base of Hitler's support.[15] Some historians, like Childers, have since argued that the basis for the middle-class movement towards the NSDAP had been established during the late 1920s, even before the onset of Depression from 1929.[16] Despite some modifications in the original emphasis, Stachura has recently emphasised that 'The NSDAP was a predominantly lower-middle-class affair'.[17] (See

Source 2.1 below.) Mühlberger, however, has taken issue with this. 'To describe the Nazi Movement as a "pre-eminently lower-middle-class phenomenon" or to characterize the NSDAP as "a predominantly lower-middle-class affair" is misleading.' Instead, the 'Nazi movement as a whole' was 'remarkably heterogeneous in social terms'.[18] (See Source 2.2.) This is a view supported most recently by Kirk.[19] (See Source 2.3.)

The differences are based on degree rather than on basics. No-one denies that middle-class support was fundamental to the rise of the Nazis; indeed, it is still possible to say that the middle classes made up the largest single proportion of Nazi support, and that their defection from their traditional parties was vitally important in converting Nazism into a mass movement. Initially they had voted in large numbers for the DDP and the DVP, although some also supported the DNVP and, if they were Catholic, the Centre. It is also possible to synthesise the arguments concerning the timing of middle-class support. The 'old *Mittelstand*', comprising artisans, small retailers and peasant farmers, formed the earlier core of the middle-class support for Hitler and were throwing their support behind him before the Depression. Theirs was a disillusionment with the structure and policies of the Republic itself. To these was added the weight of much of the 'new *Mittelstand*' – non-manual employees, civil servants and teachers – who aligned themselves with Nazism as a result of the Depression. It is possible that they were moving in this direction anyway. But the simple fact is that the NSDAP secured only 12 seats in the Reichstag election of 1928; it therefore took the Depression to convert a trickle of middle-class support into a flood.

To a class trapped between industrial capital and industrial labour, Nazi propaganda made all the difference. Hiden emphasises the diverse nature of its appeal as 'going far beyond restoration of earnings, important as these undoubtedly were'. Instead, their 'privilege and standing' would be restored; 'traditional values would be reaffirmed'; and steps would be taken to control 'large capitalists on the one hand, "Marxist" unions and parties on the other'.[20] Peukert also stresses the importance of restoring the displaced *Mittelstand*. 'The immediate social strata of an industrial society dominated by big capital and labour once more became the respected and authoritative centre-ground of a hierarchical, corporatist society.'[21] Meanwhile propaganda had also appealed to the farmers through the work of the party's Agrarian Policy Apparatus and the ideas of Walter Darré. The restoration of an urban-based middle class would therefore be accompanied by a healthy independent peasantry as an integral part of the racial community.

A more fundamental shift has occurred in explaining the relationship between Nazism and the working class. It was once strongly argued that the working class remained largely loyal to the parties of the left which, in any case, had a distinctively proletarian appeal. The KPD was especially class-based and its support actually increased during the Reichstag elections of 1930 and 1932. Although the SPD lost seats, it came nowhere near the collapse suffered by the liberal parties, clearly indicating that it retained the bulk of its support. The proletariat, by this analysis, was less drawn to Nazism because, in the words of Stachura, 'The Party was unable to establish a significant working-class constituency because it did not develop a coherent interpretation of "German Socialism"'. This was partly because Hitler's 'innate contempt and distrust of the proletariat remained paramount'.[22] Mühlberger, by contrast, emphasises the importance of recruitment from within the working class, and recent research has tended to support the view that working-class input was substantial. Studies of Nazi membership records show something like 40 per cent of the membership coming from the working class, while 60 per cent of the SA were of the same origins. Parallel research on electoral trends has, through computer analysis of statistical data, produced very similar voting results. According to Fischer, 'a good 40 per cent of the NSDAP's voters were working class, remarkably similar to the proportion of workers in the party itself'.[23] He adds: 'All in all the National Socialist Party contained a significantly higher number of workers among its voters and activists than was once believed.'[24]

What was the Nazi appeal for the working class? The growth of unemployment has been seen as one important factor, although the KPD probably attracted as many from this sector; certainly, unemployed workers were less likely to vote Nazi than were those who still had jobs. More important was the decline of trade union powers as a result of the Depression, since for many this weakened the connection with the main parties of the working class – the SPD and the KPD. As collective bargaining began to falter after 1930 in the face of the growing intransigence of industrial leaders, many workers faced a sudden decline in status. Those who saw this as an ideological issue requiring revolutionary action swelled the ranks of the KPD and its Red Front; but more were drawn to the propaganda for a new *Volksgemeinschaft* than to open class war. This enabled the Nazis to draw support widely across the whole of the working class – from the urban factory workers to the agricultural workers in rural areas – even though this support was thinner in specific regions like the Ruhr and Saxony than for the Communists and SPD. The fact that the KPD and SPD were bitter mutual enemies created disillusionment with the traditional political choice, and by 1932 had induced many to see the NSDAP as a genuine alternative.

Hence the working class never came to provide the largest body of support for Nazism; in that respect, the original interpretations seem correct. On the other hand, it is possible to overestimate the continued loyalty of the working class to the parties of the left. After 1928 substantial shifts *did* occur: the growth of the Communists was more than offset by the decline of the SPD. The latter shrank by between a quarter and a third: many of these lost votes almost certainly went straight to the Nazis. Thus, although the NSDAP was not primarily a working-class party and the majority of workers remained with the parties of the left, the inflow of working-class support for Nazism was still a vital factor in the conversion of Nazism into a mass movement.

The attitude of the social elites to Nazism has also been subject to controversy. Marxist analyses emphasise that Nazism, as a variant of fascism, was typically under the direct influence of finance capital and the great industrialists. East German historians saw Nazism as capitalism making an adjustment to the destruction of its previous economic environment, as an alliance between the elite and the middle classes to intensify the exploitation of the proletariat. Hitler was therefore the tool of big business. A less extreme version, also favoured by many non-Marxists, is that landowners, industrialists and businessmen supported and used the Nazis for their own ends. There is some truth in this. Many saw in Hitler the prospects of safety from the threat of Communism and socialism on the left. Arguably, many saw beyond this and expected Nazism to deliver over to them a disciplined and constrained workforce. They looked to Hitler to undo the pro-trade-union and welfare policies of most of the governments of the Weimar Republic. Even those who distrusted the violence and vulgarities of the Nazi movement were still likely to be supporting it indirectly. It was unlikely that the affluent levels of German society after 1929 voted in significant numbers for any party to the left of the DNVP, and the DNVP itself was in close collaboration with the NSDAP after Hugenberg assumed the leadership. Hence the Nazis benefited considerably from the respectability, publicity and, of course, funding brought by a relatively narrow but highly influential sector of society.

Three sectors within society which overlapped class boundaries have been given separate attention. These were women, youth and the churches. A considerable amount of research has been done recently on the reaction of women to Nazism,[25] with a tendency to distinguish between party activists and voters who were not party members. The former joined organisations like the German Women's Order

(DFO or *Deutscher Frauenorden*), set up in 1923. Largely uninvolved in political campaigning, their main roles were fundraising and distributing Nazi propaganda on race and the role of women in society. Although their importance was acknowledged by Goebbels, such groups developed more slowly than other party organs, and even by 1932 women constituted less than 6 per cent[26] of total party membership. The real changes came within the electorate. It has been estimated that 'at least 7 million women had supported the NSDAP in at least one election between 1930 and 1933'.[27] Several reasons could be advanced for this. Many women, of course, were the wives of male Nazi voters: this was one basis for allegiance to any political party. But others were self-motivated – perhaps as younger women who had not been involved in pre-war feminist struggles; or as family supporters with a special concern about declining expenditure on welfare and housing; or, again, as single women attracted by the Nazi undertaking to remove married women from the employment market. To some extent the NSDAP benefited from the traditional tendency of most women to support the parties to the right of centre: from 1928 onwards the DVP and DNVP, in particular, leaked votes. In one respect, however, women may actually have delayed the rise of Hitler 'by voting predominantly for Hindenburg in the two-stage presidential elections of March and April 1932'.[28]

Historians are agreed that the appeal to youth was a vital factor in the rise of Nazism. Two-thirds of all party members by 1933 were under 40, with an average age in 1930 of 31.[29] Key to the growing support from this sector was the undermining of the traditional social hierarchy by a relentless succession of war, inflation, depression and political crisis. Nazi propaganda found a ready response, with slogans such as: 'National Socialism is the organised will of youth'; 'Make way, you old ones; your time is up!'; and 'Who has Youth has the future; who has the future has Youth'. The SA attracted young workers, radicalised by propaganda, supplemented by growing numbers of middle-class students. Future support was guaranteed through the exploitation of boys in their teens, with a steady movement to the new Hitler Youth (HJ) from existing groups such as the *Bündische* Youth and the *Wanderwogel*, although there has been some controversy about whether these were actually precursors. As for the contribution of youth to the election results after 1928, many men and women in their twenties were new voters without previous party allegiances; certainly the Nazis benefited from the combination of support from first-time enthusiasts and the desertion of more traditional loyalties by longer-established voters.

It is difficult to identify with any precision the impact of confessional beliefs on the Nazi vote. One generalisation is, however, widely accepted. Support for the Nazi movement as a whole was more likely in the Protestant north than the Catholic south, where the electoral performance of the Catholic Centre and its ally, the BVP, remained remarkably consistent. In addition, traditional right-wing parties like the DVP and DNVP were overwhelmingly Protestant in their religious orientation and, as we have seen, later became a conduit for defecting support to the NSDAP. Unlike the Catholic Church, Protestantism had no international connections or influence and was more closely connected politically with the structure of the nation state. This made it easier for Protestants to adapt to the right-wing emphasis on German nationalism. It should be stated that most of the Churches, whether Protestant or Catholic, never openly advocated support for the Nazis. But neither did they do much to condemn Nazi ideas nor to influence their laity into opposing Hitler. Even the attitude of the Catholic Church can best be described as one of official reserve. Hence many German Christian believers, from whatever class and of whatever age, felt that they could vote for or even join the NSDAP without compromising their religious beliefs or their consciences. This was due largely to skill of Nazi propaganda which promised as many forms of recovery and regeneration as there were needs and hopes for them. Only after the formation of the Third Reich did the true nature of this 'regeneration' and the number of victims sacrificed to it become fully apparent.

Questions

1. Did the NSDAP achieve its core support before 1933 from the upper or lower half of German society?
2. Did the NSDAP mobilise or transcend class differences?

SOURCES

1: THE IDEOLOGY AND PROGRAMME OF NAZISM

Source 1.1: From the Programme of the German Workers' Party, February 1920

1. We demand the union of all Germans, on the basis of the right of the self-determination of peoples, to form a Great Germany.

2. We demand equality of rights for the German people in its dealings with other nations, and abolition of the Peace Treaties of Versailles and Saint-Germain.
3. We demand land and territory (colonies) for the nourishment of our people and for settling our surplus population.
4. None but members of the nation may be citizens of the State. None but those of German blood, whatever their creed, may be members of the nation. No Jew, therefore, may be a member of the nation …
7. We demand that the State shall make it its first duty to promote the industry and livelihood of the citizens of the State …
8. All further non-German immigration must be prevented …
11. [We demand] abolition of incomes unearned by work …
13. We demand the nationalization of all businesses which have been amalgamated.
14. We demand that there shall be profit-sharing in the great industries.
15. We demand a general development of provision for old age.
16. We demand the creation and maintenance of a healthy middle class …
17. We demand a land reform suitable to our national requirements …
25. That all the foregoing requirements may be realized we demand the creation of a strong central power of the Reich …

Source 1.2: From a speech by Hitler on 13 April 1923

It has ever been the right of the stronger, before God and man, to see his will prevail. History proves that he who lacks strength is not served in the slightest by 'pure law'. … All of nature is one great struggle between strength and weakness, an eternal victory of the strong over the weak. If it were any different, nature would be in a state of putrefaction. The nation which would violate this elementary law would rot away.

Source 1.3: From Hitler's *Mein Kampf*

The art of all truly great national leaders has at all times primarily consisted of this: not to divide the attention of a people, but to concentrate that attention on a single enemy. The more unified the fighting spirit of a nation, the greater the magnetic attraction of a movement, the more forceful the power of its thrust. It is part of the genius of a great leader to make it appear as though even the most distant enemies belonged in the same category; for weak and fickle characters, if faced by many different enemies, will easily begin to have doubts about the justness of their cause.

Source 1.4: Otto Strasser's recollection of a conversation with Hitler (published in 1940)

I remember one of my first conversations with him. It was nearly our first quarrel.

'Power!' screamed Adolf. 'We must have power!'

'Before we gain it,' I replied firmly, 'let us decide what we propose to do with it. Our programme is too vague; we must construct something solid and enduring.'

Hitler, who even then could hardly bear contradiction, thumped the table and barked: 'Power first. Afterwards we can act as circumstances dictate!'

Source 1.5: From a speech by Hitler at an election meeting in March 1928

We can conclude that bourgeois nationalism has failed, and that the concept of Marxist socialism has made life impossible in the long run. These old lines of confrontation must be eradicated along with the old parties, because they are barring the nation's path into the future. We are eradicating them by releasing the two concepts of nationalism and socialism and harnessing them for a new goal, towards which we are working, full of hope, for the highest form of socialism is burning devotion to the nation.

Source 1.6: Otto Strasser's record of a discussion with Hitler on the subject of socialism in 1930 (published in 1940)

Strasser: All that is very simple for you, Herr Hitler, but it only serves to emphasize the profound difference in our revolutionary and Socialist ideas. ... The real reason is that you want to strangle the social revolution for the sake of legality and your new collaboration with the bourgeois parties of the Right.

Hitler: I am a Socialist, and a very different kind of Socialist ... your kind of Socialism is nothing but Marxism. The mass of the working classes want nothing but bread and games. They will never understand the meaning of an ideal, and we

> cannot hope to win them over to one. What we have to do is to select from a new master-class men who will not allow themselves to be guided, like you, by the morality of pity. Those who rule must know that they have the right to rule because they belong to a superior race.

Questions

1. How much evidence is there in Source 1.1 that the Nazis intended to follow a policy based on nationalism?
*2. How valuable are Sources 1.4 and 1.6 to the historian studying Nazi ideology?
3. Using Sources 1.1, 1.4 and 1.6, explain the different viewpoints of Hitler and Strasser concerning the implementation of socialism.
4. Using Sources 1.1 to 1.6 and your own knowledge, discuss the view that National Socialism before 1933 was 'pragmatic rather than ideological'.

WORKED ANSWER

*2 *[The answer to this question should be confined to one – possibly two – carefully argued paragraphs. If at all possible, two sides should be presented, although these need not be evenly balanced. There is also scope for the inclusion of additional material, provided this is carefully controlled and directly relevant to the question.]*

Sources 1.4 and 1.6 provide the historian with a valuable insight into Hitler's political thinking. Source 1.4 shows that he could be strongly pragmatic: his emphasis on 'Power first!' and on acting as 'circumstances dictate' confirms his change of political strategy after the failure of the Munich Putsch in 1923. Strasser amplifies this in Source 1.6 with his references to Hitler's policy of 'legality' and 'collaboration' with the right. Source 1.6 also reveals the extent of the ideological split within the Nazi Party between Hitler's interpretation of socialism and Strasser's. Source 1.4 also provides an intriguing picture of the more impetuous side of Hitler, who 'screamed' and 'thumped the table and barked'.

There are two drawbacks of which the historian needs to be aware. The first is that Otto Strasser had every reason to give a distorted picture of Hitler's views and mannerisms. He left Germany under a cloud and wrote his accounts while in exile. Second, the impressions were actually published in 1940, over a decade after the incidents: this opens up the possibility of inaccuracy in the precise wording. He was also concerned to present himself in a positive way by using phrases such as 'I replied firmly' (Source 1.4). But these disadvantages are offset by the rarity of a frank, if hostile, view of Hitler from a Nazi colleague.

2: HISTORIANS ON CLASS SUPPORT FOR THE NAZIS

Source 2.1: From P.D. Stachura, 'The Nazis, the Bourgeoisie and the Workers during the Kampfzeit', an article published in 1983

The NSDAP's inclinations were certainly anti-labour and anti-socialist/Marxist, but to account for its rise and ultimately successful advent to power on these terms alone is totally misleading. The *Machtergreifung* was the climax of a complicated interaction of social, economic, political and historical forces of which the NSDAP's antipathy for the Left was but one. The Party was the spearhead of a broadly restorationist, anti-modernist movement of propertied, nationalist and Protestant Germany which had its genesis in the ideas and conventions of the Wilhelmine Reich. As such, the NSDAP could hardly be anything other than a product of a quintessentially bourgeois ideological and political ambience.

This conclusion does not obviate the need, of course, for further research into the sociological aspects of early National Socialism. There is considerable scope not only for more detailed analysis of the Party's growth in particular geographical locations, most pressingly in central Germany, but also for investigation of a whole range of variables relating to age, sex, generational conflict, marital status, mobility, religious beliefs and educational experience as well as of emotional–psychological impulses which conditioned the *Mittelstand*. The extent of downward mobility among the middle classes and the applicability of modernisation theories also require much further work. As for the NSDAP–worker relationship, it would be helpful, of course, to have more details of the ideological and physical factors involved on both a national and local level, but the overall character of that relationship is now firmly established ... The NSDAP was a predominantly lower-middle-class affair.

Source 2.2: From D. Mühlberger, 'Conclusion to Hitler's Followers', an article published in 1983

The presence of a sizeable working-class following in the NSDAP and SS, and especially the dominance of this social stratum within the SA and the HJ, as well as the strong contingent of support drawn from the elite element of German society by the Nazi Party, and to a lesser degree the SS, argues against the validity of the middle-class thesis of Nazism, and suggests that it would be unwise to continue to adhere to this interpretational hypothesis. To describe the Nazi Movement as a 'pre-eminently lower-middle-class phenomenon' or to characterize the NSDAP as 'a predominantly lower-middle-class affair' is misleading. The perpetuation of the middle-class thesis of Nazism in the light of the empirical evidence now available on the rank and file membership of the party, the SA and the SS, as well as the more limited data on the HJ, both at the macro and micro level, is untenable. It is clear that in the period following the re-formation of the Nazi Party in 1925 and its *Machtergreifung* eight years later the Nazi movement as a whole ... mobilized a following which was remarkably heterogeneous in social terms.

Source 2.3: From T. Kirk, *Nazi Germany*, published in 2007

The designation *Mittelstandspartei* was problematic for a number of reasons. First of all it bracketed together the established occupational groups of the 'old *Mittelstand*', such as small farmers and artisans, with those of the 'new *Mittelstand*' produced by industrialisation and urbanisation, the salaried white-collar workers whose incomes were scarcely higher, and often lower than those of skilled manual workers. All these groups, along with shopkeepers and other urban small business people, belonged to the same social stratum, between wage earners and the propertied middle classes; but clerks and craftsmen, smallholders and shopkeepers lived in social cultures that were worlds apart, and espoused irreconcilable political values. ... Secondly, the party itself explicitly sought to transcend sectional interests and appeal to the whole electorate, to be not just nationalist, but national as well. The idea of the 'national community' (*Volksgemeinschaft*) meant putting the national interest above 'selfish' materialist motives – like the more equitable distribution of wealth. The very name of the party reflected its ambition to recruit manual workers, and considerable effort was put into campaigning among them during the 1920s, albeit with such little success that it redirected its appeal very clearly towards the middle classes in the late 1920s.

By the time it reached the peak of its electoral success in July 1932, the NSDAP represented a greater range of social and economic groups than any of its competitors. Despite the diversity of the party's appeal, however, the middle classes remained over-represented both as members and as voters before 1933.

Source 2.4: From C. Fischer, *The Rise of the Nazis*, published in 1995

All in all the National Socialist Party contained a significantly higher number of workers among its voters and activists than was once believed. A proportion of 40 per cent has now become widely accepted. Had the Nazi Party's social make-up reflected that of German society perfectly the figure would have been even higher, but the most obviously under-represented part of society within the party is better defined in gender than in class terms. Women were seldom party members, nor did they receive much encouragement to join. Furthermore what under-representation of workers there was within the party was offset quite significantly by the SA's ability to recruit a much higher proportion of workers, some 60 per cent, to its ranks.

Questions

1. Compare the arguments of Sources 2.1 and 2.2.
2. How convincing is the comment of Source 2.2 on Source 2.1?
3. How far does Source 2.4 differ from Sources 2.1 and 2.2?
4. Source 2.4 is the most recent of the four. Does it take forward the debate on class-based support for the Nazis?

2

THE ACHIEVEMENT AND CONSOLIDATION OF POWER 1933–4

BACKGROUND

By 1930 the change of strategy employed by Hitler after the Munich Putsch (see Chapter 1) had begun to pay off as the NSDAP became the second largest party in the Reichstag with 107 seats. Encouraged by this apparent success, Hitler played a double game. Below the surface of German politics the SA terrorised and victimised its opponents. Officially, however, Hitler sought power through election to Germany's highest office, the Presidency in April 1932, only to be defeated on the second ballot by the incumbent, Hindenburg, by 19.4 million votes to 13.4 million. Having failed to enter government as head of state, Hitler now sought the second highest office, becoming caught up in the political complexities that involved three Chancellors and Hindenburg himself. The first of these, Brüning, was forced to resign in May 1932 and, for a while, President Hindenburg continued to underpin a minority government, this time under von Papen, by use of emergency decrees under Article 48 of the Constitution. (See Source 1.1 below.) When the Reichstag eventually challenged this, Hindenburg dissolved it and called for an election in July. This, however, failed to broaden the base of Papen's administration, as did a further election in November. Hindenburg turned to Papen's political rival, von Schleicher, who undertook to form some sort of coalition. When he failed to deliver, Schleicher requested another dissolution; this time, however, Hindenburg refused and reluctantly accepted a deal which had in the meantime been worked out by Papen. By this, Hitler would be appointed Chancellor, with Papen in a new office of Vice-Chancellor and possessing equal access to the President. Since there were only three Nazis in an otherwise ultra-conservative government, Hindenburg was persuaded that Hitler would be under careful control. Hitler assumed his post on 30 January 1933.

Within days of his appointment Hitler requested a dissolution of the Reichstag so that he could increase the number of seats for the NSDAP. During the election campaign he made use of emergency decrees, issued under Article 48 of the Constitution, to hamstring the other parties, especially the SPD and KPD; the reason given for this was the Reichstag fire, which was blamed on the Communists. Although the NSDAP did not achieve an overall majority in the election, they did succeed in increasing the number of their seats from 196 to 288. Hitler's next objective was to change the Constitution. Because of an entrenched clause this required a two-thirds majority vote in the Reichstag. In March 1933 Hitler achieved this through two measures. One was the banning of the KPD deputies from assuming their seats because of their alleged implication in the Reichstag fire. The other was a deal struck up with the Centre Party guaranteeing Catholic liberties in exchange for the absence of any opposition from the Centre party to Hitler's measures. As a result Hitler was able to secure the passage of the Enabling Act which allowed the Chancellor as well as the Reichstag to issue legislation. This measure was used to extend Hitler's already considerable powers. In April 1933 the Chancellor decreed that the local state legislatures (*Landtäge*) need not be consulted by the local state officials in issuing legislation, while in 1934 the *Landtäge* were abolished altogether. Measures were then taken against potential opponents. In May 1940 the trade union movement was to be replaced by the Nazi-organised German Labour Front (DAF) and, in June, the Reichstag was effectively cleared out by the banning of all political parties other than the NSDAP. Also in 1934 Hitler took two measures to consolidate his power. The first was the elimination of the SA leadership in the Night of the Long Knives (30 June), the second the combination of the positions of Chancellor and President into the title of Führer (August).

These changes are considered in more detail below. Analysis 1 deals with the question as to whether Hitler's appointment was in accord with the Weimar Constitution or whether, in a term the Nazis preferred, it was a '*Machtergreifung*'. Analysis 2 goes on to look at the description of 'legal revolution' as applied to the political changes made by Hitler between February 1933 and August 1934.

ANALYSIS 1: HOW 'LEGAL' WAS HITLER'S RISE TO POWER BY JANUARY 1933?

Right down to his appointment as Chancellor on 30 January 1933, Hitler had shown a preference for radical change. Chapter 1 showed how he had initially tried to seize power through the Munich Putsch (1923) but had subsequently been forced to adopt a new strategy of legality. The purpose of this was to build up broader support for the NSDAP and status for himself. Instead of achieving power through revolution, he would introduce the revolution after achieving power. Yet, while Hitler carried through the strategy of 'legality' for the party, the Nazi movement never lost its revolutionary momentum and his appointment was followed by mass marches celebrating the *Machtergreifung* – or 'seizure of power'.

How evident, therefore, is the 'legal' aspect of Hitler's rise? His appointment was certainly within the ambit of the Constitution, although the process leading up to it had been conditioned by the collapse of the parliamentary system in practice and a growing dependence on the reserve powers of the Constitution under Article 48. This meant that the actual base of power was narrowed to a *camarilla* involving the Chancellor, the President and their immediate advisors. Given this situation, two basic approaches are possible to the issue of 'legality'.

One is that a series of political intrigues meant that a distorted and undemocratic use of the Constitution virtually handed the Chancellorship to Hitler. Bracher, for example, maintains that any sign of parliamentary democracy had ended by May 1932, to be followed by a 'transitional phase' or the 'Schleicher–Papen period'. In this, three main groups held each other in stalemate – the 'outmanoeuvred democratic forces', the 'totalitarian efforts' of the Communists and Nazis, and the 'authoritarian regime of the infinitesimal minority'.[1] The result was a series of underhand and secretive intrigues. According to Bracher, Papen 'did not wish his former friend and patron Schleicher to achieve a success at his expense and was eager, for reasons of political ambition, to get back into the regime. Here lies the historical significance of the negotiations between Hindenburg and Hitler'.[2] In these circumstances the NSDAP, which was at the time 'undergoing a grave crisis as a result of internal conflicts, financial problems, and a loss of votes' was suddenly –and to its own surprise – 'taken into the political game at the highest level'.[3] Tyrell makes a similar point. 'Hitler neither seized nor conquered the chancellorship: it was handed to him in a process which could have been prevented even in the last days of January.'[4] It certainly appeared that Hitler's support had peaked before the end of 1932, as the NSDAP won 34 fewer Reichstag seats in November than they had in July. Yet, Hitler was rescued by Papen's intrigues and 'manoeuvred back on to the main road'.[5] The many historians following this approach conclude that the frequent use of Article 48, the wrangling between Papen and Schleicher, and the appointment of Hitler, although within the wording of the Constitution, were clearly against its intentions. The manner of the handover was a clear sign that the conservative establishment intended to make controlled use of Hitler and the NSDAP to destroy Weimar democracy itself and substitute a more restrictive and authoritarian regime. Hence, as Bracher maintains, 'the purely formalistic conception of a "legal" seizure of power . . . is exposed with cynical frankness'. (See Source 2.1 below.)

There is, however, an alternative approach, which, while acknowledging the backstairs intrigue, stresses that there were fundamental defects within the Constitution itself which allowed for its misuse. The basis of the problem was that the Constitution was being directed against itself because it had never been properly defined; this was because it had not been fully completed in the first place. A case in point was Article 48. It had originally been intended to include more detailed legislation defining its implementation, but this had never been drawn up. To some extent, therefore, politicians were working in the dark. In the circumstances, the fundamental change which had occurred in the orientation of German politics is more convincing in explaining the appointment of Hitler than mere backstairs intrigue. The failure of the SPD to maintain its role as the base of Weimar coalitions, especially between 1924 and 1928, meant that President Hindenburg came to be seen as the main hope for moderates; the SPD even backed him in the 1932 Presidential election, declining to run their own candidate – in contrast to the NSDAP and the KPD. Koch argues that Hindenburg found himself in a series of dilemmas and tried to live with the Constitution rather than distort it. This started with the request of Brüning for access to Article 48 in 1930. 'This Hindenburg did with the utmost reluctance, in the end persuaded only by being made aware that his predecessor Friedrich Ebert had also made use of it.'[6] Hindenburg subsequently aimed to return to parliamentary-majority government, although he wanted a government of 'centre-right rather than centre-left'. By 1932 he had become increasingly reluctant to support a government which lacked the support of the Reichstag. He had already dissolved the Reichstag twice in 1932 – but was not prepared to do it at Schleicher's request since a further election would not give the latter a majority government. Koch maintains that Hindenburg actually wanted to see 'an end to presidential cabinets, the use of Article 48 and emergency decrees'.[7] There is much to be said for this. The Presidential manoeuvres with Papen and Schleicher can be explained – at least in part – as an attempt by Hindenburg to return to normality. He was not prepared to back Papen's minority government indefinitely and therefore, in December 1932, he gave the opportunity to Schleicher, who had hoped for the support of either the SPD or the Nazis. When Schleicher failed to deliver, Hindenburg was eventually persuaded by Papen's alternative – the appointment of Hitler. Although he disliked Hitler, Hindenburg was eventually convinced that he could be controlled by Papen, and that Hitler would be little more than a figurehead with the added recommendation that he would have far more support in the Reichstag than any of his three predecessors. In the circumstances, therefore, it could be argued that the outcome was about as 'legal' as could be achieved under the Constitution. Koch, however, pushes this a step further. 'Hitler', he says, 'achieved power by perfectly legal means' and the fact that the Reichstag was not consulted was its 'own fault' for having previously abandoned its responsibilities. (See Source 2.2.)

How appropriate is the term '*Machtergreifung*' for Hitler's assumption of power in January 1933? On the one hand, it has been seen by historians such as Tyrell as a 'mislabel'.[8] After all, it has to be balanced with the deliberate attempts of the Nazis to win the moderate vote in Germany; the seats won by the NSDAP in the elections of 1932 made it easily the largest party in the Reichstag, with a legitimate claim to represent the widest cross-section of public opinion. In addition, Hitler's appointment as Chancellor was one of the alternatives to a military coup, which *would* have been a seizure of power, and which Hindenburg had already rejected as an option. If anything, 'seizure of power' could be used more appropriately to describe the *Preussenstreich*, Papen's imposition of central control over Prussia on 20 July 1932. Hence the use of the term *Machtergreifung* in January 1933 was largely propaganda, employed by the Nazis to escape from the impression of having achieved power by a backstairs intrigue.

On the other hand, we have to bear in mind the *duality* of Hitler's perception of power. 'Legality' was a strategy only; the threat of radical change always lurked just below the surface, sometimes becoming explicit in his speeches. Hitler never tried to conceal his intention to change the parliamentary system. In a public speech shortly before the 1930 Reichstag elections he stated:

> For us parliament is not an end in itself, but a means to an end. We are not a parliamentary party as a matter of principle; that would be a contradiction of our entire conception. We are a parliamentary party under duress, and what constrains us is the Constitution.[9]

Besides, the activities of the SA and SS were considered so serious a threat to peace and public order that they were banned by Chancellor Brüning in April 1932 (although this was subsequently lifted by Papen in June). In this respect the Nazis were not dissimilar to the Communists, who had a legal superstructure in the form of the KPD but a mass movement – the Red Front – and an agenda which was ultimately revolutionary. As applied to January 1933, '*Machtergreifung*' might therefore be seen as an apt description of the achievement of an aspiration if not the method by which it was achieved. It is, however, possible to extend the term beyond January and to argue that Hitler may have been handed the power that he had wanted to seize – but that once in office he proceeded to seize more than the power that had not been given. This brings us the issue of the 'legal revolution' between 1933 and 1934.

Questions

1. Did Hitler 'seize' the Chancellorship – or was he 'given' it?
2. 'Irrespective of his real motives, Hitler's appointment as Chancellor was entirely "legal" and within the scope of the Constitution.' Do you agree?

ANALYSIS 2: WAS THERE A 'LEGAL REVOLUTION' BETWEEN 1933 AND 1934?

Having, in his eyes at least, accomplished the *Machtergreifung* through the legal strategy to power, Hitler now emphasised the importance of revolutionary change to Germany. This was to be a 'revolution from above' or, as Goebbels called it, the 'national revolution'. At the same time, his options for change were limited by the initial constraints under which he operated. He had, for example, been appointed head of a cabinet in which there were only two other Nazis – Frick as Interior Minister and Goering. Others, like Hugenberg and Gürtner, were members of the DNVP or, like von Neurath and Seldte, non-party. Hence the view of Vice-Chancellor Papen was that 'we have roped him in'.[10] Hitler was also subject to the ultimate authority of President Hindenburg, who remained commander-in-chief of the armed forces. In such a situation any change by Hitler had to be gradual to avoid giving reason for his dismissal by the President or his overthrow by the army. This explains his initial emphasis on legal change, which underlies the paradoxical concept – the 'legal revolution'. Yet how apt is this term as a description of the extension of Hitler's powers after January 1933?

In some ways the changes *can* be described as 'legal'. They were accomplished, step by step, within the literal terms of the Constitution of the Weimar Republic. There are several examples of this process. The Enabling Act, passed on 24 March, contained as part of its preamble the words 'The requirements of legal Constitutional change having been met'.[11] This was a clear reference to the accomplishment of the two-thirds majority required within the Reichstag for an amendment to the Constitution itself. The Enabling Act, in turn, became the vehicle by which the Chancellor now proceeded to use his new executive powers to modify the functions of the political institutions within the Reich. The bureaucracy, for example, was brought into line with the new relationship between executive and legislature by the law of 7 April 'for the restoration of the professional civil service'; by this the civil service was purged of potential opponents and non-Aryans. Meanwhile the system of state government was being extensively reorganised by the law 'for the co-ordination of the *Länder* of the Reich' (31 March). Hitler justified these changes with the claim that they were a more effective coordination (*Gleichschaltung*) of Germany's institutions and allayed any misgivings of the army and judiciary by maintaining at least the pretence at a legal basis. The next step was the law against the new formation of parties; passed on 14 July 1933, this gave the NSDAP a permanent monopoly of political power. Finally, the Chancellorship and the Presidency were combined in the person of the Führer on 1 August 1934, following the death of President Hindenburg.

If the process can be seen as 'legal', is there any mileage in considering them 'revolutionary'? At first sight the extent of the constitutional changes introduced scarcely warrant the description 'revolution', especially by contrast with the changes brought by the Bolsheviks to Russia. Despite the changes of institutional powers, the institutions themselves remained in existence. The Reichstag and the Reichsrat, for example, remained intact as the legislature. By contrast, Lenin had decided in 1918 to remove any remaining connection with a western-style constituent assembly and to substitute a legislature based upon Soviets. Moreover, in Germany all of the previous ministries were retained and the lists of official positions within Hitler's cabinet were remarkably similar to those within the Weimar Republic: these included the Foreign Minister, Interior Minister, Finance Minister, and Ministers for Economics, Justice, Defence, Food, Posts, Labour and Transport. By this analysis the nazification of the institutions of the Weimar Republic occurred in such a way as to minimise the chance of a sudden break which might generate resistance from the conservative powers in Germany. The process was carried through step by step, each depending on the one before. There was therefore a certain inexorable logic which became increasingly difficult to challenge.

There is, however, an alternative point of view. As we have already seen, the concept of 'legal revolution' is paradoxical at the best of times. When applied to the development of Nazi dictatorship the paradox becomes perverse. The whole emphasis was on using the legal powers of the Weimar Constitution to destroy its own political authority, not to amend it. Throughout the period 1933–4 there was at best a very thinly disguised use of legality and, at worst, a blatant disregard for it.

Any actual observance of the constitution was strictly limited: the letter of the law may have been kept, but the spirit of the law was not. Hitler's objective was nothing less than the destruction of the Weimar Republic, which he achieved on three counts. First, he converted emergency powers from an exceptional safeguard into a regular process. The 1933 Enabling Act therefore turned Article 48 on its head by making permanent what had originally been conceived as a temporary power. This completely destroyed the original aim. Article 48 had been included to preserve democracy against future enemies, whereas the Enabling Act was clearly based on the premise that democracy itself was the enemy. A second principle to be torn up was the autonomous rights of the *Länder*. Laws issued under the Enabling Act abolished the powers of the *Länder* legislatures and subordinated the state Ministers-President to the Ministry of the Interior in Berlin. This destroyed the entire federal system which had been a crucial part of the Weimar Constitution. Third, the Law against the New Formation of Parties wiped out the multi-party system, a vital ingredient of the Weimar Republic. Without the element of choice the whole purpose of voting was changed as regular Reichstag elections were replaced by plebiscites on specific issues selected by the Führer himself. Any notion of legality was a mockery. A democratic constitution was imploded by anti-democrats who targeted its emergency powers inwards to destroy the remainder.

It is not even certain that the Nazis observed the *letter* of the Constitution. Hitler's 'legal' changes were forced through with a considerable degree of mobilised pressure – of the very type that the Constitution was originally conceived to prevent. Article 48 was intended for Presidential use to control mass activism against elected governments, not to be unleashed against selected constitutional targets. Hildebrand refers to 'Nazi terrorist tactics' and maintains that 'it was often difficult to distinguish terroristic from legal measures'.[12] For example, the Nazi control over the Ministry of the Interior and other key organs of State enabled them to make free use of the police apparatus. Goering went further, creating an auxiliary police force, the Gestapo, which comprised members of both the SA and the SS. The result was paradoxical: a rampage of law and order directed against political enemies of the Nazi movement – in other words, an officially sanctioned continuation of previously illegal methods. Similar violence can be seen when the SA intimidated the Social Democrat deputies during the Reichstag vote on the Enabling Bill in March 1933. Normal legal principles, ranging from constitutional law to natural equity, would consider any institutional changes to have been invalidated by such gross examples of interference.

In one respect the changes were all too obviously a 'revolution', even if it is stretching a point to describe them as 'legal'. The 'Nazi revolution' contained the element of the mass movement which was entirely incompatible with the principle of 'legality'. This was apparent in the case of several mass interventions which were partially orchestrated by the Nazi regime – before spiralling out of control. One became known as the town hall revolution, in which the SA purged local governments, making it necessary for the central government to step in and redefine the whole nature of the federal system. Another was the mass boycott of Jewish shops in April 1933. It might, of course, be argued that the real revolutionaries were the leaders of the SA and that Hitler took emergency measures against these in the Night of the Long Knives on 30 June 1934. Indeed, Röhm, as leader of the SA, had tried to urge a 'second revolution' on Hitler, arguing that otherwise the radical impetus would be lost. On the other hand, Hitler acted against this 'second revolution' not through a preference for legality, but rather for reasons of safety. If he was to remain in power, Hitler had to avoid the possibility of a military coup launched by conservatives, something which might be triggered by premature expressions of radicalism. Hitler's caution therefore had more to do with common sense and pragmatism than with legality; in any case, 'legality' can hardly be used to describe the method by which the leaders of the SA were disposed of.

Finally, the Nazi apparatus was permeated by a body which was about as far from the constitutional apparatus of the Weimar Republic as it is possible to conceive. The SS–Gestapo–SD complex came to dominate the whole regime. According to Schoenbaum, 'in one form or another the SS made foreign policy, military policy and agricultural policy. It administered occupied territories as a kind of self-contained Ministry of the Interior and maintained itself economically with autonomous enterprises'.[13] This was a revolution in the political structure of Germany which transcended all notions of legality.

Questions

1. Why did Hitler stress the importance of 'legality' in the Nazi revolution?
2. Was the 'legal revolution' anything more than the artificial contrivance of Nazi propaganda?

SOURCES

1: THE 'LEGAL REVOLUTION'

Source 1.1: An extract from the Constitution of the Weimar Republic, 11 August 1919

ARTICLE 48. In the event that the public order and security are seriously disturbed or endangered, the Reich President may take the measures necessary for their restoration, intervening, if necessary, with the aid of the armed forces. For this purpose he may abrogate temporarily, wholly or in part, the fundamental principles laid down in Articles 114, 115, 117, 118, 123, 124 and 153.

The Reich President must, without delay, inform the Reichstag of all measures taken under ... this Article. These measures may be rescinded on demand of the Reichstag.

ARTICLE 76. The Constitution may be amended by law, but acts ... amending the Constitution can take effect only if two-thirds of the legal number of members are present and at least two-thirds of those present consent.

Source 1.2: From the Law for Terminating the Suffering of the People and Nation, 24 March 1933

The Reichstag has passed the following law, which has been approved by the Reichsrat. The requirements of legal Constitutional change having been met, it is being proclaimed herewith:

ARTICLE 1. In addition to the procedure outlined for the passage of legislation in the Constitution, the government also is authorized to pass laws ...

ARTICLE 2. Laws passed by the government may deviate from the Constitution, provided they do not deal with the institutions, as such, of Reichstag and Reichsrat. The prerogatives of the President remain unchanged.

ARTICLE 3. The laws passed by the government shall be issued by the Chancellor and published in the official gazette ...

Source 1.3: Law Against the New Formation of Parties, 14 July 1933

The government has passed the following law, which is being proclaimed herewith:

ARTICLE 1. The sole political party existing in Germany is the National Socialist German Workers' Party.

ARTICLE 2. Whoever shall undertake to maintain the organization of another party, or to found a new party, shall be punished with a sentence of hard labour of up to three years, or of prison between six months and three years, unless other regulations provide for heavier punishment.

Source 1.4: Law Concerning the Head of the German State, 1 August 1934

The government has passed the following law, which is being proclaimed herewith:

ARTICLE 1. The office of President shall be combined with that of Chancellor. Thus all the functions heretofore exercised by the President are transferred to the Führer and Chancellor Adolf Hitler. He has the right to appoint his deputy.

ARTICLE 2. This law is in force as of the date of the death of President von Hindenburg.

Source 1.5: From a newspaper article by Ernst Röhm, June 1933

A tremendous victory has been won. But not absolute victory! ... In the new Germany the disciplined brown storm battalions of the German revolution stand side by side with the armed forces ... The SA and SS are the foundation pillars of the coming National Socialist State – their State for which they have fought and which they will defend. ... The SA and SS will not tolerate the German revolution going to sleep or being betrayed at the half-way stage by non-combatants ... the brown army [so called because of the SA uniforms] is the last levy of the nation, the last bastion against Communism.

Source 1.6: From the Prosecutor's speech at the Nuremberg Trial 1946

On 24th March 1933, only 535 out of the regular 747 deputies of the Reichstag were present. The absence of some was unexcused; they were in protective custody in concentration camps. Subject to the full weight of the Nazi pressure and terror, the Reichstag passed an enabling act known as the 'Law for the Protection of the People and the State', with a vote of 441 in favour.

... Thus the Nazis acquired full political control, completely unrestrained by any provision of the Weimar Constitution.

Questions

1. To what extent were the principles in Source 1.2 based on those in Source 1.1?
2. How accurately does Source 1.5 describe the role of the SA and SS in the changes made in Germany between 1933 and 1934?
3. What questions might the historian wish to ask about Source 1.6 as evidence for the political changes in Germany in 1933?
4. Using these sources, and your own knowledge, comment on the validity of the description of Hitler's constitutional changes between 1933 and 1934 as a 'legal revolution'.

SOURCES

2: HISTORIANS ON THE '*MACHTERGREIFUNG*' AND THE 'LEGAL REVOLUTION'

Source 2.1: From an article by K.D. Bracher, published in English in 1970

Here the purely formalistic conception of a 'legal' seizure of power, which has animated not only the apologies of such central participants as Papen and Meissner but also the juridical interpretations down to our own day, is exposed with cynical frankness. The persons who opened the road to power to Hitler were utterly irresponsible exponents of political and economic aims and illusions, utterly unconcerned with constitutionality. The responsible constitutional authorities, in particular the parties, the Reichstag, and the President, allowed themselves to be excluded from, or misled by, these activities.

Source 2.2: H.W. Koch on Hitler's appointment as Chancellor (from *Aspects of the Third Reich*, published in 1985)

Hitler achieved power by perfectly legal means. That members of the Reichstag had not been consulted was not unconstitutional; rather, this omission was the Reichstag's own fault, for its impotence left Hindenburg with no other choice. Hindenburg has often been accused of making concessions to Hitler which he denied to Schleicher, such as the dissolution of the Reichstag, a presidential government based on Article 48, new elections and an Enabling Law. The crucial difference is that these concessions if made to Schleicher would not in the end have produced a government backed by a parliamentary majority, whereas a Hitler cabinet would have that majority. However, everyone had underestimated Hitler. They acknowledged his great talent for public oratory, but they assumed that once burdened with governmental responsibility he would quickly burn himself out and become Papen's willing follower ...

Source 2.3: A comment by C. Leitz in 1999 on the use of the term '*Machtergreifung*'

On 30 January 1933, Adolf Hitler, leader of the largest party in the Reichstag, was made Reich Chancellor of the Weimar Republic. Hitler's appointment, a constitutional act, has frequently been mislabelled as *Machtergreifung*. Hitler, clearly, did not seize power. However, the rapid progress of events which began with Hitler's appointment and ended on 2 August 1934 with the union of the offices of president and chancellor in the person of 'the Führer and Reich Chancellor Adolf Hitler' did amount to a seizure of complete power. In quick succession, Hitler and his fellow Nazi leaders implemented radical policies in order to make Germany's government their own, thus turning democracy into dictatorship.

Source 2.4: H.W. Koch on Hitler's Enabling Act (from *Aspects of the Third Reich*, published in 1985)

Enabling laws, by which Parliament gives the government the right to legislate for a period of time, were nothing new in Germany's constitutional history. After the outbreak of the First World War the Reichstag had enabled the *Bundesrat* to legislate in the economic sphere for the duration of the war. The first great coalition under Stresemann as well as his successor passed Enabling Laws on 13 October and on 8 December 1923, to stabilise Germany economically, that is to end inflation. *In practice* all presidential cabinets between 1930 and 1932 acted on the basis of enabling laws, that is, emergency decrees. While in 1930 a total of 98 laws were enacted, in 1931 the number of laws had been reduced to 34 compared with 42 emergency decrees. In 1932, 5 laws were passed, and 60 emergency decrees enacted. Hitler had made an Enabling Law one of the conditions of his chancellorship.

Source 2.5: K.D. Bracher's views on the term 'legal revolution' (from *The German Dictatorship*, first published in English in 1970)

The slogan of legal revolution offers the key to the character and development of the National Socialist power seizure. National Socialist propagandists, politicians, and constitutional experts all along emphasized that although Hitler's takeover was the beginning of a revolution that would profoundly affect all aspects of life, it was a completely legal, constitutional process. The paradoxical concept of a 'legal revolution' artificially linked two contradictory axioms of political action and behaviour. The significance of this legality tactic with revolutionary aspirations was in fact more than a mere propaganda gimmick and should not be underestimated. In examining specific components of the political process, we find that this tactic played a decisive role in surrounding this new type of totalitarian power seizure with its seductive aura of effectiveness and made all legal, political, or even intellectual resistance so difficult, and, in the opinion of many, well-nigh impossible.

Questions

1. Compare the arguments of the following extracts:
   *a Sources 2.1 and 2.2
   b Sources 2.4 and 2.5
2. Who presents the stronger case: Bracher (Sources 2.1 and 2.5) or Koch (Sources 2.2 and 2.4)?
3. Does the view of Leitz (Source 2.3) eliminate the need for the term 'legal revolution'?

WORKED ANSWER

*1a *[Comparison involves finding similarities and differences. It is important to avoid describing the contents of the two sources; instead, there should be an integrated comparison of several distinct points drawn from the passages. The two arguments are clearly different – but try to identify at least one or two similarities as well. Extracts should be used from the sources, but placed – in quotation marks – in the context of* *your own sentences. Finally, be aware of the limits to the question. You are not asked to comment on the validity of the arguments or to explain* why *they differ. These issues are addressed in other questions.]*

Sources 2.1 and 2.2 both deal with the issue of whether Hitler's assumption of power in January 1933 was 'legal'; but they do so from different angles. Bracher (Source 2.1) refers to a 'legal' seizure of power as a 'purely formalistic conception' which was 'exposed with cynical frankness' both at the time and 'down to our own day' (Source 2.1.). Koch, on the other hand, refers to Hitler achieving power 'by perfectly legal means' in terms of the constitution (Source 2.2). Secondly, both consider the Reichstag responsible for Hitler's appointment – but in different contexts. Bracher names it as one of the participants, along with other 'constitutional authorities' such as 'the parties' and 'the President' (Source 2.1). Koch, on the other hand, places heavier responsibility on the Reichstag than on the President; Hindenburg had not consulted the Reichstag because of the latter's 'impotence'. Indeed, Hindenburg had 'no other choice' but to make 'concessions to Hitler' that he had previously 'denied to Schleicher' (Source 2.2). The implication is therefore that the President was trying to uphold the constitution in the absence of any Reichstag initiative – in contrast to Bracher's condemnation of both the Reichstag and the President who were 'utterly unconcerned with constitutionality'. Finally, both historians see the appointment of Hitler in a negative light and as a sign of the collapse of democracy in Germany. But Bracher condemns the 'utterly irresponsible' attempts to achieve certain 'political and economic aims and illusions' (Source 2.1); the implication is that such 'exponents' were trying to exploit Hitler as much as he was them. Koch, however, places more stress on the attempt to control Hitler rather than to use him; their assumption was that, 'once burdened with governmental responsibility', he would become 'Papen's willing follower' (Source 2.2).

3

THE NAZI DICTATORSHIP

BACKGROUND

The two diagrams (*Figures 2 and 3*) indicate the main changes between the Weimar Republic and the Third Reich. Figure 2 shows a clear distinction in the Weimar system between legislature and executive, and between central and state institutions. This dichotomy largely disappears in *Figure 3*, indicating the emergence of a more centralised and authoritarian Nazi regime.

In *Figure 2* the legislature represents the Republic in two main layers. Centrally, the Reichstag is the elected body for the Reich as a whole and the Reichsrat the appointed representative of the individual states, or *Länder*, which made up the Reich. The *Länder* also have their own elected state assemblies, or *Landtäge*. *Figure 3*, by contrast, shows that there are no longer elections to the Reichstag and that the Reichsrat and the *Landtäge* have been abolished altogether. The role of the electorate – extensive in *Figure 2* – has been reduced in *Figure 3* to participation in the occasional plebiscite.

There is also a change in the executive. *Figure 2* shows a dual leadership, comprising a directly elected President and a Chancellor with the confidence of the elected Reichstag. In *Figure 3* the leadership has narrowed to a single Führer, who is no longer subject to election. In central government most of the ministries are retained in *Figure 3*, but with the addition of new Nazi special deputies. A new Chancellery has also been added, its offices all serving the Führer direct. The local or state executives, autonomous in *Figure 2*, continue in *Figure 3* to be headed

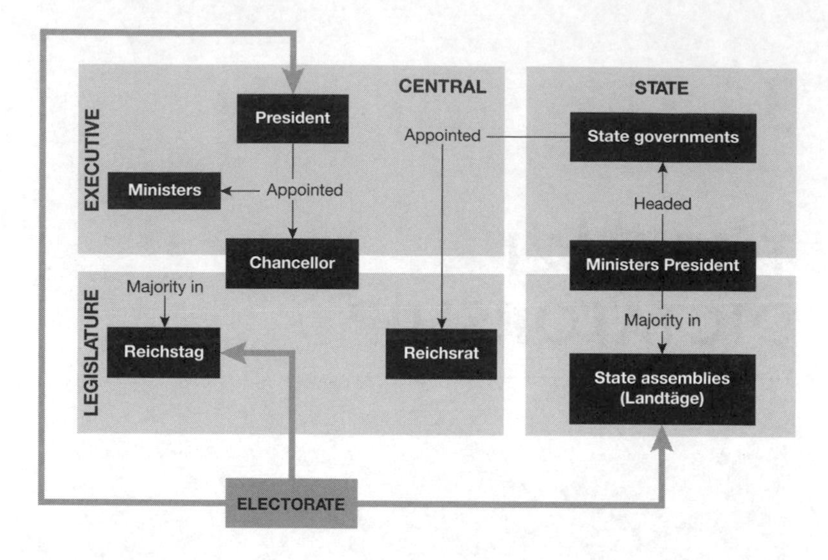

Figure 2 Political structure of the Weimar Republic

by their Ministers but, at the same time, are also under the authority of new Nazi officials – the Reich Governors (*Reichsleiter*).

Finally, *Figure 3* shows the addition of new special agencies in the Third Reich, each responsible directly to the Führer. These include the SS–Gestapo–SD complex, the SA and the Four Year Plan Office. None of these are shown in *Figure 1* since they had no part to play in the Weimar system; indeed, before 1933, the SA and SS were organisations contained within the Nazi movement itself.

How these changes came about was explored in Chapter 2, Analysis 2. Chapter 3 explains how they characterised a political dictatorship (Analysis 1) and whether they were necessarily efficient (Analysis 2).

ANALYSIS 1: HOW WAS GERMANY GOVERNED BETWEEN 1933 AND 1939?

Germany was governed between 1933 and 1939 by a permanent dictatorship which contained some traditional institutions while imposing sweeping changes upon them. Although some of the original features were retained, their functions were distorted to establish the basis of an incontestable political authority. This had the following features, all explored in greater detail below. The constraints imposed by the Weimar Constitution of 1919 were gradually dismantled; the legislature was weakened at the centre and destroyed in the *Länder*; the executive, by

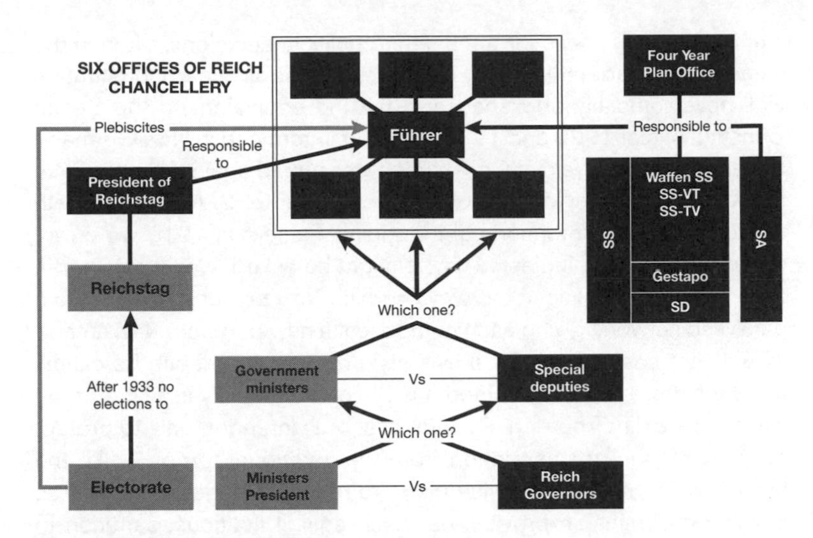

Figure 3 Political structure of the Third Reich

contrast, was strengthened and personalised in the name of the Führer; this involved the destruction of the federal structure which had been an integral part of previous German constitutions; it also meant the destruction of the independence of trade unions, judiciary and professional bodies. The whole process was accomplished by a policy of enforced coordination (*Gleichschaltung*) which imposed officials from the NSDAP into all layers of the system; this meant the building of new structures – political, economic, and policing. The whole purpose of these changes was to build a people's community (*Volksgemeinschaft*) which rested on racial principles and targeted minorities that had been ideologically 'rejected'.

Like any permanent dictatorship, the Nazi regime cut itself free from the constraints of a constitution. The purpose of the Weimar Constitution had been the protection of democracy: for this purpose it had imposed limits on arbitrary political power, although allowing the exercise of executive authority to prevent revolution and the collapse of the Republic. In effect, this meant that 'temporary' dictatorship was possible to preserve democracy – but only within the limits allowed by the constitution; even during the period of 'presidential dictatorship' in 1931 and 1932, President Hindenburg did not give up all hope of returning to the normal use of the Constitution. With permanent dictatorships, especially Fascist Italy, Nazi Germany and Stalinist Russia, the reverse applied. Whatever its theoretical status, the constitution was circumscribed by actual political power; as such, it became little more than the process for transmitting political decisions, often in the name of the leadership itself. It is true that the Weimar Constitution was never officially abolished and that no equivalent to the Soviet Constitutions of 1922 and 1936 was ever introduced in Nazi Germany. Nevertheless, the Weimar Constitution was turned against itself in what the Nazis called the 'legal revolution' (see Chapter 2, Analysis 2) with the result that the intentions of its original framers in 1919 were rendered entirely meaningless. Why, it might be asked, was it retained it at all? The answer lies in the way in which Nazi power crept across a paralysed network, giving each component a new purpose. Nazi authority was not based on a Bolshevik-style revolution, despite its claims to *Machtergreifung* (examined in Chapter 2, Analysis 1), but on claims to legality. This 'legality', however, was intended only to protect the new regime against action from the traditional forces – like the army – which might otherwise claim to represent legality. Hence, as Bracher maintains, in providing a quasi-legal, if fictitious, sanction to acts of government, 'it was highly effective in deceiving and mollifying a legalistically oriented civil service and judiciary'.[1]

The first casualty in any permanent dictatorship is the legislature – even though this is not necessarily abolished. The Reichstag was retained but its powers were substantially altered in the ways explained in Chapter 2, Analysis 2. Its monopoly on legislation was withdrawn by the Enabling Act of March 1933 and its role as the forum of party representation and debate was ended by the Law Against the New Formation of Parties (July 1933). Total control by the NSDAP was officially declared on 14 July 1934 and the presidency of the Reichstag was declared under Goering. This meant an overall change in function as well. The Nazi constitutional lawyer, Huber, maintained that the Reichstag was 'an institution that expresses the political agreement of nation and Government', intended to 'document the unity of Führer and nation'. Indeed, it would be 'impossible for the Reichstag to propose and pass a law that did not originate with the Führer or at least had not been approved by him beforehand'.[2] Elections were not continued beyond March 1933 since all parties other than the NSDAP were banned. Instead, the opinion of the electorate was sought as an expected endorsement of the government's policies in the form of plebiscites to give approval for decisions already taken. Altogether five of these were held in the period 1933–8. These included popular votes on Germany's withdrawal from the League of Nations in 1933, Hitler's powers as Führer (August 1934), the reunification of the Saar with Germany (January 1935), Hitler's reoccupation of the Rhineland (March 1936) and the Anschluss (April 1938). State (*Länder*) representation was given shorter shrift. The Reichsrat was abolished by the Nazi-controlled Reichstag with the intention of removing the remnants of the federal system (see below) and to prevent the possibility of local political influences resisting the spread of the Nazi political system. As for the constitutional system of checks and balances – this was now seen as an expression of the political uncertainty of liberal democracy. Since the Nazi regime intended to do away with all such uncertainty and hence throw out any such constraint, the legislature needed only one central chamber.

The key characteristic of a dictatorship is an executive unfettered by a potentially hostile legislature. During the Weimar period the Presidential emergency powers could be used under Article 48 but these could be challenged by the Reichstag. As we saw in Chapter 2, Analysis 2, Hitler, as Chancellor, exercised these powers in February 1933 and then effectively had them transferred to the Chancellor through the Enabling Act of March 1933. This conferred on the executive the same right as the Reichstag to initiate legislation. The remaining obstacle, however, was the existence of a dual head of state – in the form of the President and Chancellor. Some dictatorships managed to coexist with this situation. Fascist Italy, for example, retained the duality in the form of the *Duce* (Mussolini) and the King (Victor Emanuel III). In Nazi Germany, however, Hitler was reprieved from a similar situation by the death of Hindenburg in 1934. This was followed in August by the Law concerning the Head of State of the German Reich, which combined the Chancellorship with the Presidency, centralising both offices under Hitler as Führer. From this new title emerged personalised dictatorship with the hydra of *Führerprinzip* examined below.

No dictatorship finds it easy to coexist with a federal system. The Nazi regime faded it out altogether. The process started with action against state governments in the 'town hall revolution' of March 1933. Particularly affected were Hamburg, Hesse, Lübeck, Bremen, Baden, Saxony and Württemberg. This was followed – belatedly in terms of the 'legal revolution' – by legislation in the Reichstag in March and April 1933 – the First and Second Laws for the Co-ordination of the Federal States – which created the office of Reich Governor (*Reichsstatthälter*) and imposed Nazi Party control. The next stage was the formal abolition of the federal structure by the abolition of the Reichsrat in January 1934 and the disappearance of the state parliaments, or *Landtäge*, in 1934. The state Ministers-President remained but they came under the control of central government and were rivalled by Nazi functionaries. All this was in contrast with the Soviet system. The latter introduced, in Stalin's 1936 Constitution, the fiction of federalism through the Union of Soviet Socialist Republics, even though the constitutional structure was dominated throughout by the centralised Communist Party. Hitler preferred to take the short cut of abolishing the fiction of federalism and confirming the actuality of centralism. Perhaps there was not a great deal of immediate difference between two versions of totalitarianism.

No dictatorship is able to tolerate independence in the civil service, trade unions, judiciary or professional bodies. The Law for the Restoration of the Professional Public Service (April 1933) secured the dismissal of civil servants not of 'Aryan' descent or unwilling to guarantee unconditional allegiance to the Nazi regime. Eventually all civil servants of any influence were required to be loyal members of the NSDAP. This radicalisation reversed the previous pattern of the Weimar Republic, where the personnel within the civil service had provided an underlying continuity – albeit a conservative one – between the changing political composition of the different governments. A month later, in April 1933, the Nazis abolished the trade union movement, substituting a new German Labour Front or DAF (*Deutsche Arbeitsfront*); the Beauty of Labour or SdA (*Schönheit der Arbeit*) and Strength Through Joy or KdF (*Kraft durch Freude*) were added in November 1933 (see Chapter 7, Analysis 3). In the Weimar Republic the judiciary had been independent of government control, even if it did have a reputation for favouring individuals and groups on the political right while acting harshly against those on the left. The Nazis changed the official status of the judiciary, establishing the People's Court in 1934 to deal with crimes against the state, while new guidelines were issued by Hans Frank for the handling of legal cases. Judge Roland Freisler summed up the new approach in the words: 'Just is that which is useful to the German people.'[3] Finally, all professional bodies were replaced by Nazi equivalents and tied to the relevant central ministry, usually the Ministry of Education or the Ministry for People's Enlightenment and Propaganda. Examples included the National Socialist Teachers' League (NSLB) and the German News Agency (DNB); these are dealt with in Chapter 4.

All of these changes involved the process of *Gleischaltung* – variously interpreted as 'coordination', 'overlapping' or 'forced integration'. Existing state structures were merged into or linked with new part organs. All the central government departments were kept – for example the Ministries of Foreign Affairs, Interior and Education – as was the civil service. Several new ones were added, including the Ministry for People's Enlightenment and Propaganda under Goebbels (March 1933) and the Ministry of Churches under Kerrl (July 1935). At the same time, new offices were added at both central and local levels. Centrally, Special Deputies were introduced, such as the General

Inspector for German Roads and the Youth Leader of the Reich. These were more distinctively Nazi organisations, often fulfilling similar functions to the Departments. Locally, the *Gauleiter* were given greater power as state Governors, who often overlapped with the Ministers-President. In addition to the traditional institutions and the parallel offices, a third layer emerged, which was independent of both. These included the office of the Deputy Führer, the Four Year Plan Office (along, confusingly, with its six ministries), and the SS–Gestapo–SD complex under the authority of Himmler.

All of these came under the direct control of the Führer, who was seen as the personal embodiment of the state. Oaths of allegiance were taken to him by the army, the judiciary and civil servants and his powers were enhanced by the development of a cult of personality and the *Führerprinzip*. Within the new system, Hitler was the fount of Nazi ideology and the rationale for action and power; other Nazi leaders – Hess, Goebbels, Himmler, Goering, Heydrich, Ley, Rust, von Schirach, Frank, Bormann and Rosenberg – all acted in his name. The *Führerprinzip* was upheld by all the organs of a totalitarian state. The Ministry of People's Enlightenment and Propaganda manipulated his image on radio, in films and in the press, the Hitler Youth focused upon him the loyalty of youth and the RAD ordered the lives of the workforce to fit his vision of society. But the extent to which Hitler was personally involved in directing the new structure was another matter. As will be shown in Analysis 2, a vacuum developed at the centre of power, resulting in conflicts and chaos which – paradoxically – were both the antithesis and the hallmark of the personalised dictatorship of Nazi Germany.

The Nazi state differed from most others in one important respect – it represented only a selected part of the population. Those Germans who were defined by racial criteria as Aryans were considered to be integral to the *Volksgemeinschaft*. Others were excluded: social 'deviants', hereditarily 'diseased', 'undesirable' groups and racial 'inferiors' – especially Romanies and Jews. For some of these the state exercised punitive powers, for others the protection normally conferred by the state on behalf of its citizens was removed altogether. The implications were huge, with the passing of discriminatory legislation such as the Nuremberg Laws (1935), the growth of a network of concentration camps, the compulsory sterilisation of targeted individuals and groups, and, in extreme cases, the application of 'euthanasia'. Above all, a policy of extermination was adopted from 1941 onwards. In the Nazi dictatorship the role of the state was therefore not only that of 'selector', but also of 'eliminator'. This is the most extreme function – or malfunction – that any state is capable of fulfilling.

Questions

1. In what ways did the Nazi dictatorship differ from the 'Presidential dictatorship' of the last two years of the Weimar Republic?
2. To what extent did the Nazis change Germany institutionally after 1933?

ANALYSIS 2: HOW EFFECTIVE WAS THE NAZI POLITICAL SYSTEM?

The nazification of the whole system of government in Germany might suggest that the organisation was tight and carefully structured. The precision with which the Nazi legal revolution occurred also infers that Hitler had full control over the whole process. The Third Reich, in other words, might be seen as a model of efficiency precisely because the effort taken to establish it had been so minimal.

Such an approach would, however, be open to fundamental question and a number of historians have presented a very different picture. It is generally argued that, far from being orderly, the Nazi dictatorship was actually prone to internal conflict which resulted in a surprising degree of chaos. The basic problem was that the Third Reich was a hotchpotch of overlapping institutions and structures. This was the result of the minimalist approach to constitutional change. Instead of knocking down the old structure, the Nazis had simply constructed another on top of it. The effect was the duplication of functions and the conflict between officials in central and local government. This was apparent even to contemporaries; Otto Dietrich, Hitler's press chief, later wrote in his Memoirs: 'In the twelve years of his rule in Germany Hitler produced the biggest confusion in government that has ever existed in a civilized state.' (See Source 1.3 below.)

Examples abound of the overlapping of traditional and new institutions creating a web of conflicting structures. At the centre the process was especially pronounced. Special Deputies were appointed in parallel to the heads of the old government ministries, often performing similar functions to them. For example, the General Inspector for German Roads, a newly appointed official, overlapped some of the functions of the traditional Minister for Posts and Transport: the result was frequent conflict between the respective incumbents, Todt and von Rubenach. The Youth Leader of the Reich, von Schirach, similarly duplicated the functions of the Minister of Education, Ley. The confusion was compounded by the development of a third layer of personnel, who were outside the scope both of the normal ministries and of the parallel party functionaries. These included the office of the Deputy Führer, the Four Year Plan Office, and the SS–Gestapo–SD complex under the authority of Himmler. All this resulted in widespread inefficiency. The main problems were the duplication of functions between agencies and growing conflict between officials. On numerous occasions appeals were made to the Führer himself to arbitrate in disputes between them. His response was to distance himself from routine disputes and to rely upon Hess as a mediator. Faced with this sort of problem, it is hardly surprising that there was a threat of creeping inertia among subordinates as officials at all levels shied away from taking responsibility through fear of making a mistake – not of policy but of jurisdiction.

Much the same problems applied in the area of local government. Each of the *Länder* retained its traditional official, the Minister-President, or Prime Minister. After the legislation of 1934 had ended the autonomous powers of the state legislatures, the Minister-President became the local official subordinate to the Ministry of the Interior. This would seem a logical enough process: the consolidation of Hitler's dictatorship through the process of centralisation. But the whole thing became more cumbersome with the addition of ten Reich governors, appointed by the regime from the most important of the Party *Gauleiter*. Again, their function was to ensure the full implementation of the Führer's policy, but again they came into conflict with existing officials. Overall, Noakes and Pridham argue, the state authorities were a façade, 'the substance of which was progressively being eaten away by the cancerous growth of the new organization under individuals appointed by Hitler'.[4]

Explaining this complex process has produced a major historiographical debate. There are two broad possibilities, the historians expounding them being loosely categorised as 'intentionalists' and 'structuralists'.

The 'intentionalists' argue that Hitler exploited this confused state of affairs in order to maintain his own authority; in this sense, Nazi Germany was based on a monocratic power structure, albeit an inefficient one. Jäckel, for example, refers to the 'sole ruler' in the Nazi regime (*Alleinherrschaft*): 'the essential political decisions were taken by a single individual, in this case by Hitler'.[5] In the process, Hitler deliberately set Nazi institutions and officials against each other in order to maintain his own position as the only one who could manoeuvre between them. Bracher argues that Hitler remained detached from the struggles between officials and that: 'the antagonisms of power were only resolved in the key position of the omnipotent Führer'. Hence 'the dictator held a key position precisely because of the confusion of conflicting power groups'.[6] Hildebrand makes an essentially similar point. 'The confusion of functions among a multitude of mutually hostile authorities made it necessary and possible for the Führer to take decisions in every case of dispute, and can be regarded as a foundation of his power.'[7]

In contrast to this approach, the 'structuralists' (or 'functionalists') stress that the institutional chaos in Nazi Germany was entirely *un*intended. Instead, it was the result of confusion, neglect and sheer incompetence. The basis of the argument is the polycratic nature of power in the Third Reich, rather than Hitler's monocratic dictatorship. Hitler's power was only one element of a 'multidimensional' power structure incorporating all the components seen above. Far from being able to distance himself effectively from competing officials in order to maintain his position, Hitler simply showed incompetence and hence administrative weakness. Broszat argues that: 'The authoritative Führer's will was expressed only irregularly, unsystematically and incoherently.'[8] Far from sowing discord to maintain his own power, Hitler simply refrained from any coherent regulation. Sometimes this was because he saw rivalry as a natural – darwinistic – function of power, only occasionally requiring the intervention of the Führer. More often it was because he could not be bothered with the tedious routine of administration – unless something specific caught his attention. According to Mommsen, 'Instead of functioning as a balancing element in the government, Hitler disrupted the conduct of affairs by continually acting on sudden impulses, each one different, and partly by delaying decisions on current matters'.[9] Such 'Führer Decrees' and 'Führer Directives' gave 'the force of law' to 'throw-away remarks by the dictator' and 'reflected the interests of whatever influences were in the ascendant at any particular moment'.[10]

At the height of the original debate, these two sets of interpretations seemed mutually exclusive. To some extent the boundaries between them have blurred since the 1980s and a judicious combination of their main elements is therefore possible. There is no doubt that Hitler did whatever he could to fragment potential opposition: indeed, he had already welcomed the partial collapse of the party while he was in Landsberg prison. It is not, therefore, beyond the realms of possibility that he welcomed discordance within the State in order to regulate his subordinates and prevent the emergence of 'over-mighty' barons. The 'intentionalists' therefore have a point. On the other hand, it is difficult to imagine this being *planned*. The deliberate projection of chaos carries enormous risks which may seem justifiable in retrospect but which can hardly have been chanced at the time. In any case, if the original 'legal revolution' had been 'planned' on the basis of the simplest and most direct route to dictatorship, what would have been the logic in complicating the process by deliberately creating overlapping bureaucratic layers? The balance of credibility therefore switches here to the 'structuralists'.

This deals only with the *origins* of the chaos. Once we focus on its *continuation*, we have two further possibilities. In one respect, Bracher's perspective makes more sense. Conceding that the chaos was unintended, what possible motive could Hitler have had for tolerating it – unless it was in his interests to do so? Would it be too much to assume that, having adjusted his approach to taking power by 1933 and to consolidating it by 1934, Hitler would have been unable to correct any aberrations thrown up in the process? It is more likely that it suited Hitler to live with the chaos which had emerged despite his efforts, because this was an effective way of cancelling out troublemakers within the party. On the other hand, it could also be argued that Hitler had no choice in the matter. His own lack of interest in administration meant that the sheer complexity of involvement in a polycratic structure was beyond his limited skills: Broszat is therefore also convincing on this score.

There is a final approach, which also combines facets of both approaches. In 1934 Werner Willikens, State Secretary in the Reich Ministry of Agriculture, warned delegates not to expect constant direction from above. Instead, 'it is the duty of everybody to try to work towards the Führer along the lines he would wish'.[11] (See Source 1.2 and Kershaw's comments in Source 1.6.) The instruction of Willikens might be seen as support for the 'intentionalist' position in maintaining the 'will of the Führer' as the overall defining process, even to the extent of competing interpretations of what that will was; after all, they were expressed as policies which were based on monocratic principles. On the other hand, the motives for invoking the 'will of the Führer' and 'working towards the Führer' were usually pragmatic – based either on individual ambition or on departmental interests. The emphasis here would be more 'structuralist' since it highlighted the complexities of polycratic rivalries and clashes.

Whatever the combination of 'intentionalist' and 'structuralist' interpretations, one thing is certain. The chaos within the Nazi regime extended to the key decisions made by it during the twelve years of its existence. The result was the growing radicalisation of economic measures, foreign policy, social measures and – above all – anti-Semitism. The 'intentionalist'/'structuralist' debate therefore reappears in different forms in other Chapters in this book.

Questions

1. In administrative terms, did the Weimar Republic ever give way completely to the Third Reich?
2. Does the notion of 'ordered chaos' make any sense when applied to the political system of Nazi Germany?

SOURCES

1: THE FUNCTIONING OF POLITICAL INSTITUTIONS IN NAZI GERMANY

Source 1.1: From a communication from the Minister of the Interior to the Chancellor, 4 June 1934

If we are to stick to the idea of a central and unified leadership of the Reich through the Reich Chancellor and the departmental ministers assisting him, who corporately together with the Reich Chancellor form the Reich Government, then it is impossible to leave differences of opinion between a departmental minister on the one hand and a governor on the other ... to be decided by the Reich Chancellor. On the contrary the decision of the Reich Minister who represents the Reich Government in his area of responsibility must be accepted by the Reich Governor without allowing him a form of legal redress against the decision of the Reich Minister in the field of legislation.

Source 1.2: From a statement by Werner Willikens, State Secretary in the Reich Ministry of Agriculture, to a meeting of state agricultural representatives, February 1934

Everyone who has the opportunity to observe it knows that the Führer can hardly dictate from above everything which he intends to realize sooner or later. On the contrary, up till now everyone with a post in the new Germany has worked best when he has, so to speak, worked towards the Führer. Very often ... it has been the case ... that individuals have simply waited for orders and instructions. Unfortunately, the same will be true in the future: but in fact it is the duty of everybody to try to work towards the Führer along the lines he would wish. Anyone who makes mistakes will notice it soon enough. But anyone who really works towards the Führer along his lines and towards his goal will certainly both now and in the future one day have the finest reward in the form of the sudden legal confirmation of his work.

Source 1.3: From the Memoirs of Otto Dietrich, Hitler's press chief, published in 1955

In the twelve years of his rule in Germany Hitler produced the biggest confusion in government that has ever existed in a civilized state. During his period of government, he removed from the organization of the state all clarity of leadership and produced a completely opaque network of competencies. It was not laziness or an excessive degree of tolerance which led the otherwise energetic and forceful Hitler to tolerate this real witch's cauldron of struggles for position and conflicts over competence. It was intentional. With this technique he systematically disorganized the upper echelons of the Reich leadership in order to develop and further the authority of his own will until he became a despotic tyrant.

Source 1.4: From K.D. Bracher, *The German Dictatorship*, published in English in 1970

The Führer constituted the only definite link between and above the jurisdictional thicket of party agencies and state machinery. The omnipotence of his position rested not least on the ill-defined relationship of party and state; he alone was able to solve the costly jurisdictional conflicts which were part of the system. Regardless of whether this was an unavoidable dilemma of totalitarian dictatorship or a consciously wielded tool of dictatorial rule, the widespread idea about the better organized and more effective 'order' of totalitarian one-man rule is a myth all too easily believed in crisis-ridden democracies. It is the lie that animates all authoritarian movements, then and now; its matrix is an ideology of order which vilifies the pluralistic character of modem society, subjugating it to a misanthropic as well as unreal ideal of efficiency modelled on technical perfection and military order.

Source 1.5: From an article by H. Mommsen, 'National Socialism – Continuity and Change', published in 1991

Throughout his reign, Hitler was fearful of institution-backed power; he certainly never displayed the slightest understanding of any attempts towards setting it up. His aversion from any institutional restriction may indeed be explained by the circumstances of his life; in some respects an element of personal insecurity seems to be involved ...

Instead of acting as a balancing element in the government, Hitler disrupted the conduct of affairs, partly by continually acting on sudden impulses, each one different, and partly by delaying decisions on current matters. His totally unbureaucratic type of leadership, nothing being dealt with in writing, his frequent absences from Berlin, his utter lack of contact with departmental ministers, his dependence on advice from outsiders (often given by chance-comers and usually incompetent), and his dismissal of officialdom as too unwieldy to carry out political necessities – all this gave his government an aura of instability and sometimes of self-contradiction.

Source 1.6 From an article by I. Kershaw, 'Working towards the Führer: reflections of the nature of the Hitler Dictatorship', published in 1997

'Working towards the Führer' may be taken in a literal, direct sense with reference to Party functionaries, in the way it was meant in the extract cited. In the case of the SS, the ideological executive of the Führer's will, the tasks associated with 'working towards the Führer' offered endless scope for barbarous initiatives, and with them institutional expansion, power, prestige, and enrichment. The career of Adolf Eichmann, rising from a menial role in a key policy area to the manager of the 'Final Solution', offers a classic example.

But the notion of 'working towards the Führer' could be interpreted, too, in a more indirect sense where ideological motivation was secondary, or perhaps even absent altogether, but where the objective function of the actions was nevertheless to further the potential for implementation of the goals which Hitler embodied. Individuals seeking material gain through career advancement in Party or State bureaucracy, the small businessman aiming to destroy a competitor through a slur on his 'aryan' credentials, or ordinary citizens settling scores with neighbours by denouncing them to the Gestapo, were all, in a way, 'working towards the Führer'.

Questions

*1. What can be inferred from Source 1.2 about the problems which the State Secretary in the Reich Ministry of Agriculture was attempting to resolve?

2. How useful and reliable would Sources 1.1 and 1.3 be to the historian studying the political structure of Nazi Germany?

3. According to Haffner, Hitler's power over the Nazi political and administrative system was based on his use of 'controlled chaos'. Comment on this view in the light of Sources 1.1 to 1.6.

WORKED ANSWER

*1 *[The answer to this question needs to be confined entirely to the material in the Source. At the same time, the reasoning behind the statements should be analysed. The emphasis therefore needs to be on inferences from the Source rather than supplements to it.]*

The advice provided to agricultural representatives by Secretary of State Willikens is expressed in a positive way; this would, however, have been a response to certain negative perceptions. The initial statement that 'the Führer can hardly dictate from above everything' would have been a criticism of those who expected constant and direct leadership. Hence those who 'simply waited for orders and instructions' would need to be more willing to exercise their initiative. At the same time, any such responsibility would need to be more in accordance with the official policy. Closer co-ordination was therefore necessary since 'it is the duty of everybody to try to work towards the Führer along the lines he would wish'. There is also an implied criticism of the low level of some of the work carried out since the Secretary of State saw it as necessary to point out that those making mistakes 'will notice it soon enough'. The overall tenor of the Source is the need for greater responsibility in decision-making, undertaken in the spirit of proper delegation: this would receive 'the finest reward' through 'sudden legal confirmation'.

4

INDOCTRINATION AND PROPAGANDA

BACKGROUND

Indoctrination and propaganda were the means by which the Nazis aimed to secure voluntary support for the new regime; coercion and terror were reserved for those individuals or groups who failed to respond or who were not included within the scope of the People's Community or *Volksgemeinschaft*. The former process was dominated by Joseph Goebbels, the latter by Heinrich Himmler (see Chapter 5).

Goebbels had started his political career as Gauleiter of Berlin in 1926, progressing to Party *Reichspropagandaleiter* from 1929. After the rise of the Nazis to power, he made a considerable contribution to the process of *Gleichschaltung* in the administration (see Chapter 3) and headed the new Ministry of People's Enlightenment and Propaganda. This took over various functions of other Ministries, especially the Interior, its task made easier by the nazification of the civil service and the imposition of controls on the media. Goebbels made his overall intention clear from the start. He told a press conference on 15 March: 'It is not enough for people to be more or less reconciled to our regime, to be persuaded to adopt a neutral attitude towards us; rather we want to work on people until they have capitulated to us, until they grasp ideologically that what is happening in Germany today not only must be accepted but also can be accepted'.[1] He also emphasised the need to take full advantage of the latest technology in order to achieve maximum saturation to create complete loyalty and subservience.

This chapter looks at the impact of his policies on youth and the remainder of the population. The former were subject to the dual impact of educational changes from the Ministry of Education under Bernard Rust, and the initiatives from the Hitler Youth headed by Baldur von Schirach. Analysis 1 considers the extent to which the Nazis succeeded in their efforts to transform the curriculum and teaching methods, as well as the administrative conflicts between the Ministry of Education and the Hitler Youth movement. The latter had been established within the Nazi movement in 1926 and, for a while, had to compete with rival organisations set up by the Catholic Church and the Centre Party, the Communists and Social Democrats on the left and the DNVP on the right; this was in non-political youth movements. By 1933 the Hitler Youth was still in a minority but the banning of other groups soon inflated its numbers. In 1939 all Germans between the ages of 10 and 18 were compulsorily recruited. Below the age of 10 boys joined the *Pimpf*, between 10 and 14 the German Young People (*Deutsches Jungvolk* or DJ) and from 14 to 18 the Hitler Youth itself (*Hitler Jugend*, HJ). The equivalent for girls between 10 and 14 was the League of German Girls (*Jungmädelbund* or JM) and League of German Maidens (*Bund Deutscher Mädel*, BDM). Analysis 1 also deals with the impact of the HJ and examines recent views on the importance of its contacts with the SS.

The rest of the population were controlled through other organisations, all of which were under the Minister of Labour, Robert Ley. The workforce were regulated by the Reich Labour Front and its subordinate sections, Beauty of Labour (*Schönheit der Arbeit* or SdA) and Strength through Joy (*Kraft durch Freude* or KdF); these are dealt with in Chapter 7. But the overall coordination of indoctrination came through the Ministry of People's Enlightenment and Propaganda under the personal direction of Goebbels. Within this was the Reich Chamber of Culture (*Reichskulturkammer*), along with a series of sub-chambers for press, radio, theatre, music, creative arts and film. In theory the regime had the power to apply negative censorship in whatever form it considered necessary and, more constructively, to shape the development of culture at all levels. Analysis 2 is divided into two main parts, the first considering the impact of the mass media and the second dealing with the Nazi attempts to transform the various components of German culture.

In assessing the effects of these changes and institutions, a distinction needs to be made between 'propaganda' and 'indoctrination'. To an extent these were connected, since the long-term indoctrination of the population involved regular exposure to official propaganda. Yet propaganda was on the whole more directly related to the use of channels such as the radio, cinema and press, while indoctrination was a process carried out in education, the youth movements, the work place and the armed forces. Propaganda provided the highlights, indoctrination the main body.

ANALYSIS 1: ASSESS THE IMPACT OF NAZI INDOCTRINATION ON GERMANY'S YOUTH

In a speech made in 1933 Hitler said: 'When an opponent declares, "I will not come over to your side," I calmly say, "Your child belongs to us already".' He added: 'What are you? You will pass on. Your descendants, however, now stand in the new camp. In a short time they will know nothing else but this new community.'[2] This indicated the priority of the Nazi Party and Nazi regime. The emphasis of the former on youth had always been apparent during Hitler's rise to power; this would now continue into the future, creating a commitment to the new ideals of the *Volksgemeinschaft* undiluted by any lasting influences from the past. Hence, although indoctrination was a long-term process, it could be applied most rapidly and effectively to Germany's youth – within the two main areas of education and youth movements.

The role of indoctrination in schools was extensive. The Law of 20 March 1933 provided for the separate education of boys and girls, ended confessional schools and placed curbs on private education. Schools also experienced a radicalisation of the curriculum which saw the introduction of race study, eugenics and health biology, all used as vehicles for imparting Nazi ideology. According to Hitler in *Mein Kampf*, 'No boy and no girl must leave school without having been led to an ultimate realisation of the necessity and essence of blood purity'.[3] Conventional subjects, such as History and even Mathematics were given a twist: they were geared at every possible opportunity to enhancing Nazism. According Rust, the Minister of Education, the purpose of textbooks was 'the ideological education of young German people'.[4] For example, 22 out of the 76 pages of the official Mathematics textbook contained ideological references such as calculations of the cost to produce lunatic asylums as opposed to workers' housing.[5] Another radical departure from the past was the preparation of boys and girls for separate and obviously stereotyped roles; in the process, matriculation options for girls were restricted to modern languages or home economics, compared with the options for boys of modern languages, science or classics. Meanwhile, 'elite' schools were established to mould the future leadership of the

Volksgemeinschaft. Particularly important were *Nationalpolitische Erziehungsanstalten* (or *Napolas*), for the education of future government officials and military personnel; the Adolf Hitler Schools and the Castles of Order (*Ordensburgen*).[6] Underlying all the changes was the emphasis on race and anti-Semitism. Jews were forced out of German schools and allowed only to attend Jewish schools – until these were abolished in 1942. Finally, the teaching profession was also carefully reorganised: the Nazi Teachers' League (NSLB) – established in 1929 – accounted for 97 per cent of the total teaching force by 1937, as compared with 25 per cent in 1935.

Sweeping though these changes were, the process of indoctrination through Germany's school system proved in several ways to be badly flawed. In the first place, there was extensive conflict between the various agencies involved. For example, the Ministry of Education continued to use the guidelines of the Weimar Republic largely because it argued interminably with the Party headquarters about the shape to be taken by their replacement. The conflict between Ley and Rust on the one hand and Bormann and Hess on the other meant that the new regulations for elementary education were delayed until 1939, while secondary schools were served little better. Such differences had three unfortunate side-effects. One was that the content of the curriculum was diluted by more traditional influences than was originally intended. Part of the problem here was that it took until the late 1930s for many of the new textbooks to come into the school system, partly because of the difficulty of coordinating authors, publishers, the Ministry of Education and the Censorship Office under Philipp Bouhler. The second was the persistence of confusion within the schools themselves as to the precise means of delivering the curriculum. Gestapo reports contained numerous examples of unsatisfactory teachers, many of whom were quite probably confused rather than deliberately uncooperative. And, third, there was a gradual change in the attitudes of teachers. At first the Nazis had received widespread support from teachers. But, as Pine observes, 'in the end teachers became one of the most disillusioned groups'. The promised reforms were not delivered, the 'rhetoric of the NSLB and the regime was empty' and educational aims were subordinated to 'the desire to disseminate Nazi ideology'.[7]

Meanwhile, the constant intrusion of ideology – and especially of racism – caused an inevitable decline in standards, whether in mathematics, the sciences or the humanities. This, in turn, affected the intake into universities, the latter frequently complaining about the poorer quality of their students. Even the elite schools were affected by the indifferent levels of education and delivered nothing like the quantities of leadership originally anticipated. Nazi schools were ample evidence that 'education' becomes weaker in direct proportion to the strengthening of indoctrination.

Universities were similarly affected as the Nazis undertook a major redefinition higher education. Instead of pursuing academic excellence through academic freedom, the universities were to complete the process, started in schools, of embedding the spirit of the *Volksgemeinschaft* in the mind of the people. The result was a major upheaval in university tradition, although there were already indications that something like this might happen with the rapid spread of the National Socialist German Students' Association from 1926 onwards. The main manifestations of change, however, came from May 1933, with an outbreak of book-burning throughout Germany, to which student bodies contributed with enthusiasm.

As with schools, serious problems soon became apparent. For one thing, there was an alarming decline in student enrolment: from 127,580 in 1932 to 92,622 in 1934 and 58,325 by 1937.[8] After 1939 higher education looked in danger of fading away altogether. What kept it going was the rapid increase in numbers of women students, who were permitted to take up places as a result of the conscription of the men; in this way higher education survived despite Nazi policy – not because of it. It could even be argued that the dilution – or pollution – of the sciences, especially Physics, had a damaging effect on Germany's capacity for advanced weapons technology during the war years. Martin Heidegger, Rector of the University of Freiburg from April 1933, had originally had expectations of 'conquering the world of educated men and scholars for the new national political spirit'.[9] Even more than in the schools, however, the distortion of the curriculum and the constant purges undermined academic standards – without delivering a reservoir of future leaders.

Indoctrination through a revised educational system was reinforced by mobilisation through the youth movements. Collectively referred to as the Hitler Youth, their numbers were initially unimpressive. At the beginning of 1933, Communist and Socialist youth movements had 80,000 members (of whom about 50,000 belonged to the SAJ of the Social Democrats), the right-wing parties had 253,000, the Centre 35,000 and the less politicised *Bünde* about 70,000. These compared with the 120,000 members of the Hitler Youth.[10] Thereafter, expansion was rapid, the result of the banning of other groups in 1933 and the Hitler Youth Law of 1 December 1936. Membership reached 2.3 million by the end of 1933, 3.6 million in 1934, 5.4 million in 1936 and 7 million in 1938. At the end of 1933 membership of the Hitler Youth accounted for 30.4 per cent of the total population between the ages of 10 and 18; by 1938 the proportion was 77.2 per cent.[11]

How have historians interpreted the activities, influence and effectiveness of the Hitler Youth? Initial post-war views assumed that the will of the state was all-embracing and that a whole generation was brought under the full controls of the totalitarian state, in line with the objectives expressed by Hitler in 1938: 'These young people learn nothing else but to think as Germans and to act as Germans.'[12] (See Source 2.1.) Writing in the 1950s, Jarman emphasised the seductive nature of the Hitler Youth which so 'captured the imagination' that it was 'a real punishment to remain, for any reason, outside'. 'Children wanted to march and sing and salute, they wanted to go to the Nazi camps, they wanted to enjoy the wonderful, exciting life that was organized for them.'[13] There is some truth in this; the Hitler Youth carried widespread appeal, initially appearing as a challenge to more conservative forms of authority and giving youth a sense of collective power. But more recently, historians such as Burleigh, Wippermann,[14], Bessel[15] and Peukert[16] have emphasised the partial loss of this appeal as the Hitler Youth authorities came to be seen as part of a new establishment. According to Peukert, for example, 'The thesis that the Hitler Youth successfully mobilised young people fits only one side of the social reality of the Third Reich'.[17] (See Source 2.3.) The experience of war, especially, had a varied impact on the attitude of youth. Many remained enthusiastic to the end. Others became increasingly disillusioned and did their best to avoid being drawn into yet further obligations to an organisation they now found onerous. But, perhaps most surprising of all, was the increasing numbers of 'dissident youth' which, according to Burleigh and Wippermann, resulted in 'a specifically anti-National Socialist youth resistance movement'.[18] Particularly important were the Edelweiss Pirates – who frequently picked conflicts with the Hitler Youth – and 'swing' groups, who opted for jazz from the United States, even though the Nazi regime condemned this as 'decadent' and 'degenerate'. The importance of dissent among youth is considered further in Chapter 6, Analysis 2.

But perhaps the pendulum has swung too far the other way. There has now been a partial return to the 'impact' theories, although usually in more specific ways. A good example is the work of Rempel,[19] who sees the Hitler Youth as one of the successes of the Nazi regime. 'The social, political, and military resiliency of the Third Reich is inconceivable without the HJ.' It acted as 'the incubator that maintained the political system'; it renewed the Party and prevented 'the growth of mass opposition'. Particularly important, however, was the relationship between the HJ and the SS, both of which replenished and reinforced the whole Nazi system. 'After 1933, when many old fighters were slowly growing weary and fat, eager to enjoy the comforts and pleasures of power, the SS and HJ provided a wellspring of youthful élan. Without them Hitler could not have withstood the sceptical old officers of the army.'[20] Similarly, 'The SS could not have become a state within a state if the alliance with the HJ had not been struck in 1936'.[21] A more detailed exposition of Rempel's views is provided in Source 2.5 below, and further comments of the connection between the HJ and the SS in Chapter 5, Analysis 2.

ANALYSIS 2: ASSESS THE CHANGES MADE BY THE NAZIS IN THE MASS MEDIA AND CULTURE, AND THE IMPACT OF THESE ON THE GERMAN PEOPLE

If indoctrination had a significant but limited impact on youth, could the same be said about the effect of propaganda on the rest of the population? A further distinction needs to be made at this point between the development of propaganda channels in the mass media – such as radio, cinema and press – and the attempts to influence cultural output in literature, art and music, where contact with the public was less constant and direct. Both sectors, however, came under the control of the Reich Chamber of Culture, established within the Ministry of People's Enlightenment and Propaganda.

The mass media

The potential of radio was quickly grasped by Goebbels, who considered it 'the most modern and the most important instrument of mass influence'.[22] He brought the different radio organisations into a centralised and state-controlled Reich Radio Company. This was controlled by the Radio sub-chamber of the Ministry of People's Enlightenment and Propaganda. Priority was given to political broadcasts, of which Hitler made 50 in 1933 alone; these created the impression of personal contact between the people and their leader, thereby enhancing the effectiveness of the Führer cult. Collective listening was organised at the workplace, in blocks of flats and in public places, radio wardens being given the task of setting up loudspeakers. (See Source 1.3.) But Goebbels also considered light entertainment important, especially light music and the operettas of Lehar and Johann Strauss. Women were particularly targeted with a wide variety of programmes to reinforce their contribution to the *Volksgemeinschaft*. Housewives were to be compensated for being confined to the home and encouraged to bring their household management into line with the autarky principles of the Four Year Plan.

In some ways the experiment was a considerable success. The manufacture of cheap radios, payable in instalments, meant that the ownership of sets increased from 25 per cent of households in 1932 to 70 per cent by 1939; this was the largest proportion anywhere in the world. For the vast majority of the population, the radio provided the most abiding impression of the Führer that they were ever likely to have, and frequent exposure to the airwaves greatly enhanced Hitler's personal popularity – a key factor in developing support for the regime (See Chapter 6, Analysis 1.) During the war years, however, several drawbacks became apparent. Many Germans listened to foreign radio stations, even though this was banned. This was probably the widest form of illegal activity but one of the most difficult for the Gestapo to track down. It was also a reflection on the unwillingness of a large part of the population to believe the blatant lies which were used to try to cover up the growing military failures after 1943.

The Nazis ended the golden period of cinema which had existed during the period of the Weimar Republic. Many leading directors emigrated, along with film stars like Peter Lorre and Marlene Dietrich. Instead, Goebbels reconstructed the film industry, bringing it under the control of the Reich Film Chamber and imbuing it with new principles and a new intensity. The Third Reich produced 1,097 feature films, of which about one-sixth were openly political.[23] These fulfilled a variety of purposes: promoting the *Führerprinzip*, reinforcing the *Volksgemeinschaft* and the anti-Semitic message, and instilling patriotism and self-sacrifice. Some films were about Germany's past; examples included *Bismarck* and *Friedrich Schiller* (1940), *Der Grosse König* (1942) about Frederick the Great, and *Paracelsus* (1943). But Goebbels also promoted entertainment as a form of escapism, especially during the war years.

How effective were these changes? The most accomplished film was not necessarily the most influential. Riefenstahl's *Triumph of the Will* (*Triumph des Willens*) was commissioned by Hitler himself as a record of the Nuremberg rallies of 1934. Technically a brilliant achievement, it created a multi-layered image of Nazism which brought in all elements of society and directly fostered the Führer cult. On the other hand, it was too long for most audiences, who sometimes reacted negatively to the repetition of the same types of scene. During the war, film-based propaganda was radicalised and the anti-Semitic component became more extreme. But it soon became apparent that Hitler's vision of what was likely to engage the public was less effective than Goebbels's. *The Eternal Jew* (*Der ewige Jude*), commissioned by Hitler, was directed by Hippler, whose view was that in the cinema 'the spectator should know whom to hate and whom he should love'.[24] But the principle was taken too far: the message was so crudely blatantly expressed that 'the spectators' reacted by hating the images more than the people they represented. The anti-Semitic message was conveyed more effectively through a feature film, *Jew Süss* (*Jud Süss*). Goebbels was more subtle in his approach, using propaganda as a subliminal message within the context of a story with which the viewers could identify. This applied also to his attempts to engender a spirit of resistance to the Allies with *Der Grosse König* and *Kolberg* (1945). But the latter came too late to affect the morale of a population facing imminent defeat. Indeed, it actually impeded the war effort by drawing off 187,000 troops from military duties. Overall, the regime made full use of a modern medium but its leaders seemed uncertain as to how to strike the balance between indoctrination and escapism; hence the surprisingly strong influence from Hollywood. Even as propaganda, there were no great productions to rival those made in the Soviet Union – no equivalent to Eisenstein's *Great October* or *Ivan the Terrible*. The only director who came close was Leni Riefenstahl.

Channelling the press for propaganda was also problematic. Because it was based on a more traditional technology, it had had longer than radio to develop within the structure of private ownership; radio, by contrast, could be taken over relatively easily by the State. The proliferation of newspapers during the liberal era of the Weimar Republic accentuated the difficulty: by 1933 there were about 4,700 daily newspapers in Germany, representing a wide variety of political and regional views and loyalties. Examples of political papers included the *Red Flag* (*Rote Fahne*) of the Communists, *Forwards* (*Vorwärts*) of the SPD and *The Day* (*Der Tag*) of the DNVP. After coming to power the Nazis removed most of these and the *People's Observer* (*Völkischer Beobachter*) became the most important.

To an extent, the regime achieved effective administrative control through the Press Chamber, under Amann, and the overall press chief, Otto Dietrich. Between 1933 and 1945 the number of State-owned newspapers increased from 2.5 per cent of the total to 82 per cent. The German News Agency (*Deutsches Nachrichtenbüro* or DNB) provided an effective control over the means whereby news was to be presented; news agencies were amalgamated to ensure a single source of information; and journalists were made responsible to the State rather than to their editors. Daily press conferences ensured that an official line was maintained in reporting. But, with the exception of virulently racist papers such as Streicher's *Der Stürmer* and *Das Schwarze Korps* of the SS, the result was a bland form of journalism which placed safety and political correctness above controversy. The inevitable result was a decline in public interest and readership; Goebbels failed in his attempts to promote newspapers with slogans such as 'Who Reads Newspapers Gets Ahead Faster!'[25] Throughout the whole period, the regime was never able to use the press to generate mass support and enthusiasm. The emphasis of its censorship was therefore preventive rather than creative.

Culture

The Nazi relationship with culture was ambivalent. On the one hand, it distrusted some of the traditional content while, on the other, never quite succeeding to provide an alternative. In the three major cases of literature, art and music, censorship created a contemporary vacuum, which a new and distinctive Nazi culture was intended to fill. The results differed in intensity. Literature produced a complete void; music was less affected; and the vacuum of art was most filled – but with work of distressingly low quality.

The focus on literature was preventive censorship. All literary activity was controlled by the Reich Chamber of Literature, which also maintained checks on 2,500 publishing houses and 23,000 bookshops. Some 2,500 German authors were placed on the list of banned books, including all Jewish writers and left-wingers, such as Ossietzky and Mühsam. Libraries were ransacked by students and the SA, followed by massive book-burning sessions. (See Source 1.5 below.) The extent to which the ideology was taken in all this is evident in the banning of Baumann's *On Swabia's Past: Swabian Customs* for trying 'to identify German folklore with religious endeavors' and 'ecclesiastical institutions as part of German customs'. This 'folkloristic confusion' should be 'sharply resisted' at a time when German folklore was being 'systematically described and analyzed in relation to its special racial characteristics'.[26] Even Schmitt's *Mountain Fate* was declared 'undesirable' on the grounds that it contained 'foul comments on Italian mountain guides'[27] – at a time, of course, when Hitler was improving his diplomatic relations with Mussolini. The gaps were partially filled by pro-Nazi writers such as Beumelberg and Hans Grimm (who wrote a long novel entitled *People Without Living Space*). Others, like Jünger, kept their heads down and depoliticised their work. Overall, the literary poverty of

Nazi Germany was obvious – and hardly surprising since Nazism itself was anti-intellectual. It discouraged any diversity of viewpoints and individual experience, seeking instead to stereotype collectivism. Within this atmosphere, any chance of creating an 'official' literature disappeared – even supposing that the population would have been allowed any time to read it.

If the Nazis gave up on literature as a form of propaganda, they made a deliberate effort to use the visual arts to put across basic blood and soil values. This meant the end of the Weimar experiment conducted by painters such as Nolde, Barlach, Beckmann, Grosz, Hoech, Dix, Klee and Kokoscka – all of whom were now described as 'degenerate' – and the elimination of trends such as Expressionism and Dadaism. Some 42,000 practising artists had to be registered with the Reich Chamber of Visual Arts under Ziegler and authorisation to paint could be withdrawn. An example of one of the 1,400 artists affected by this was Schmidt-Rottluff, who was informed by a letter from Ziegler that his paintings 'did not contribute to the advancement of German culture in its responsibility toward people and nation'. It concluded: 'I hereby expel you from the National Chamber of Fine Arts and forbid you, effective immediately, any activity – professional or amateur – in the field of graphic arts'.[28] Exhibitions of 'degenerate' art opened in Munich, Dortmund and Cologne, to which a number of Schmidt-Rottluff's works were added. These were contrasted with officially approved work exhibited in the German Art Exhibition held in Munich between 1937 and 1944. The whole purpose was to remove abstract influences and create a new sense of 'order' which would reflect that of the *Volksgemeinschaft*. Painters like Kampf, Ziegler, Erler, Spegel, Bastanier, Peiner, Diebitsch and Hilz produced pictorial stereotypes of racial appearance, of women as mothers and home-minders, and of men in a variety of martial roles. Such images reinforced the roles inculcated through the institutions of youth indoctrination, such as the BDM and the HJ. The result was a form of art which was bland and lacking in any obvious talent. Much of Nazi 'art' was derivative and eclectic: for example, Kampf's study of Venus and Adonis was a thinly disguised copy of earlier masters such as Rubens and David. The effect of such plagiarism on the public cannot have been anything more than peripheral, especially since there was always more interest in exhibitions of 'degenerate' art.

The Reich Chamber of Music ended the period of musical experimentation which had been a major cultural feature of the Weimar Republic. The works of Schoenberg, Weill, Hindemith and Berg were considered 'degenerate' and un-German, while from 1937 all new productions in music required the approval of the Censorship Reading

Panel. Particular targets were atonality and 'modernism'. All Jewish composers and musicians were banned and popular trends which were officially deplored by the regime included American jazz and 'swing'; these were considered deeply 'corrupting' and a 'cancerous growth'. Yet the actual volume of change was less in music than in art or literature. The majority of German or Austrian composers were unaffected and retained their place as part of Germany's cultural heritage. Contemporary composers like Richard Strauss and Carl Orff managed to coexist with the regime. Strauss, for example, escaped censure for elements of atonality in his music and was even President of the Chamber of Music until 1935. The Nazis also used prominent nineteenth century composers to spearhead their cultural penetration: foremost among these was Wagner, whose *Ring* cycle was seen by Hitler as the musical embodiment of *völkisch* values. Even the musical *bête-noir* survived. During the war years Goebbels was dubious about the regime's attempts to enforce a ban on jazz, fearing this would affect civilian commitment and morale; he therefore had to be content with targeting the most radical forms, especially 'hot' jazz. Even so, the Gestapo had problems dealing with the numerous instances of 'antisocial behaviour' by 'swing youth' (see Chapter 6, Analysis 2). Overall, there was less success in creating a monolithic approach to music, and output remained more eclectic than, for example, that of artists or writers. As a result, the quality of Reich's musical output was superior to the work of painters like Kampf and Ziegler – but the result was less distinctively Nazi.

There is a tendency to associate Nazi culture with philistinism, for which there has always been plenty of evidence; some of this has been given above. But, according to Steinweiss, 'there is a danger in overstating the vacuousness of German culture under the Nazis'. The reality is that the whole cultural process was complex. The Nazis may have had ideological priorities, but they were also pragmatic in their application. This meant that many links with the past were permitted and that even the 'degenerate' influences were not entirely eliminated, since the Nazis themselves had 'certain modernistic elements'.[29] Yet the cumulative effect of the regime was to lower rather than raise the sum of Germany's cultural parts. There was no real equivalent to the achievements of the Soviet Union, which had a more genuine claim – especially in music – to have added to the already formidable record of Russian culture.

The ultimate test of the success of Nazi controls over the media and culture must be the degree to which the people of Germany could be brought to accept the experience of war. Throughout the Nazi era there were really two levels of propaganda. One level put across Hitler's basic ideology, the other made pragmatic adjustments to fit the needs of the moment. During the period 1933–9, pragmatism frequently diluted ideology, giving rise to considerable theoretical inconsistency in Hitler's ideas. During this period Hitler was presented as a man of peace and yet all the processes of indoctrination and propaganda emphasised struggle and its martial refinement. The period 1939–45 tended to bring the man and his ideas closer together. This occurred in two stages. The first was the acclimatisation of the people to the *idea* of war, achieved through the emphasis on *Blitzkrieg,* or 'lightning' war. Logically this fitted in with the notion of easy conquest achieved by the 'master race', and while it lasted it was a considerable success: Hitler probably reached the peak of his popularity in 1940, at the time of the fall of France.

During the second stage, however, propaganda had to acclimatise the people to the *experience* of war. At first Goebbels scored a propaganda success in his 'total war' speech, but in the longer term there was a clear decline in popular enthusiasm. From 1943, the main characteristic shown by German civilians was fortitude in the face of adversity and destruction, not a fanatical desire to achieve a world vision. By this stage, Nazi propaganda and indoctrination had not so much failed. They had become irrelevant.

Questions

1. Which areas did the Nazis most successfully control in (a) the mass media and (b) culture?
2. Was there a Nazi 'information and cultural revolution'?

SOURCES

1: THE ORGANISATION OF PROPAGANDA

Source 1.1: From a speech by Goebbels, 15 March 1933

The most important tasks of this Ministry must be the following. Firstly, all propaganda ventures and all institutions for the enlightenment of the people throughout the Reich and the states must be centralized in one hand. Furthermore, it must be our task to instill into these propaganda facilities a modern feeling and bring them up to date. Technology must not be allowed to proceed ahead of the Reich: the Reich must go along with technology. Only the most modern things are good enough. We are living now in an age when the masses must support policies ... It is the task of State propaganda so to simplify complicated ways of thinking that even the smallest man in the street may understand.

Source 1.2: Goebbels speaking to a meeting of radio officials on 25 March 1933

The Ministry has the task of achieving a mobilization of mind and spirit in Germany. It is, therefore, in the sphere of the mind what the Defence Ministry is in the sphere of defence. Thus, this Ministry will require money and will receive money because of a fact which everybody in the Government now recognizes, namely that the mobilization of the mind is as necessary as, perhaps even more necessary than, the material mobilization of the nation.

Source 1.3: From the local paper in Neu-Isenberg near Frankfurt, 16 March 1934

Attention! The Führer is speaking on the radio. On Wednesday 21 March, the Führer is speaking on all German stations from 11.00 to 11.50 a.m. According to a regulation of the Gau headquarters, the district Party headquarters has ordered that all factory owners, department stores, offices, shops, pubs and blocks of flats put up loudspeakers an hour before the broadcast of the Führer's speech so that the whole work force and all national comrades can participate fully in the broadcast. The district headquarters expects this order to be obeyed without exception so that the Führer's wish to speak to his people can be implemented.

Source 1.4: From official instructions issued at the daily press conferences in the Propaganda Ministry, 6 April 1935

The Propaganda Ministry asks us to put to editors-in-chief the following requests, which must be observed in future with particular care.

Photos showing members of the Reich Government at dining tables in front of rows of bottles must not be published in future, particularly since it is known that a large number of the Cabinet are abstemious. Ministers take part in social events for reasons of international etiquette and for strictly official purposes, which they regard merely as a duty and not as a pleasure. Recently, because of a great number of photos, the utterly absurd impression has been created among the public that members of the Government are living it up. News pictures must therefore change in this respect.

Source 1.5: From a description by Louis P. Lochner, head of the Associated Press Bureau in Berlin, May 1933

The whole civilized world was shocked when on the evening of 10 May 1933 the books of authors displeasing to the Nazis, including those of our own Helen Keller, were solemnly burned on the immense Franz Josef Platz between the University of Berlin and the State Opera on Unter den Linden. I was a witness to the scene.

All afternoon Nazi raiding parties had gone into public and private libraries, throwing on to the streets such books as Dr Goebbels in his supreme wisdom had decided were unfit for Nazi Germany. From the streets Nazi columns of beer-hall fighters had picked up these discarded volumes and taken them to the square above referred to. Here the heap grew higher and higher, and every few minutes another howling mob arrived, adding more books to the impressive pyre. Then, as night fell, students from the university, mobilized by the little doctor, performed veritable Indian dances and incantations as the flames began to soar skyward.

Source 1.6: From an article in the *Daily Express*, written by David Lloyd George, 17 November 1936

I have just returned from a visit to Germany. ... I have now seen the famous German Leader and also something of the great change he has effected.

... It is true that public criticism of the Government is forbidden in every form. That does not mean that criticism is absent. I have heard the speeches of prominent Nazi orators freely condemned. But not a word of criticism or of disapproval have I heard of Hitler. He is as immune from criticism as a king in a monarchical country.

Questions

1. How far are the points expressed in Sources 1.2 and 1.3 a logical application of the ideas expressed in Source 1.1?
2. To what extent does Source 1.4 show the ease with which the Nazi regime was able to control the German press?

3. Using Sources 1.1 to 1.6, and your own knowledge, would you agree that the creation of loyal Nazis was achieved by 'negative' rather than by 'positive' means?

2: HISTORIANS ON THE HITLER YOUTH

Source 2.1: Hitler in 1938 on the Hitler Youth

These young people learn nothing else but to think as Germans and to act as Germans; these boys join our organisations at the age of ten and get a breath of fresh air for the first time; then, four years later they move from the *Jungvolk* to the Hitler Youth and here we keep them for another four years. And then we are even less prepared to give them back into the hands of those who create our class and status barriers; rather, we take them immediately into the Party, into the Labour Front, into the SA or the SS. And if they are there for eighteen months or two years and have still not become real National Socialists, then they go into the Labour Service and are polished there for six or seven months, and all of this under a single symbol, the German spade. And if, after six or seven months, there are still remnants of class consciousness or pride in status, then the Wehrmacht will take over the further treatment for two years and when they return after two or four years then, to prevent them from slipping back into the old habits once again we take them immediately into the SA, SS etc., and they will not be free again for the rest of their lives.

Source 2.2: From T.L. Jarman, *The Rise and Fall of Nazi Germany* (first published in 1956)

At every stage of development the Nazis sought to mould and influence the young with the object of creating a race of splendid Germans, a true *Herrenvolk.* Little boys and girls had their own Nazi organizations, and at fourteen the boys joined the *Hitlerjugend.* The Nazi youth movement undoubtedly captured the imagination of the children; it was a real punishment to remain, for any reason, outside. Children wanted to march and sing and salute, they wanted to go to the Nazi camps, they wanted to enjoy the wonderful, exciting life that was organized for them. And no other youth movement was allowed to compete for their loyalty. Children became, from an early age, the devoted followers of the *Führer* ... Then for the young men there came six months of compulsory labour service in a camp before their two years' military service. The labour service had as its object to let manual labour break down the barriers of social class, mould the character still further to the Nazi pattern, and strengthen the physique of the potential soldier and worker. Outdoor manual labour and military drill (with spades instead of rifles) were the means. The physical training of the young began to make its mark on the whole nation; the Germans carried off many of the prizes at the Olympic Games held in 1936 in Berlin, and the foreign visitors were impressed both by German athletic prowess and by the splendid spectacle offered in the German capital. There was before their eyes a new Germany: of youth, of power, of faith – though its future was in the hands of one man whose megalomania would lead its people to disaster.

Source 2.3: From D.J.K. Peukert, *Inside Nazi Germany* (first published in German in 1982)

The thesis that the Hitler Youth successfully mobilised young people fits only one side of the social reality of the Third Reich. The more the Hitler Youth arrogated state powers to itself, and the more completely young people were assimilated into the organisation, the more clearly visible became an emergent pattern of youth nonconformity. By the end of the 1930s thousands of young people were declining to take part in the leisure activities of the Hitler Youth and were discovering their own unregimented styles in spontaneous groups and gangs. Indeed, they defended their autonomous space all the more insistently as the Hitler Youth *Streifendienst* and the Gestapo applied ever more massive pressure. ... The leadership could no longer get out of this by saying that the people involved had been conditioned by the Weimar 'system', by Marxism, clericalism or the old youth movement. The 14- to 15-year-olds who made up this opposition in the late 1930s and early 1940s were boys (and to a lesser extent girls) whose socialisation in school had largely taken place under National Socialist rule. It was the very generation, indeed, on whom Adolf Hitler's system had operated unhindered that turned out so many 'black sheep'.

Source 2.4: From M. Burleigh and W. Wippermann, *The Racial State: Germany 1933–1945* (published in 1991)

The growing political and ideological influence of the Hitler Youth was accompanied by a clear diminution of its attraction to many young people. It had become identified with ideological indoctrination, paramilitary training, and the exploitation of the labour potential of young people in the service of war. ... Young people reacted to the onset of compulsion in various ways. While many were enthusiastic up to the end, joining special military units consisting of fourteen- to eighteen-year-olds and throwing away their lives in expectation of 'final victory', others became progressively disillusioned, recalcitrant, and rebellious. Rebelliousness was regarded as resistance, and hence a crime, by the terroristic institutions of the Third Reich, and was dealt with accordingly. Measures taken by the State provoked further protest and resistance, which began to assume organised forms. National Socialist youth policy therefore resulted in a specifically anti-National Socialist youth resistance movement, which was taken seriously by the leadership of police and state, who combated it with exemplary savagery and harshness.

Source 2.5: From G. Rempel, Hitler's Children: *The Hitler Youth and the SS* (published in 1989)

The social, political, and military resiliency of the Third Reich is inconceivable without the HJ. It was the incubator that maintained the political system by replenishing the ranks of the dominant party and preventing the growth of mass opposition. It may be impossible to define the influence millions of young people had on parents, teachers, and adults in general, but there can be little doubt that the uniformed army of teenagers had something to do with promoting the myth of Hitler's invincible genius. When the war began, the importance of the HJ as the cradle of an aggressive army became apparent to military leaders and to the creators of the combat wing of the SS.

... Besides the Labor Front, two of the most important instruments of the policy of social integration after the SA had been broken were to be the SS and the HJ. After 1933, when many old fighters were slowly growing weary and fat, eager to enjoy the comforts and pleasures of power, the SS and HJ provided a wellspring of youthful élan. Without them Hitler could not have withstood the skeptical old officers of the army. The army needed the HJ as well. ... The Nazi movement could not have expanded and kept its youthful character without SS terrorism and without the HJ becoming an important element in the movement before the assumption of power. As a mass organization, incorporating nearly the entire younger generation in the twelve years that followed, the HJ sustained the movement's vitality. ...

There is no way the SS could have become the most significant single element in the Nazi system without the HJ alliance, because that alliance provided the Black Corps with a steady stream of committed loyalists and ideologically pure functionaries and soldiers. The SS could not have become a state within a state if the alliance with the HJ had not been struck in 1936 ...

Questions

1. Compare the arguments of Sources 2.2, 2.3 and 2.4.
*2. How far – according to Sources 2.2 to 2.5 and your own knowledge – were the aims set out by Hitler in Source 2.1 actually achieved?

WORKED ANSWER

*2 *[This type of question requires careful handling. It is important not merely to 'describe' the content of the sources in turn, and then proceed to 'thus it can be seen that ...'. Several key points need to be drawn from Source 2.1 and compared with their equivalent in the other sources. 'Own knowledge' covers additional material, including comments on the views in the passages or knowledge of background history and historiography. This can be either integrated into the other comments (as is done here) or added separately at the end, as in the Worked Answer on pages 83–4. Normally more substantial and complex answers are needed when dealing with secondary sources than with primary sources. This is because the former are more likely to feature at A2 or in higher education, while the latter are a feature at AS. This answer is therefore longer than that on pages 83–4.]*

The aims set out in Source 2.1 concern indoctrination through innovation and a permanent reorientation to new roles. Whether or not these were achieved depends on the viewpoint of the authors of the other four sources. Jarman (Source 2.2) considers that most were; Peukert (Source 2.3) maintains that most were not, as do Burleigh and Wippermann (Source 2.4); Rempel (Source 2.5) turns the argument the other way around.

Hitler's emphasis on indoctrination is apparent in his desire to make young people 'think as Germans and to act as Germans'. This is to be done through involvement in 'our organisations' at an early age and the promotion of enthusiasm for something new – from which they 'get a breath of fresh air for the first time'. Source (2.3) argues that the process succeeded: that it 'undoubtedly captured the imagination of the children' and that it was a 'real punishment to remain, for any reason, outside'. Jarman presents a view which was common during the 1950s and reflects the images provided in the Riefenstahl's *Triumph of the Will*. Source 2.3, however, questions the appeal of the Hitler Youth. Peukert is more interested in the 'emergent pattern of youth nonconformity', as are Burleigh and Wippermann who refer in Source 2.4 to the Hitler Youth's diminishing 'attraction to many young people'. By the 1980s and 1990s a considerable amount of research had been carried out to emphasise the importance of rebellious youth sub-cultures in Nazi Germany, challenging the earlier emphasis on successful indoctrination. Rempel adjusts the focus from the attractions – or otherwise – to the impact of the Hitler Youth on other sectors (Source 2.5). In so doing he restores at least some acknowledgement that the indoctrination of youth must have been successful. This is an example of the historiographical pendulum swinging partially back from a revisionist position.

Hitler also aimed at permanent reorientation through the Hitler Youth, followed by 'the Party', the 'Labour Front', the 'SA or the SS' and the 'Wehrmacht' – all intended to 'prevent them from slipping back into the old habits' (Source 2.1). Again, this is taken more or less at face value by Jarman, who refers to the success of these organisations and the persistence of Hitler's vision: 'There was before their eyes a new Germany: of youth, of power, of faith'. Peukert, on the other hand, stresses that it was the very system by which Hitler hoped to create a new generation that had 'turned out so many "black sheep"' (Source 2.3). Burleigh and Wippermann, too, refer to disillusionment, recalcitrance and rebelliousness, which meant that Hitler's policy resulted in 'a specifically anti-National Socialist youth resistance movement' (Source 2.4). Rempel, however, deals with wider issues, examining the progression of those who were successfully indoctrinated by the Hitler Youth rather than those who were not. He sees the Hitler Youth as 'the incubator that maintained the political system' and 'the cradle of an aggressive army'. Above all, it established a direct connection with the SS so that together they 'provided a wellspring of youthful élan' (Source 2.5). Although it is possible to overstate the impact of the Hitler Youth on other organisations, Rempel's argument is a necessary corrective to the view that it was widely rejected. The power of indoctrination has, after all, been described in all areas of the Nazi system. Bartov, for example, has shown how youthful combatants, recently from the Hitler Youth, could be turned into ruthless killers in the *Einsatzgruppen* of the SS and Police Battalions of the *Wehrmacht*. These were a necessary part of the Final Solution and the most extreme example of Hitler's aim to indoctrinate youth to the acceptance of a new order.

5

THE SS AND GESTAPO

BACKGROUND

The SS complex grew from three strands to form a network which covered all areas of policing and security. The three were initially separate. The SS (*Schutzstaffeln*) originated in 1925 as the elite within the SA; the SD (*Sicherheitsdienst*) was set up in 1931 as the NSDAP's internal police force; and the Gestapo (short for *Geheime Staatspolizei*, or secret state police) was established in Prussia by Goering in April 1933 and was initially accountable to the Ministry of the Interior.

Gradually these components came together as the SS infiltrated the leading positions of the State police system in line with Hitler's decree of 17 June 1936 providing for the unification of 'police duties in the Reich'. From this stage onwards the SS expanded even further. They penetrated the army by means of the SS Special Service Troops (*SS-Verfügungstruppe* – SS-VT), from which were eventually recruited the military units, the *Waffen SS*. They took over from the SA the organisation of the concentration camps, staffing them with the Death's Head Formations (*SS-Totenkopfverbünde* – SS-TV), while the genocide programme from 1941 came under the control of the Reich Security Main Office (*Reichssicherheitshauptamt* or RSHA).

The Gestapo was initially separate from the criminal police (*Kriminalpolizei* or Kripo) but in 1939 these were formed into two branches of Sipo (*Sicherheitspolizei*) under the *Reichssicherheitshauptamt*. This centralised the leadership of all branches of the state police force, although the Gestapo acquired the strongest reputation and were the most directly feared by the German people.

The man most directly connected with the SS structure is Heinrich Himmler. He was appointed head of the SS in 1929 at a time when it was still within the SA and confined to the role of Hitler's bodyguard. In masterminding the 1934 purge of the SA, however, he ensured that the SS would become an independent organisation, and that he would be one of the key functionaries of the Nazi regime. Henceforward he increased the scope of the SS and accumulated a range of offices for himself. In November 1934, he was recognised by Goering as the effective head of the police and was appointed overall *Reichsführer SS* in 1936. By 1943 he had also become Commissar for the Consolidation of German Nationhood and, in 1943 he added the post of Interior Minister to his portfolio. He was closely involved with the spread of the concentration camp system, which the SS had taken over from the SA, and with the establishment of the extermination camps during the war (see Chapter 8). He was strongly committed to racist policies, believing firmly in an 'Aryan physical ideal'.

For much of the period 1933–41 he was assisted by Reinhard Heydrich, who had joined the SS in 1931 and become head of the SD in 1932. Himmler's deputy from 1933, Heydrich was appointed head of RSHA in 1939, with oversight of all the police services, before being given the post of Reich Protector of Bohemia and Moravia in 1941. Unlike Himmler, Heydrich was strongly pragmatic, although equally ruthless. He was entrusted by Goering with the overview of the extermination of Europe's Jews, a 'responsibility' that was ended by his assassination at the hands of the Czech resistance in 1942. This role fell to Ernest Kaltenbrunner, who became head of the RSHA in 1943 – under the ultimate control of Himmler.

The SS structure expanded within the Nazi system until it came to be seen as a 'state within a state'; the reality of its power and influence is considered in Analysis 1. Whether the Gestapo deserved its fearsome reputation is the theme of Analysis 2.

ANALYSIS 1: HOW FAR WAS THE NAZI REGIME DOMINATED BY THE SS STRUCTURE?

The SS comprised a complex set of institutions collectively known as the SS–Gestapo–SD complex. As explained in the Background, it grew from comparatively small origins to provide, in the view of Noakes and Pridham, 'a separate organizational framework for the enforcement of the will of the regime'.[1] The following analysis is based on the general premise that this framework came to dominate the regime, but that it suffered nevertheless from several inherent faults.

In the opening years of the Third Reich, the SS acted in what was very much a supporting role, seeing off the apparent challenge of the SA and the attempt by Röhm to launch a 'second revolution'. As far as the Nazi system was concerned – and, for that matter, the population at large – the SS had acted against attempted radicalisation, with discipline and total obedience to the Führer. In the process, the SS had assisted Hitler in preserving the delicate balance of Nazi control implicit in the 'legal revolution' (see Chapter 2, Analysis 2). Himmler seemed content at this stage to play a subordinate role and, throughout the remainder of the 1930s, Hitler regarded the *Reichsführer SS* as his 'loyal Heinrich'. The general expectation was that the SS would remain subordinate to the twin structures of Party and State.

But what actually happened was very different. The SS expanded rapidly to fill the vacuum left by the contraction of the SA. The latter's role became predominantly ceremonial as it lost control over public order and the newly-established concentration camps. The SS, by contrast, reversed its original role to become the principal agent in the very process of radicalisation: it was Himmler, not Röhm, who accomplished a 'second revolution'. The earliest measures included control over all police functions, whether security through the SD, political through the Gestapo, or criminal through Kripo and Sipo. These were accompanied by the rapid growth of the concentration camp system. Based on the original Dachau model, this came to include new centres at Sachsenhausen near Berlin, Flossenbürg near Czechoslovakia, Buchenwald outside Weimar, Mauthausen in Austria, and Ravensbrück in Mecklenburg. The SS also imposed extensive social controls and enforced the regime's racial policies. Both underpinned the *Volksgemeinschaft* – making the SS the most important connection between the Nazi state and the population.[2] While extending the area of its administrative competence, the SS became the guardian of the race and struggle ideology of the Nazi movement, and was consistently the main force behind its radicalisation. In some respects, Himmler went even further than Hitler. This applied especially to his views on Christianity. In 1937 he sanctioned the view that 'It is part of the mission of the SS to give the German people over the next fifty years the non-Christian ideological foundations for a way of life appropriate to their character'.[3] Then, during the period of war, the SS organised the whole network of conquered territories as well as the programmes for slave labour. It implemented the programme for the extermination of Jews in occupied areas, at first through the *Einsatzgrüppen*, then in the main extermination camps at Auschwitz-Birkenau, Sobibor, Maidenek, Chelmo, Belzec and Treblinka. Meanwhile the SS had also infiltrated the entire political structure. By 1939 it was already a source of new Party functionaries and replenishing manpower in the key departments of State.

All this has led some historians to believe that by 1941 the Nazi State had been transformed into an SS State. To the 'functionalist/structuralist' historians, this carried all the implications for the conflicts examined in Chapter 3, Analysis 2: in its competition with the other agencies, the SS contributed greatly to the chaos inherent within the polycratic system. By contrast, Bracher considers that the SS were perhaps the exception to the 'intentionalist' argument. Of all the agencies within the Third Reich, 'Only the SS were able to develop an independent position as the avant-garde of the National Socialist empire'.[4] Browder goes further: although Hitler 'did not have to be persuaded to adopt a police-state system like the one Himmler offered', he did have to abandon his customary principle of divide-and-rule and 'to concentrate enormous powers in Himmler's hands'.[5]

There was, of course, still conflict between the SS on the one hand and State and Party functionaries on the other. But when these occurred, the SS usually got its way; indeed, it was the instrument chosen to implement key policies during the war years, even forcing the State and Party into line. This can be illustrated by the Wannsee Conference, held on 20 January 1942. Fully aware of tensions between the SS and government ministries, *Reichsmarschall* Goering instructed General Heydrich, effectively number two in the SS, to secure full cooperation in finding a 'total solution of the Jewish question in the German sphere of influence in Europe'.[6] It was, however, clearly an SS operation. Among the representatives at the Conference were Heydrich himself, Eichmann from the RSHA, General Müller (head of the Gestapo), General Hofmann (Race and Settlement Main Office), and Schoengarth and Lange (both from the Security Police). From the various government departments and agencies outside the SS were Kritzinger (Reich Chancellery), Meyer and Leibbrandt (East Ministry), Stuckart (Interior Ministry), Freisler (Justice Ministry), Bühler (Government General), Neumann (Office of the Four Year Plan) and Luther (Foreign Office). The Nazi Party was represented by Klopfer from the Party Headquarters. There was no question as to the purpose of the Conference. The decision for the secret extermination (the euphemism used throughout the meeting was 'evacuation') using gas chambers, had already been taken and the SS were now bringing the rest of the administration into line.

No historian has seriously questioned the influence of the SS structure on Nazi policy. There have, however, been debates as to its rationale. Höhne believes that:

> the SS world was a bizarre nonsensical affair, devoid of all logic . . . history shows that the SS was anything but an organization constructed and directed on some diabolically efficient system: it was the product of accident and automatism. The real history of the SS is a story of idealists and criminals, of placeseekers and romantics: it is the history of the most fantastic association of men imaginable.[7]

This probably goes too far: after all, might the last point not apply to the story of Nazism generally? But given that the 'fantastic' occurred, the SS was a vital structural part in its realisation: this surely makes more sense than seeing it as a fantastic part of the Nazi system. A different approach is provided by Browder, who emphasises that the SS actually provided the means whereby Hitler could implement his most extreme intentions. Himmler developed the SS into a system which went beyond anything originally envisaged by Hitler. A police state may well have come into existence in 1933, but the 'relatively uncontrolled terror of 1933–1934 could be neither maintained nor used effectively for Nazi imperialism or genocide. These required the SS-police state'. Indeed, Browder goes a step further, intimating that the SS helped shape Hitler's policy. 'Hitler had not yet formulated clear lines of action that required the existence of the SS-police system.' Therefore, 'It was only after the emergence of that machinery that the potential for radical solutions to "racial problems" came into view as a correlated result'.[8] This argument makes the SS structure essential for the radical drive of the whole Nazi system, a view which is now widely accepted. Whether or not Hitler can be sidelined in the process is more contentious. There is much to be said here for Kershaw's belief that Hitler's officials 'moved towards the Führer' in their own way, interpreting his will in the process (see Chapter 3, Analysis 2).

In all this, it is important not to ignore the internal problems experienced by the SS. One was the growing difference between the racial 'idealism' of Himmler and the more ruthless and self-seeking opportunism of Heydrich. Himmler, for example, was fully committed to the 'biological' basis of 'racial purity'. He said to the Reich Peasant Congress on 12 November 1935: 'The first principle for us was and is the recognition of the values of blood and selection.'[9] By contrast, Heydrich's attitude to the SS was purely pragmatic. According to his wife, 'My husband did not play with ideas. His tasks were concrete and clear and depended on the day-to-day events'. In any case, 'Each person interpreted National Socialism as it suited them. There were as many ideologies as there were members'.[10] Another problem was the sheer complexity of the SS – its constant shifts, changes of shape and subdivisions. Historians have also questioned the extent to which these sub-structures within the SS complex were fully competent. What, for example, was the real function of the SD? Did this become more and more amorphous? And how effective was the Gestapo? (See Analysis 2.)

To sum up, the SS complex became integral to the functioning of the Nazi regime, changing its shape and purpose after 1936 and rising above the polycratic chaos experienced by that regime. Indeed, the SS gradually established itself as an alternative, especially after 1939, with Himmler influencing Hitler at least as much as the other way round. Even so, there was still evidence of chaos and conflict within the SS; in some ways it was less coherent and cohesive than Stalin's NKVD. Yet the Soviet Union had no equivalent to the SS – the most completely totalitarian part of the Nazi regime. Certainly, Himmler came closer than the official administration to giving effect to the incoherent ramblings of Hitler's *Mein Kampf.*

Questions

1. Why was the development of the SS structure so complicated?
2. Was the SS the logical development of the Nazi State system – or a 'bizarre' departure from it?

ANALYSIS 2: HOW EFFECTIVE WAS THE GESTAPO?

The Gestapo was originally seen as an unqualified success, as the epitome for sinister, all-embracing power. Passant, for example, maintained that 'any resistance of a political kind became impossible, and, within a few years, a general (Fritsch) or an industrialist (Thyssen) was little more safe from Himmler's Gestapo than the most proletarian Communist'.[11] Crankshaw considered them a 'highly professional corps'.[12] According to Schulz, 'scarcely a politically significant initiative against the National Socialist regime went undetected'.[13] Delarue maintained: 'Never before, in no other land and at no other time, had an organisation attained such a comprehensive penetration of society, possessed such power.'[14] This has been given recent reinforcement by Allen: 'the Gestapo became extraordinarily efficient by reason of rumours and fears' and 'given the atmosphere of terror, even people who were friends felt that they must betray each other in order to survive'.[15]

It is true that the Gestapo was widely respected and generally feared by the German populace; also that this fear assisted the Gestapo in its efforts to maintain widespread control. Heydrich, for example, said in 1941: 'The secret police, the criminal police and the security forces are shrouded in the whispered secrets of the political crime novel.'[16] But was this fear based on the power of an organisation that was able to impose itself directly on all layers of society? Was compliance based on the certainty of retribution by an 'omniscient' force? Or was the key issue the fear of a more limited force being activated by neighbours or even family members? Has the power of the Gestapo, in other words, been overstated – or at least misunderstood?

According to a number of recent historians, it has: some argue that the reputation of the Gestapo is something of a myth deriving from its own propaganda. To some extent this goes back to the period 1933–45. Gellately points out that 'some accounts of working-class resistance exaggerate the role of the Gestapo as an explanation for the failure of workers' resistance'.[17] Taken further, an 'omniscient' Gestapo might be a convenient explanation for the way in which the German people as a whole were gripped by the Nazi system. Mallmann and Paul add that the Gestapo did everything it could to promote the illusion: 'The aura of a perfectly operating secret police was preeminently an image created by means of propaganda, which was meant to intimidate but also to conceal its own structural deficits.'[18]

What were these deficiencies? One was certainly the haphazard nature of its evolution during the 1930s. Browder states that the Gestapo 'grew so rapidly that it remained overwhelmed by its responsibilities'.[19] One result was gross inefficiency within the system. According to Mallmann and Paul, 'Bickering over the demarcation of authority, paper war and the sheer bureaucratic waste of energy generated permanent frictions that reduced efficiency and appears often to have produced an effect exactly the opposite of what was intended'.[20] Even more serious was inadequate numbers; at local levels, the Gestapo 'was hardly an imposing detective organization, but rather an under-staffed, under-bureaucratized agency, limping along behind the permanent inflation of its tasks'.[21] In 1937, for example, there were 126 Gestapo officials in Düsseldorf, a city with a population of 500,000, while Essen had only 43 to cover 650,000.[22] Other major cities, such as Duisburg, Oberhausen, Dortmund, Hanover, Bremen and Würzburg were similarly affected. The beginning of the war aggravated the problem with a further decline in the number of staff. According to Gellately, 'By the end of 1944 there were approximately 32,000 persons in the force, of whom 3,000 were administrative officials, 15,500 or so executive officials and 13,500 employees and workmen'.[23] Even at the time, the head of the SD, Ohlendorf, estimated that only between a quarter and a third of the Gestapo's numbers were 'specialists'.[24] Inexperienced officials replaced those who had been conscripted, and the use of torture tended to increase, along with general thuggery.

Yet, despite, these problems, German society proved easier to police than many other countries in Europe – especially the Soviet Union. The Gestapo was able to identify dissidents and send them to concentration camps; its victims included writers, critics from the clergy, unauthorised religious sects, and a wide range of individuals with opinions that were considered in some way dangerous to the state. It reinforced the ban on other political parties and crippled internal organisations of Communists and Social Democrats. It took sweeping measures against 'social undesirables' such as homosexuals, alcoholics, itinerants and 'deviant' youth groups. The extent to which these groups continued to pose a problem is dealt with separately in Chapter 6. And finally, it helped reinforce the racial state and *Volksgemeinschaft*, tracking down Jews who had escaped the racial net and, from 1942, coordinating with the SS the measures necessary to implement the 'Final Solution'.

How, therefore, did the Gestapo manage to impose this grip? Some historians have seen the answer to this question in a largely complicit and 'self-policing' society which compensated for defects within the Gestapo structure. A key element here was the volume of information which poured into the Gestapo offices. Two sources were particularly important. One comprised agents and spies planted in the workplace and recruited from volunteers; these were not, however, as numerous as was once thought. The other were the denunciations received from the public at large. In Düsseldorf, 26 per cent of Gestapo actions originated from information from the public, compared with 17 per cent from other 'control organizations' (which also depended on public denunciations), 15 per cent from Gestapo informants and 13 per cent from interrogations.[25] The pattern was repeated throughout Germany as information received covered a wide range of issues such as Jewish sympathies, anti-social behaviour, defeatism, public offences, and comments against the Führer. In addition to 'public spiritedness', motives might include revenge, conflicts with neighbours or within the family, search for advancement or financial profit and, of course, acting first to avoid being denounced by others. The disturbing implication of this is that the Nazi regime depended upon a large amount of voluntary support – even from the very classes where loyalty to the KPD and SPD had been strongest in the years before 1933. In this respect, Gellately raises the vital point about the Gestapo was an 'instrument of domination' – that 'it was one which was constructed within

German society and whose functioning was structurally dependent on the continuing cooperation of German citizens'.[26] Of course, there was a downside to the sheer volume of information received. At times the Gestapo was inundated with huge quantities of material which it classified as trivia and had to appeal for greater discrimination from informants. Mallmann and Paul see the situation created as a paradox. On the one hand, the denunciations 'compensated for the Gestapo's considerable investigative deficiencies' while, on the other, they caused 'a great deal of the overloading of the Gestapo capabilities and frequently harnessed district offices to the pursuit of personal interests'. Hence denunciations were both 'dysfunctional' and 'indispensable'.[27]

Some historians consider that this line of reasoning has gone too far. Johnson believes that the emphasis on complicity and denunciations threatens 'to underestimate and obscure the enormous culpability and capability of the leading organs of Nazi terror, such as the Gestapo, and to overestimate the culpability of ordinary German citizens'.[28] Evans is also critical of references to the Gestapo functioning within a bottom-up 'self-policing society'. This, he argues, 'understates the element of top-down terror and intimidation in the functioning of the Third Reich'.[29] In any case, 'it was not ordinary German people who engaged in surveillance'; after all, 'nothing happened until the Gestapo received a denunciation'.[30] There should therefore be less emphasis on voluntary denunciation and more on the 'network of local officials of the regime'. Evans also questions the view that the Gestapo aimed their terror 'exclusively against small and despised minorities'; instead, the threat 'loomed over everyone in the Third Reich'.[31] Burleigh, too, argues that we have now heard too much about the Gestapo as 'desk-bound policemen, almost buried under the avalanche of denunciations from ordinary citizens': this view, he adds, appears to 'normalise Gestapo practice' and 'underestimate the extent of its operations'. Above all, the Gestapo actually relied most on special agents, or *V-Leute*, 'as distinct from casual denouncers, informants and *agents provocateurs*'.[32]

The debate on the Gestapo is a good example of the way in which the historical pendulum swings. The initial position was the state of terror imposed by the Gestapo on the population as a whole. This was substantially revised by a new wave of interpretation emphasising the extensive cooperation of much of the population and the targeting of minorities. The most recent position seems to have settled somewhere between the two, restoring the 'top-down' view of the Gestapo as the instigator of widespread terror while, at the same time, allowing for a greater public contact with the Gestapo as part of the widespread support for the regime. Further light will be thrown on this in Chapter 6.

QUESTIONS

1. Jäckel maintained that 'Hitler's dictatorship over the Germans in no way only and at no time predominantly rested on terror'.[33] Do you agree with this assessment?
2. Was Nazi Germany a 'self-policing' society?

SOURCES

1: THE SECURITY SYSTEM OF THE SS

Source 1.1: From the *Völkischer Beobachter* (*People's Observer*), 27 January 1936

The Secret State Police is an official machine on the lines of the Criminal Police, whose special task is the prosecution of crimes and offences against the State, above all the prosecution of high treason and treason. The task of the Secret State Police is to detect these crimes and offences, to ascertain the perpetrators and to bring them to judicial punishment. … The next most important field of operations for the Secret State Police is the preventive combating of all dangers threatening the State and the leadership of the State. As, since the National Socialist Revolution, all open struggle and all open opposition to the State and to the leadership of the State is forbidden, a Secret State Police as a preventive instrument in the struggle against all dangers threatening the State is indissolubly bound up with the National Socialist Leader State.

Source 1.2: Heydrich on his promotion to Himmler's deputy, 1933

Now we no longer need the Party. It has played its role and has opened the way to power. Now the SS must penetrate the police and create a new organisation there.

Source 1.3: Himmler and the values of the SS in a speech at the Reich Peasant Congress, 12 November 1935

The first principle for us was and is the recognition of the values of blood and selection. … We went about it like a seedsman who, wanting to improve the strain of a good old variety which has become crossbred and lost its vigour, goes through the fields to pick the seeds of the best plants. We sorted out the people who we thought unsuitable for the formation of the SS simply on the basis of outward appearance.

The nature of the selection process was to concentrate on the choice of those who came physically closest to the ideal of nordic man. External features such as size and a racially appropriate appearance played and still play a role here …

The second principle and virtue which we tried to instil in the SS and to give to it as an indelible characteristic for the future is the will to freedom and a fighting spirit …

The third principle and virtue are the concepts of loyalty and honour.

The fourth principle and virtue that is valid for us is obedience, which does not hesitate for a moment but unconditionally follows every order which comes from the Führer or is legitimately given by a superior, obedience … which obeys just as unconditionally and goes into the attack even when one might think in one's heart one could not bring oneself to do so.

Source 1.4: Heydrich's attitude to the SS, as described by his wife during the 1950s

Himmler was obsessed by ideas, kept developing new ones, at first only in theory, but then he tried to realize them. My husband did not play with ideas. His tasks were concrete and clear and depended on the day-to-day events. Naturally, he identified himself with the ideological framework. This framework was, however, regarded as self-evident and hardly bothered my husband, at least in those days. When he joined the SS the order had not yet become what Himmler with his ideas was to turn it into. Each person interpreted National Socialism as it suited them. There were as many ideologies as there were members. As far as my husband was concerned, the idea of a Greater Germany naturally played a decisive role – the rebirth of Germany. But that was really something obvious rather than being a matter of ideology. The German nation was for him more a geographical rather than a racial concept and his concrete tasks developed with the tasks of the Reich as Hitler projected it.

Source 1.5 : Hitler's response to the plea of Frick (Minister of the Interior) for a regulation on who was to control the police, 17 June 1936

To unify the control of police duties in the Reich, a chief of the German police shall be appointed within the Reich Ministry of the Interior, to whom is assigned the direction and executive authority for all police matters within the jurisdiction of the Reich and Prussian Ministries of the Interior.

1. The Deputy Chief of the Prussian Gestapo, Reichsführer SS Himmler, is hereby nominated Chief of the German police in the Reich Ministry of the Interior.
2. He is personally and directly subordinate to the Reich and Prussian Ministers of the Interior.
3. For matters within his jurisdiction he represents the Reich and Prussian Ministers of the Interior in the absence of the latter.
4. He carries the service title; Reichsführer SS and Chief of the German Police within the Reich Ministry of the Interior.

Source 1.6: From a speech by Himmler to SS leaders in Posen, 4 October 1943

One basic principle must be the absolute rule for the SS man: we must be honest, decent, loyal and comradely to members of our own blood and to nobody else. What happens to a Russian or a Czech does not interest me in the slightest What the nations can offer in the way of good blood of our type we will take, if necessary by kidnapping their children and raising them here with us. Whether nations live in prosperity or kick the bucket interests me only in so far as we need them as slaves for our culture. ... Whether 10,000 Russian females fall down from exhaustion while digging an anti-tank ditch interests me only in so far as the anti-tank ditch is finished.

Questions

1. How much evidence is there in Sources 1.2, 1.3 and 1.4 to support the view that ideology was more important to Himmler than to Heydrich?
2. How useful and reliable would the historian find Source 1.4 as an insight into the role of Heydrich in the SS?

*3. Using Sources 1.1 to 1.6, and your own knowledge, how true would it be to say that the SS became a 'state within a state'?

WORKED ANSWER

*3 *[In the answer to this question, it is important to focus on the issue of 'state within a state' from the two directions of 'Sources 1.1 to 1.6' and 'your own knowledge'. One way of doing this and ensuring* *maximum marks is to use two separate paragraphs and to specify which material comes from the sources, and which from elsewhere. The alternative is to integrate 'own knowledge' into the analysis of the sources, as is done in the Worked Answer on pages 70–1.]*

The sources show that the SS certainly seemed to expand into a role much greater than that originally given to it by the State. In theory, the SS were encompassed within the state institutions. Indeed, Source 1.1 emphasises the importance of the SS complex as 'a preventive instrument in the struggle against all dangers threatening the State'. However, Minister of the Interior Frick was clearly concerned about the emergence of a new power as a possible rival to the institutions of the State. This necessitated Hitler's rationalization of the 'control of police duties in the Reich' within 'the jurisdiction of the Reich and Prussian Ministers of the Interior' (Source 1.5). This did not prevent the emergence of an organisation conscious of a separate identity – and of being an elite with a special mission to create racial purity, as shown by Himmler in Source 1.3. Less ideological, but more blatant, was Heydrich's view that the SS might penetrate deeply into the State now that 'we no longer need the Party' (Source 1.2).

Other material can be used to back the views of the sources. The way in which the SS evolved was itself an example of the growth of a huge power bloc within the State. Emerging from within the SA, it took over the SD and Gestapo (initially intended as the Prussian State police), before expanding its role in the *Wehrmacht* in the form of the *Waffen SS*. During the Second World War it was responsible for the implementation of the racial programme in its most extreme phase – the extermination of the Jews. It also administered the Eastern territories and therefore assumed direct responsibility for the implementation of *Lebensraum*. Historians have increasingly emphasised the conflict between State and Nazi institutions. The best example of this so-called polycratic tension is the growth of the SS from humble origins into almost total ascendancy.

2: HISTORIANS ON THE GESTAPO

Source 2.1: From E. Crankshaw, *Gestapo: Instrument of Tyranny* (published in 1956)

There was no organised resistance by the time Himmler had taken over. The last time the braver and soberer German masses made their voices heard was during the March elections in 1933, when, after over a month of S.A. rule, there were still 22 million Germans out of 39 million with the courage to vote against Hitler. With the banning of political parties three months later, and the smashing of the Trade Unions, there was no more sectional opposition. But there was incessant grumbling and a great deal of sporadic underground activity, which, but for the vigilance of Heydrich, would soon have made itself felt. All over Germany groups of anti-Nazi workers were meeting in secret, and it was the job of Heydrich's S.D., with its fabulous network of honorary informers, to smell out this activity. Then, as a rule, it was the job of Himmler's Gestapo to investigate more closely, often by insinuating one of its own agents into a group of dissidents, before taking action. There were many actions of this kind between 1934 and 1939 of which the outside world heard nothing, and the prisons and concentration-camps were filled with the victims.

Source 2.2: From R. Gellately, *The Gestapo and German Society: Enforcing Racial Policy 1933–1945* (published in 1990)

The Gestapo's reputation for brutality no doubt assisted the police in the accomplishment of its tasks, but brutality alone ... does not provide a satisfactory explanation for its effective functioning. While the Gestapo certainly intensified the pressure to attain compliance with Nazi anti-Semitism, for example, it could not on its own enforce even the more rudimentary racial policies designed to isolate the Jews. From the case-files it appears that many individuals, especially members of official and semi-official organizations and associations, members of the Nazi Party, and others in positions of authority (such as medical doctors, nurses, welfare officials), collaborated with the Gestapo in the endeavour to enforce racial policy. When it came to separating the Jews from other persons in Germany, a great deal of such volunteered information *was* forthcoming. Much of this assistance was not required by law or by orders from above. While Gestapo officials intensified their efforts to bring pressure to bear, to achieve National-Socialist ends, the Gestapo's operations would have been seriously hampered without the provision from non-official sources of information on suspected deviations from the new behavioural norms.

Source 2.3: From the editor's introduction to an article by K. Mallmann and G. Paul, 'Omniscient, Omnipotent, Omnipresent? Gestapo, society and resistance' (published in 1994)

Ever since 1933, the Gestapo has been the ultimate symbol of that typically twentieth-century nightmare, the totalitarian police state. In the following article, Mallmann and Paul show, however, that the popular image of the Gestapo is a 'myth' originally propagated by the Gestapo leaders themselves. After the war, historians perpetuated this myth of the 'omniscient, omnipotent, omnipresent' Gestapo by taking the Gestapo leaders' statements of aims and ambitions as accurate reflections of everyday Gestapo practices. The 'myth' of the Gestapo also gave the mass of ordinary Germans a convenient alibi; their failure to engage in serious resistance to the Nazi dictatorship could simply be seen as the inevitable consequence of the Gestapo's awesome power.

Mallmann and Paul dissolve these widely circulated images of Gestapo omnipotence and popular impotence by showing just how ill-equipped most Gestapo district offices were to perform the role of totalitarian 'Big Brother'. Local Gestapo offices simply did not have the manpower necessary to put into practice the increasingly grandiose directives issued by the Berlin central office. Indeed, the Gestapo would have been virtually 'blind', had it not been able to draw upon the information produced by a 'flood' of denunciations made by ordinary Germans against their relatives, friends and neighbors. … Most denunciations were generated not by political or ideological conviction but by anger, greed, hate and prejudice. Ordinary Germans used the Gestapo to settle scores with neighbors or relatives, to rid themselves of inconvenient spouses or to acquire Jewish property.

Source 2.4: Extracts from M. Burleigh, *The Third Reich: A New History* (published in 2000)

Much of the modern literature on the Gestapo has conveyed the impression of desk-bound policemen, almost buried under the avalanche of denunciations from ordinary citizens, particularly regarding violations of racial legislation. This may be so. But this approach has its own limitations. In their desire to normalise Gestapo practice, some historians have claimed that there was no difference between Gestapo 'excesses' and those of policemen in America or Britain, although no comparative evidence is cited in support of this opinion, which derives from a remark made by Himmler and is of course completely ridiculous.

The Gestapo's primary task was to destroy political and clerical opposition. It was clearly highly effective, for the Communist underground was smashed in waves of arrests, before sinking without trace between 1939 and 1941 as an inconvenience to Soviet foreign policy. The Gestapo did not simply stumble upon Communist networks. Apart from opening mail or tapping telephones, the most effective resource were contact agents, or *V-Leute*, as distinct from casual denouncers, informants and *agents provocateurs.* Opponents facing coercion or incarceration sometimes agreed to become Gestapo agents within underground organisations, with a boldly devious minority then operating as double agents, and ending up confused. … But fear was not the sole motivation. Some agents had grudges against erstwhile comrades … It is misleading to imagine that only the marginal or disgruntled small fry worked for the Gestapo. The best agents had lengthy backgrounds in Communist (or Social Democrat) politics, and the most effective of all, those in senior positions, could help the Gestapo roll up underground networks.

Source 2.5: Extracts from R.J. Evans, *The Third Reich in Power 1933–1939* (published in 2005)

To speak of a self-policing society understates the element of top-down terror and intimidation in the functioning of the Third Reich. Those cases that landed up on the Gestapo's desks constituted only a tiny proportion of criminally liable statements in any given year. The vast majority were never denounced by anybody. Denunciation was the exception, not the rule, as far as the behaviour of the vast majority of Germans was concerned. … Moreover, it was not ordinary German people who engaged in surveillance, it was the Gestapo; nothing happened until the Gestapo received a denunciation, and it was the Gestapo's active pursuit of deviance and dissent that was the only thing that gave denunciations meaning. After they had broken labour movement resistance, the Gestapo turned to suppressing a far broader range of less ideological forms of dissent, and the consequences for those whom it brought in for questioning and prosecution could be serious indeed, beginning with brutal violence and torture meted out by Gestapo officers themselves, or under their supervision, in the course of interrogation, and ending in the courts, the prisons and the camps. In this process, the Gestapo called on a network of local officials of the regime, from the Block Warden upwards, and the very existence of such a network, with the Gestapo at its centre, was in itself an incentive to denunciation. Nazi officials knew that failure to pursue dissent could easily land them in trouble themselves; they also knew that bringing it to the Gestapo's attention could earn them approbation as true servants of the Third Reich. Ultimately, it was the Gestapo and the agencies it employed, exploited or worked alongside, who kept Germans under surveillance, not the Germans themselves. … The truth is that far from Nazi terror being levelled exclusively against small and despised minorities, the threat of arrest, prosecution and incarceration in increasingly brutal and violent conditions loomed over everyone in the Third Reich ... Fear and terror were integral parts of the Nazis' armoury of political weapons from the very beginning.

Questions

1. Compare the views of Sources 2.3 and 2.5 on Nazi Germany as a 'self-policing' society.
2. To what extent has Source 2.4 returned to the argument in Source 2.1 by comparison with that in Source 2.2?
3. Do Sources 2.1 to 2.5, and your own knowledge, show that the Gestapo 'dominated' the German people?

6

SUPPORT, OPPOSITION AND RESISTANCE

BACKGROUND

Historians have carried out a considerable amount of research into the attitudes of individuals, classes and sectors within Germany to the Nazi regime. The results seem to show that there was more widespread support, especially for Hitler himself, than was once thought. This is the theme of Analysis 1, which also overlaps Analyses 1 and 2 in Chapter 4 and Analysis 2 in Chapter 5. Paradoxically, research has also shown widespread discontent with Nazism although, as Analysis 2 shows, this was more apparent as small-scale 'dissent' and 'opposition' over specific issues than as overall 'resistance' to the regime itself.

ANALYSIS 1: HOW EXTENSIVE WAS THE SUPPORT FOR HITLER AND NAZISM?

Support can be active or tacit, positive or negative. It can mean direct commitment through personal conviction or, alternatively, the absence of opposition through fear of the consequences. Both types existed in Nazi Germany.

The main reason for positive support was the personal popularity of Hitler. To many he was a direct successor to the populist vision of the Kaiser during the Second Reich. There had been no equivalent during the Weimar Republic, with the possible exception of Hindenburg. Hitler therefore filled a gap and greatly extended the leadership cult. His appeal also had a chameleon nature: he offered something different to each class and yet pulled them all together with the uniqueness of his own vision for the future. Kershaw stresses that he was seen as 'representing the national interest, putting the nation first before any particularist cause and wholly detached from any personal, material or selfish motives'.[1] He struck a chord with the widespread disillusionment with the institutions, parties and leaders of the Weimar Republic. He had, of course, the considerable advantage of a monopoly of the media, and Goebbels maintained that the Hitler myth was his greatest success in propaganda. But in a sense Hitler transcended the manufactured image; indeed, he could be seen as more important to propaganda – as an overall synthesiser of Nazi messages – than propaganda was to him.

The main reason for his popularity – and this may seem surprising – was that he was seen as a moderate. After all, he made sure that his political changes were technically constitutional; he emphasised that he was upholding traditional virtues; and, at least until the late 1930s, he professed to be deeply religious. There was considerable unease about the Nazi movement, especially about the thuggish tendencies of some of its members like Röhm and Streicher. But Hitler was perceived as the moderate who would tame the radicals. For this reason, he was seen 'practically as a hero' after the Night of the Long Knives in 1934.[2] In 1934 a secret report for the Social Democratic Party in Exile (*Sopade*) reluctantly conceded: 'A general phenomenon that has been noticeable for some time is still evident: Hitler is generally exempted from criticism'.[3] (See Source 1.3 below.) Another public manifestation of his strength was his detachment from politics. According to Welch, 'By appearing to stand above the day-to-day realities of the regime, Hitler acted as a kind of medieval monarch, as a positive symbol, a focus of loyalty and of national unity'.[4] Hitler was also able to reassure: in addition to 'moderating' the internal excesses of the Nazi movement, he appeared to guarantee peace externally, using it as a constant theme in his speeches until 1939. And, above all, he delivered results. A *Sopade* report in the spring of 1939 maintained that the key to Hitler's popularity was the drop in unemployment and his growing success in foreign policy. It should, of course, be said that he was fortunate here: he benefited from opportunities, which he seized. One was the upturn in the economy after 1933, which was projected to a grateful population as his doing rather than a cyclical phenomenon which was affecting other countries as well. He also gained considerable ground in his quest for revisionism against the Versailles settlement: the population compared the rather slow developments of the Stresemann era with Hitler's success in remilitarising the Rhineland in 1936 and annexing Austria and the Sudetenland in 1938 – all without recourse to war. Then, when war did come, he achieved a series of stunning *Blitzkrieg* victories, especially the defeat of France in June 1940. It is hardly surprising that at this stage Hitler reached the highest point of his popularity and reputation.

Not all Germans were taken in by the Führer cult; many saw through the projection of his image as an apparent moderate. Yet for those who were not swept along in professed support for the system, there were too many negative constraints on action. The constitutional changes, especially the Law Against the New Formation of Parties of July 1933, had removed the possibility not only of voting for an established opposition but even the possibility of setting up a new one. Besides, the step-by-step approach of the 'legal revolution', whereby all structural changes to Germany's institutions were made to appear within the scope of the Constitution, made opposition appear increasingly illogical. Why should it be justifiable now when earlier steps taken by the Nazis within the same process had not been resisted? As a result, opposition was no longer seen as a vital component of democracy, but rather as synonymous with disloyalty and treason. It therefore came within the scope of the terror applied by the SS and Gestapo, which was intended both to create object lessons and to isolate individuals by smashing the organisation which might have given them voice. Terror worked well because it affected only a minority but, at the same time, deterred the majority from speaking out over issues that did not immediately affect them. Overall, it made sense for most Germans to accept a trend which seemed inexorable rather than to make themselves a target for certain and terrible retribution.

Looking at the different sectors of the population has, in the past, produced a number of stereotypes. The upper and middle classes, for example, were seen as enthusiastic supporters of the regime, having brought Hitler to power in the first place. The working class, by contrast, were oppressed by the Nazi system and had to grow to accept it in the absence of the parties which they traditionally supported, the SPD and the KPD. The female population was repressed but compliant; the army was split between fervent Nazi supporters and a substantial layer of higher officers, usually Prussian, who held the Nazis in barely concealed contempt; and the churches were deeply disturbed about the whole basis of the Nazi *Machtergreifung*. Much of this has now been modified by recent historical research which has used a more distinctively bottom-up approach in examining the details of social behaviour and everyday life during the Third Reich.

The upper middle class, especially the business sector, had initially supported the Nazi Party out of fear of Communism. During the Third

Reich, the great industrialists threw in their lot with Hitler because the regime delivered to them a disciplined workforce which was deprived of any effective means of collective bargaining. Although Marxist historians have tended to exaggerate the 'monopoly capital' influence on Nazism, there remains little doubt that the industrial barons and the regime saw eye-to-eye with each other. Mobilisation for war brought an even closer identity, and many major industrial enterprises, such as Krupp and I.G. Farben, became fully implicated in the worst excesses of Nazi occupation in wartime.

The bulk of the middle classes are more difficult to disentangle. Some benefited greatly from Nazi rule and became a key element in the support of the regime. But others were more marginalised. The latter included the small landowners or peasantry. Theirs was an ambiguous position. On the one hand, Hitler built up the peasantry as the basis of the Nazi blood-and-soil policy, therefore as the most crucial component of the *Volksgemeinschaft*. On the other hand, the peasantry probably experienced the least benefit from the economic recovery from 1933, and had to suffer interference from the State in the form of the Reich Entailed Farm Law preventing the subdivision of estates. Nevertheless, any resentment remained quiescent and there was no direct opposition from this sector. Small businesses also had a mixed record. Those which were reasonably efficient thrived in the atmosphere of the mid-1930s, while those which were struggling went to the wall. Hence the successful artisanate tended to worship Hitler, while that sector which failed was in effect proletarianised and had to settle for being nazified through the institutions aimed at the working class. At least they were not absorbed into the Communist ethos which remained a concern to them. The salary-earning and white-collar sector of society, the so-called 'new' middle class, were less attracted by the 'blood-and-soil' or 'small self-made man' ethos of the Nazi appeal. They were, however, more responsive to the increased opportunities which accompanied economic revival and the rapidly growing bureaucratic complex which was Nazi Germany. The Nazi State was administered by huge numbers of officials who sank their individual identity into an authoritarian and impersonal system.

It was once argued that the working class remained more resistant to Nazi influences under the *Volksgemeinschaft*. It is true that the workers were less affected than the middle classes by the Führer cult and that they benefited far less from the economic recovery after 1933. After all, their wages were pegged, their working hours increased and their contributions to the GNP unacknowledged. They therefore had cause for grievance. Yet the fact is that the vast majority settled down into tacit support. According to Overy, the working class was not 'homogeneous', and therefore open to Nazi efforts to take it over. 'Nazi propaganda played up working-class patriotism and racialism, creating in important ways some kind of identity of interest between rulers and ruled.'[5] Hence workers were drawn into the activities and diversions offered by the 'Strength through Joy' (KdF) and 'Beauty of Labour' (SDA) movements. Increasingly they felt a sense of equality with other classes rather than a crisis of conflict with them; indeed, for many, the *Volksgemeinschaft* transcended class altogether. The regime was generally credited with their economic recovery during the mid 1930s. Mason argues that Nazi economic policies convinced many workers that 'things were getting better, especially as, for most of them, the point of reference was not the best years of the Weimar Republic but the more recent depths of the Depression'.[6] By the late 1930s most accepted the adjustment of work to mobilisation for war, which, according to Crew, confirmed that 'firm integration into traditional socio-cultural milieux' had been 'shaken'.[7] All this made it increasingly difficult for the opposition cells of Social Democrats and Communists to recruit members of a resistance organisation. (See Analysis 2.) Indeed, according to another *Sopade* report, 'There is no mistaking the enormous personal gains in credibility and prestige that Hitler has made, mainly perhaps among workers'.[8]

Women were for many years seen by historians as a distinct group, forced into compliance to the Nazi regime. Mason, for example, argued that, when it came to dealing with women, Nazism was the 'most repressive and reactionary of all modern political movements'.[9] By this approach, compliance was the result of unrelieved repression.

Others, however, point to substantial gains made by women during the Nazi era. Haffner considers that their status 'made great leaps forward'.[10] Recent historiography, to which major contributions have been made by women, has also integrated them more fully into the mainstream of German life: as such, women would have experienced the full range of views about Hitler. Nazism would, on the one hand, have exercised an appeal based on the family and home, reinforced by improved provision for maternity, family benefits, financial assistance, help with chores, and visits from welfare workers and nurses.[11] This all added up to a strong emphasis on the importance of the family and the central role of women in this. Against this, of course, was the resentment caused by the removal of women from many sectors of employment, especially the professions. But this was often offset by the creation of new roles within party and public organisations, with which many women became actively involved. Hence for some women the Nazi regime actually brought further opportunities than had been available under the Weimar Republic. This applied especially to women who had few formal qualifications but who wished to be involved in political activism. By 1935 about 11 million out of the country's 35 million females belonged to the Nazi Women's Movement (*NS-Frauenschaft*) and were willing to support the ideas and beliefs of Nazism. Not all of these were meekly subservient: some, who were actually Nazi activists, challenged the official line on gender subordination. For example, a Nazi feminist, Sophie Rogge-Berne, argued in 1937 that it was misguided to remove women from the professions since 'Women doctors could give aid and comfort to fatigued mothers. Women teachers would be most suited to instruct adolescent girls. Women jurists would be most qualified for dealing with cases involving children'.[12] Overall, women are now accredited with a more active role in Nazi Germany, although this places more emphasis on their complicity with, rather than their compliance to, the regime.

The army has always been seen as largely dominated by the Nazi political system, but there has been some shift in interpretations concerning its complicity in German war crimes. The bulk of the army was systematically taken over. Until 1934, at least, it always had the option of removing Hitler, and Hindenburg, of course, remained its commander-in-chief until his death. But Hitler won its support by stealth rather than by the confrontation preferred by Röhm, who wished to submerge the field grey into the 'brown flood' of the SA. The army was grateful for the action taken by Hitler during the Night of the Long Knives and, on the death of Hindenburg, backed his claim to the presidency. The support of the army was also institutionalised to an unprecedented degree in an oath of allegiance, making any future opposition an act akin to treason: 'I swear before God to give my unconditional obedience to Adolf Hitler, Führer of the Reich and of the German People, Supreme Commander.'[13] But the influence went further. Every attempt was made to nazify the army through the adoption of the swastika insignia on uniforms and through a prolonged process of indoctrination. The introduction of the *Waffen SS* as the elite corps was considered crucial for the invasion and conquest of much of Europe.

For many years the view was that it was the SS, not the *Wehrmacht*, which committed the atrocities in the occupied territories. More recent research, however, has shown that the army played an integral part in the shooting of civilians in Poland and the Ukraine. Indeed, Bartov has argued that even members of the working class, who had once supported the SPD or KPD, could be transformed into 'brutalized and fanaticized soldiers'.[14] It has also been argued that the army was partly responsible for the rise of the SS. Boehnert has shown that after the silencing of the threat from Röhm and the SA, significant numbers of retired army officers joined the SS, helping to establish the respectability of the latter.

> In a more direct manner the retired officers provided invaluable assistance in shaping the military branch of the SS. By doing so they inadvertently helped to create the branch of the SS which in a few years would successfully challenge the military's traditional right as the sole bearer of arms.[15]

Finally, the Christian churches gave a cautious initial welcome to the Nazi regime. Neither the Catholic Church nor the various Protestant organisations had been ardent supporters of the Weimar Republic; both disliked the materialism and decline in spiritual values they accused the Republic of fostering and both saw a threat from the 'godless' left of socialism and, even worse, Communism. Catholic and Protestant leaders reacted positively to Hitler's assurance on 23 March 1933 that Christianity was 'the unshakeable foundation of the moral and ethical life of our people'.[16] Catholic goodwill was strengthened by the Concordat, signed on 20 July 1933 by Cardinal Pacelli and Franz von Papen. Catholic bishops undertook to swear loyalty to the state, Catholic trade unions were to be dismantled and the clergy were to be prevented from participating in political activity. In exchange Catholics were guaranteed freedom of worship, the right to distribute pastoral letters and state protection for denominational schools. This seemed to satisfy the main needs of the Catholic Church, and Bishop Berning made a public statement on 21 September 1933: 'The German bishops have long ago said Yes to the new State, and have not only promised to recognise its authority . . . but are serving the State with burning love and all our strength.'

Protestant leaders were even more willing to accept the new regime. At first this was largely voluntary. There had been extensive distrust of the Weimar Republic because of the Catholic influence exercised through the Centre Party; where they had been politicised, ardent Protestants had tended to support the parties of the right, especially the DVP and the DNVP, and many had found the switch to the NSDAP relatively easy. According to Steinbach, many of the Protestant clergy welcomed the Nazi 'seizure of power because they mistook it for the reestablishment of "order" and traditional state authority'.[17] The Protestant structure was taken over in July 1933, when 28 provincial churches were incorporated into a single Reich Church; two years later this was placed under Hans Kerrl, the Minister of Church Affairs. In its most extreme form, Protestantism was directly nazified, in the form of the 'German Christians', an organisation whose members readily combined Christianity with racism, anti-Semitism and Führer-worship. But such examples of initial cooperation with the regime did not mean total surrender. Both Catholics and Protestants began to speak out, first against government policy on specific issues, then against the regime itself: this is dealt with in Analysis 2.

Overall, there has been a recent shift in interpretation about the extent to which the regime was voluntarily supported by the population. More emphasis is now placed on complicity with the Nazi regime at all levels. Three historians present a particularly disturbing picture. Mallmann and Paul[18] argue that the Gestapo relied predominantly on information volunteered by large numbers of people – from all sections of society, including the working class. (See Chapter 5, Analysis 2.) Goldhagen goes further by insisting that a substantial portion of the German army were willing agents in the slaughter of Jews in the Ukraine and Russia.[19] It is, of course, possible that the pendulum has swung too far in the other direction and that more notice needs to be taken of the opposition which developed to the regime. To this we now turn.

Questions

1. How 'genuine' was the support within Germany for Hitler and the Nazi regime?
2. Did the appeal of Hitler and the Nazi regime break class barriers?

ANALYSIS 2: EXAMINE THE OPPOSITION AND RESISTANCE TO THE NAZI REGIME

The original focus on 'opposition' was political, primarily on 'resistance' to the regime; this applied in both parts of post-war Germany. According to the East German historian, Mammach, 'The most consistent political force of this movement, the KPD, carried out from the first day of the fascist dictatorship, organized, and centrally directed, the struggle against imperialism . . .'.[20] The emphasis was therefore on Communist defiance at the expense of other movements. West German writers, meanwhile, pointed to the importance of the political and military plots formed against Hitler in wartime. Both approaches are now seen as too narrow, and more attention is now given to the widespread nature of opposition and resistance. This is due partly to the increase of specialist studies on all areas of the Third Reich and partly to the influential thesis that the Nazi system was less efficient than was originally thought. (See Chapters 3 and 5.) The incomplete nature of German totalitarianism meant that opposition was not only possible; it was a reality, and affected many different areas of society.

The problem is that 'opposition' and 'resistance' have become more difficult to define. Historians have used them in different ways, sometimes exclusively, sometimes interchangeably. One of the definitions that makes most sense is that of Stibbe, who makes a distinction between resistance (defined as 'politically organised action aimed at the overthrow of the National Socialist system') and opposition (or 'any type of behaviour that was intentionally non-conformist or that showed contempt for the Nazi regime and its policies').[21] Kershaw distinguishes between 'resistance', 'opposition' and 'dissent'. Resistance meant 'active participation in organized attempts to work against the regime with the conscious aim of undermining it or planning for the moment of its demise'. Opposition was a 'wider concept', which involved 'many forms of action with partial and limited aims'. It was 'not directed against Nazism as a system' and sometimes came from 'individuals or groups broadly sympathetic towards the regime and its ideology'. Dissent meant 'the voicing of attitudes frequently spontaneous and often unrelated to any intended action'.[22] Other historians have made further distinctions between actions that were 'defensive' or 'offensive', 'self-interested' or 'principled'.

The categorisation to be used in the rest of this Analysis is based on the following. There were widespread social manifestations of 'opposition' to various aspects of the regime. The most common but least threatening to the regime itself were grumbling and minor dissent. Another area, more controversial and difficult to assess precisely, was 'deviant behaviour', which might or might not be aimed directly at the Nazi system. Third, there was opposition over specific issues, where people were provoked into taking a stand for a particular reason without, however, aiming to bring down the regime. The fourth category moves into the area of 'resistance' where the aim of banned political groups from the SPD and KPD was to bring down the Nazi regime altogether. During the period of war, a fifth element came to the fore as a variety of groups sought to remove Hitler from power and to seek a settlement with the Allies. These ranged from organised conservative political groups, principled individuals – both religious and secular – and military conspiracies.

'Opposition'

Despite the levels of support given to the Nazi regime and the adulation in which Hitler himself was held, grumbling and minor dissent were quite widespread. Kershaw argues that:

> The acute perception of social injustice, the class-conscious awareness of inequalities . . . changed less in the Third Reich than is often supposed. . . . The extent of disillusionment and discontent in almost all sections of the population, rooted in the socio-economic experience of daily life, is remarkable.[23]

There was, for example, considerable oral dissent about the lack of wage increases, or increased working hours, or compulsory activities within the KdF, or the increasing subordination of the consumer market to rearmament. Yet the type of discontent remained remarkably low key, certainly when compared with the resistance of the peasantry to collectivisation in the Soviet Union. There was little chance of discontent ever being converted into something stronger. *Sopade* reports indicated that most grumbling was sparked by economic conditions, and not by more fundamental reservations about the nature of the regime. 'This is especially so among the *Mittelstand* and the peasantry. These social strata are least of all ready to fight seriously against the regime because they know least of all what they should fight for.'[24] Most Germans were therefore never likely to turn against a system which, for all its inconveniences, they still preferred to the Weimar Republic.

In contrast to undirected grumbling, formal complaints might be made about specific issues or as a matter of conscience. These might involve individuals, small groups or major institutions. Individual women, for example, made a stand over aspects of social legislation which impinged on the interests of their families. Jehovah's Witnesses refused the call to military service and, as a result, many were sent to concentration camps. More generally, there was at least some disquiet about the treatment of the Jewish population, which meant individual Germans protested to authorities or helped Jews evade the measures taken against them. This, however, involved the risk of investigation by the Gestapo, followed by public disgrace, prosecution and imprisonment. Most Germans, therefore, kept their heads down and did nothing – even at the time of *Kristallnacht* in 1938. Even so, the regime was sufficiently aware of popular concerns about the later killing of Jews to change to a policy of secret extermination.

The most organised and concerted 'opposition' over specific issues came from the churches, which clashed with the regime on three occasions before 1939. One was Pastor Niemoller's objection to the establishment of the Nazi-dominated Ministry of Churches under Hans Kerrl. (See Analysis 1.) The second instance was the Catholic protest against the government order to replace crucifixes by portraits of Hitler in Catholic schools. A third, and the most significant, stance was taken in opposition to the regime's euthanasia programme from 1939 onwards. These complaints varied in the degree of their success. The Protestant opposition was less likely to succeed than the Catholic, owing to the fragmentation of Protestantism into a number of different sects and the fundamental issue on which that opposition was being expressed: the regime could hardly be expected to reverse a major constitutional change. The Catholic Church, by contrast, was a centralised structure, with considerable capacity for exerting pressure at certain specific points. It succeeded over the two issues it contested: the programmes to nazify Catholic schools and to conduct the clandestine euthanasia programmes were both temporarily suspended. On the other hand, the more general complaints made by the Pope in his 1937 encyclical *Mit brennender Sorge (With Deep Anxiety)*, that the regime had broken the provisions of the Concordat across the board, were less likely to succeed. There is little doubt that Christianity proved most effective not as a general impetus for opposition but as a residue for the nation's conscience. Despite efforts at the end of the 1930s to eradicate it through the paganism of the Nazi Faith Movement, the majority of Germans remained either Catholic or Protestant, and the incidence of church attendance actually increased after 1939.

One category of opposition greatly puzzled the authorities. Social deviance was most apparent among younger Germans, especially from the working class, and pointed to the deficiencies of the Hitler Youth as a channel of indoctrination. As the whole structure became more bureaucratised and less imaginative, some of the earlier attractions began to wear off. The Hitler Youth came to be seen increasingly as part of the establishment rather than as a rival to it. Hence there developed alternative, even oppositional, cultures and groups among youth. Deviant behaviour among adolescents during the Third Reich was much wider than was once thought. In 1942 the Reich Youth Leadership stated:

> The formation of cliques, i.e. groupings of young people outside the Hitler Youth, has been on the increase before and, particularly, during the war to such a degree that one must speak of a serious risk of the political, moral and criminal subversion of youth.[25]

Examples included the Navajos, centred largely on Cologne, the Kittelbach Pirates of Oberhausen and Düsseldorf, and the Roving Dudes of Essen. These were all sub-groups within the broader Edelweiss Pirates. They were antagonistic to authority and in particular to the Hitler Youth, patrols which they would ambush and beat up: indeed one of their slogans was 'Eternal War on the Hitler Youth'. They also defied restrictions on movement during the war by undertaking extensive hikes, and they maintained a much more liberal attitude to sexuality than the authorities liked. Some also supported the Allies during the war or offered help to German army deserters. Less militant and more cultural in its emphasis was the Swing Movement. This was aimed more against the cultural indoctrination of the Reich and it adopted influences from British and especially American jazz. This was particularly provocative to the authorities, who regarded jazz as 'negro music' and therefore as 'degenerate'. In all cases the authorities were seriously concerned, but frequently did not know what to do – apart from the occasional salutary public hanging of Edelweiss Pirates. At the same time, the activities of the Edelweiss Pirates and Swing Movements lacked the organisational edge to be anything more than an embarrassment to the regime. Social deviance was, therefore, never likely to amount to serious political challenge.

'Resistance'

Resistance was aimed at changing the regime itself rather than at specific measures taken by it. At first this was largely 'political', as the parties of the left – the Social Democrats and Communists – continued to oppose the Nazi regime legally until they were banned and many of their activists imprisoned. From the middle of 1933 they went underground or into exile and legal opposition became treasonable resistance. Until 1939 there were few other instances of resistance except for courageous individuals who protested against Nazi racial policies. During the war years, however, a second wave of resistance occurred, especially after the invasion of the Soviet Union in 1941 and the threat of defeat on the eastern front from 1942 and 1943. This consisted of 'conservative' political organisations, military conspiracies, and small secular or religious groups acting for reasons of conscience.

Left-wing resistance developed at the outset of the Third Reich. The KPD and SPD were left in isolation by the capitulation of the other parties. The SPD had been the only party to vote against the Enabling Act, the Communist deputies having been banned from taking up their seats won in the March Reichstag election. Both parties were banned after refusing to take the course of voluntary liquidation adopted by the others. Even then, neither gave up, setting up organisations abroad and attempting to foster resistance within Germany.

But this had disappointing results. The Communists tried to fight the Nazi regime as they had the Weimar Republic – but failed badly. This was due in part to the success of the Gestapo in identifying and eradicating

Communist cells. As a result, something like 10 per cent of the whole Communist membership were killed, and Thälmann, the leader of the KPD, was arrested as early as 1933. There were also unpredictable shifts in Communist policy. Initially strongly antagonistic to the SPD, they rejected the latter's feelers for joint collaboration against the Nazi regime. Then, in 1935, they reversed this in response to instructions from Comintern – only to find that the SPD had started to distance themselves from the far left. Further changes came as a result of direct influence from the Soviet Union. The Nazi–Soviet Non-Aggression Pact (August 1939) prevented any remaining resistance until Hitler's invasion of the Soviet Union in 1941. The Communist regime in East Germany that followed Hitler's eventual downfall was more the result of direct Soviet occupation than of home-bred Communist resistance to Nazism, despite the argument by East German historians that it was a combination of both.

The SPD experienced changes which were a mirror-image to those of the Communists. After a relatively inactive first year, the Social Democratic Party in Exile (*Sopade*) issued in 1934 a Manifesto from its headquarters in Prague, drafted by Rudolf Hilferding. This argued that 'The answer is total revolution – moral, intellectual, political and social revolution!' The battle to bring down the Nazi regime 'cannot be waged in any other way'. It was also essential to collaborate with all other opposition groups, including the Communists, since 'The unification of the working class is a necessity imposed by history itself'.[26] But by the time the Communists were willing to accept the need for a united anti-fascist front, the SPD had begun to move away from a revolutionary leftist stance. The strategy of the Social Democrats was being changed by information in *Sopade* reports about the popularity of Hitler with many sections of the working class, even in working-class heartlands. Hence *Sopade* began from 1935 to look to longer-term cooperation with exiled politicians from the bourgeois liberal parties.

The result was a disunited front. There were attempts to bring the two together, but these were not generally welcomed by the leadership of the SPD. In terms of actual resistance, the Communists were more active during the 1930s, the SPD generally being more restrained and cautious, influenced as they were by the more accurate information they had from *Sopade* reports on the attitudes of German workers. The success of the Gestapo in infiltrating Communist cells meant that professional agitators were replaced by inexperienced local volunteers and neither they nor the Social Democrats succeeded in making any major inroads into the working classes. As we have already seen, there was plenty of grumbling but little chance of persuading workers to risk their livelihood or families in the expression of political opposition.

Later initiatives were partly political and partly military. There was also more widespread individual and small-group resistance, for example, from Dietrich Bonhoeffer and student organisations like *Weisse Rose* (for which Hans and Sophie Scholl and fellow students distributed leaflets at Munich University against Hitler's leadership after the failure at Stalingrad in 1943). Increasingly organised resistance aimed to remove the regime altogether. Realistically, this could be done only by a 'coup' from within the power structure, since all the constitutional channels had been blocked by Hitler's changes between 1933 and 1934, and the Communists and Social Democrats had shown that a broader-based 'revolution' was impossible.

The key to any chance of success was the army. This had, however, been won over by the process of gradual nazification during the 1930s. Hence the only possibility was the defection of disillusioned elements and their linking up with individuals and groups prepared to risk everything on a political substitution. The army elements had always been there. General Beck, for example, had tried to persuade the General Staff to remove Hitler in 1938, and unsuccessfully urged the British government to resist Hitler's demands over the Sudetenland. He was followed by other courageous individuals who went directly against the overwhelming weight of loyalty to the Führer. Ironically, they were nearly always members of the Prussian aristocracy, deeply conservative in their outlook and, in some instances, former enemies of the Weimar Republic. But this should not be taken to the usual extreme view that the conservative forces within the army were generally anti-Nazi. Many, as we have already seen, welcomed Nazism without reservation. This was one of the basic reasons for the failure of armed resistance: there was simply no depth in numbers to offset the failure of individual attempts on Hitler's life, such as that made by Tresckow and Schlabrendorff on 13 March 1943 and the Stauffenberg bomb plot in July 1944.

Other leading members of the resistance movements were strongly conservative, comprising members of the traditional right, many of whom had served Hitler at one time or another. Gradually, however, some elements of the conservative right had lost influence to the new Nazi functionaries and Nazism came to be seen as an alien force challenging deeply-held traditional precepts. None wanted a return to the Weimar Republic, whose political system had so patently failed to maintain stability. But there were significant differences in what they *did* want. Younger conservatives dominated the Kreisau Circle, led by Count von Moltke and Count von Wartenburg. This aimed at achieving a decentralised post-Hitlerian Germany where the emphasis of political parties would be replaced by that on small communities and a system of direct elections at the lower (*Kreis*) levels followed by indirectly elected *Länder* and Reichstag; ideally, Germany would also be part of a federal Europe.[27] Older conservatives included men of some experience, for example Goerdeler (former mayor of Leipzig), von Hassell (former ambassador to Rome) and von Popitz (former Prussian finance minister). These were traditional – even Wilhelmine – in outlook. Certainly, they were no democrats, wanting a system much more authoritarian than that of the Weimar Republic, including an executive able to govern by decree and reversible only by a two-thirds majority in the legislature. In many ways they reflected the aims of the conservatives in the final years of the Republic.

Ultimately, however, all such resistance failed in its objective – which was to replace Hitler's regime and to negotiate an armistice with the Allies. There would be no repetition of the situation in October and November 1918, since Hitler himself was head of state and was not open to any attempts to do a deal. Even in the final year of the regime, resistance was on a smaller scale than elsewhere in Nazi-occupied Europe or in Italy, which produced more powerful anti-fascist organisations. The various organisations also had unrealistic or divided aims. The conservatives rejected both totalitarianism and democracy, hoping to step back into a pre-democratic era, while the military resistance experienced an apparently generational split between cautious and impulsive officers. There were also problems over communication. There were, it is true, links between civilian and military resistance – for example between Goerdeler and Beck – and the Stauffenberg plot involved the support of a substantial number of conservatives. But difficulties occurred over maintaining security, or in agreeing a different system after the removal of Hitler from power. Hence, according to Broszat, 'The history of military resistance represents a unique example of the conflict between politics and warfare'.[28] Foreign governments also played a part in impeding resistance within Germany. At first they compromised with the regime, thereby enhancing its reputation and undermining any chance of effective opposition to it. Examples included the Papal Concordat with Germany in 1933, the Anglo-German Naval Agreement (1935), the Munich Agreement (1938) and the Nazi–Soviet Non-Aggression Pact of 1939. After 1941 the opposite occurred as foreign governments refused to negotiate in any way. The Allies' insistence on Germany's unconditional surrender removed an important component from the programme of the German resistance movement; this meant that Nazism could be removed only by conquering armies, not by an internal coup. The reasoning of the Allies was that, by 1944, the Führer, once Nazi Germany's main asset, had become its greatest liability.

Questions

1. How much genuine 'opposition' was there within Germany to the Nazi regime?
2. Was 'resistance' at any stage a viable proposition in Nazi Germany?

SOURCES

1: POPULAR SUPPORT?

Source 1.1: An extract from *Mein Kampf*

Mass assemblies are also necessary for the reason that, in attending them, the individual who felt himself formerly only on the point of joining the new movement, now begins to feel isolated and in fear of being left alone as he acquires for the first time the picture of a great community which has a strengthening and encouraging effect on most people. Brigaded in a company or battalion, surrounded by his companions, he will march with a lighter heart to the attack than if he had to march alone. In the crowd he feels himself in some way thus sheltered.

Source 1.2: The dedication, by Goering, on the first page of a photograph album entitled *Adolf Hitler*, published in 1936

My Führer, we are not able to express our thanks in words. Nor are we able to show our loyalty and affection for you in words. Our entire gratitude, love for, and trust in you, my Führer, is shining upon you today from hundreds of thousands of eyes. Today the entire nation, the entire people feels strong and happy, because in you not only the Führer but also the saviour of the nation has appeared.

Source 1.3: From a report by *Sopade*, 1934

A general phenomenon that has been noticeable for some time is still evident: Hitler is generally exempted from criticism …

A correspondent from Berlin puts the point in more detail. In general we can say that Adolf Hitler is exempted from criticism, his aims are conceded as honourable and people think that he cannot be blamed for the mismanagement of his subordinates. This is partly the result of the systematic Führer propaganda, but is also undoubtedly the effect of his personality. His personality impresses simple people, and Hitler still has a lot of personal support among the workers.

Source 1.4: From a report by *Sopade*, 1935

KdF events have become very popular. Even ordinary workers can afford these walking trips, since they are generally cheaper than private hikes.

Almost all national comrades rate KdF as one of National Socialism's really creditable achievements. KdF sport courses are enjoying greater and greater popularity even among older people. Everyonc can take part.

Source 1.5: From a report by *Sopade*, 1935

It became clear that the effects of the economic crisis on the inward resistance of the workers were more appalling than had previously been thought, We see it time and time again; the most courageous illegal fighter, the most relentless antagonist of the regime, is usually the unemployed man who has no more to lose. Whereas if a worker gets a job after years out of work, then – however bad his pay and conditions – he at once becomes apprehensive. Now he does have something to lose, however little, and the fear of the renewed misery of unemployment is worse than the misery itself. The National Socialists have not conquered the factories. The standing of the National Socialist 'shop stewards' has constantly fallen, while that of the old free union works committees has risen in corresponding degree. But the National Socialists have destroyed the workers' self-confidence: they have crushed the forces of solidarity and crippled their will to resist.

Questions

1. How useful and reliable would Sources 1.3, 1.4 and 1.5 be to the historian studying the popularity of the Nazi regime?
2. 'Support for Hitler after 1933 existed for a variety of different reasons.' Comment on this view in the light of these sources and of your own knowledge.

2: CATHOLIC OPPOSITION?

Source 2.1: A public statement made by Bishop Berning, 21 September 1933

The German bishops have long ago said Yes to the new State, and have not only promised to recognise its authority ... but are serving the State with burning love and all our strength.

Source 2.2: From an official report, 1937

The fact is that thirty to forty villagers got into the unlocked school on the night of 6 January 1937 to hang the crucifix back in its old place. Against the explicit advice of the witness R. that the crucifix had been taken down by the order of the government and that the break-in would constitute a breach of the peace if they contravened this order, the accused B.A. (with the help of a ladder which he fetched), hung the crucifix right up beside the picture of the Führer, which had been put in this newly assigned place. Everyone then left the school.

The court of Rhaunen, on 9 January 1937, ordered a custodial sentence against B.A.

Source 2.3: From the Papal Encyclical *With Burning Anxiety*, 14 March 1937

With burning anxiety and mounting unease we have observed for some time the way of suffering of the Church, the growing harassment of the confessors who stay true to it in spirit …

He who singles out race, the people of the State, the form of State, the bearers of State power or other basic element of human social organisation … he who singles out such elements from this worldly scale of values and sets them up as the highest norm over all, including over religious values, and reverences them with idolatry, he distorts and falsifies the God-created, God-demanded order of things. Such a person is far from real belief in God and from a conception of life that corresponds to such a belief.

Source 2.4: Cardinal Galen's protest against police measures, 13 July 1941

Justice is the state's foundation. We lament, we regard with great concern, the evidence of how this foundation is being shaken today, how justice – that natural Christian virtue, which is indispensable to the orderly existence of every human society – is not being plainly implemented and maintained for all. It is not only for the sake of the rights of the Church, not only for that of the rights of the human personality, it is also out of love for our nation and out of our profound concern for our country that we beg, ask, demand Justice! Who is there among us who does not fear for the survival of his home when the foundations are being sapped7

The regular courts have no say over the jurisdiction by decree of the Secret Police. Since none of us know of a way that might give us an impartial control over the measures of the Gestapo – its expulsions, its arrests, its imprisonment of fellow Germans in concentration camps – large groups of Germans have a feeling of being without rights, and what is worse, harbour feelings of cowardly fear. Great harm is being done to the German community in this way.

The obligation of my episcopal office to defend the moral order, and the loyalty to my oath, which I swore before God and the government's representative, to prevent to the best of my ability any harm that might come to the German body politic, impel me, in view of the Gestapo's actions, to say this publicly.

Source 2.5: From a letter sent by the Bishop of Limburg to the Minister of Justice, 13 August 1941

Perhaps 8 km from Limburg, on a hill directly above the little town of Hadamar, there is an institution which used to serve a variety of purposes. Most recently it was a religious and nursing institution. It has been converted and kitted out as a place in which (according to popular opinion) euthanasia has been carried out systematically for months – since around February 1941. The fact is well known throughout the government district of Wiesbaden, because death certificates are sent from a registry in Hadamar-Mönchberg to the home districts concerned ...

All God-fearing people feel this extermination of the helpless is an almighty crime. And if this is the same as saying that Germany cannot win the war if there is still a just God, then these statements are not caused by a lack of love for the Fatherland, but rather from deeply concerned frame of mind about our Volk. The population just cannot understand that systematic actions are being carried out which, according to section 211 of the statutory law book, are punishable by death. The authority of the government as a moral concept is suffering a dreadful trauma because of these events.

Source 2.6: Bishop Würm to the Head of Hitler's Chancellery, 20 December 1943

In agreement with the judgement of all truly Christian people in Germany, I must state that we Christians feel this policy of destroying the Jews to be a grave wrong, and one which will have fearful consequences for the German people. To kill without the necessity of war, and without legal judgement, contravenes God's commands even when it has been ordered by authority, and, like every conscious violation of God's law, will be avenged, sooner or later.

Source 2.7: From a sermon given by Bishop Galen in 1944

In this hour I must direct a word of greeting and acknowledgement to our soldiers. I wish to express our gratitude to them for the loyal protection they have furnished the Fatherland and its borders at the price of unspeakable strains and sheer superhuman effort. In particular for the defence against the assaults of godless Bolshevism! And a word of deep-felt remembrance for those who, in the performance of their duty, have offered their lives and their last drop of blood for their brothers. May these all-sacrificing efforts succeed in winning for us an honourable and victorious peace!

Questions

1. According to Sources 2.2 to 2.6, over what issues did the Catholic Church oppose government policies?
2. What evidence is there in Sources 2.1 to 2.7 that the Catholic Church in Germany was 'patriotic'?
*3. What other types of source would be of use to the historian investigating how widespread was opposition to Nazi policies from the Catholic Church?
4. 'The opposition of Catholics to the Nazi regime steadily strengthened between 1933 and 1945.' Examine this view in the light of Sources 2.1 to 2.7 and of your own knowledge.

WORKED ANSWER

*3 *[This asks for types of source rather than specifically named sources. The important thing is to achieve a variety.]*

All but one of the sources provided are of a single type: they are produced by Church leaders. A variety of other sources would be needed to supplement these, always supposing that these had survived destruction in the last stages of the war. One type would be the official responses of government departments to the complaints of Bishop Würm, the Bishop of Limburg and Cardinal Galen. Another would be the parish records indicating church attendance: did this increase or decline during the Nazi era? A third would be the attitudes of other members of the clergy at different levels: how many other letters of complaint were sent to the departments, or letters of support to Galen? A fourth would be material linking the Catholic Church to political opposition or to the emergence of the Christian Democratic

Union in the immediate postwar era. Finally, do the *Sopade* reports contain any reference to Catholic dissidents? All of these would help to establish the extent of support for the initiatives of the few leaders shown in the Sources.

3: HISTORIANS ON LEFT-WING RESISTANCE

Source 3.1: An extract from Klaus Mammach's work on the German anti-fascist resistance, published in East Germany in 1974

The German anti-fascist resistance movement, especially the KPD and the forces allied with it, embodied the progressive line of German policy. The most consistent political force of this movement, the KPD, carried out from the first day of the fascist dictatorship, organized, and centrally directed, the struggle against imperialism and preparation for war in which it was supported by the Communist International and the other fraternal parties and in which it constantly sought to incorporate new allies. The anti-fascist, democratic programme worked out by the KPD with help of the Communist International represented a true alternative to fascist barbarism and war. ... The expression of the victory of the resolute anti-fascists after the smashing of fascism by the Soviet Union and the other states of the Anti-Hitler Coalition and the defeat of German imperialism is the existence of the GDR in which the legacy of the best of the German people who gave their lives in the anti-fascist struggle was realized.

Source 3.2: An extract from Matthew Stibbe's *Women in the Third Reich*, published in 2003

By far the largest and best organised of the anti-Nazi groupings in Germany before 1933 were the left-wing political parties, the Social Democrats and the Communists, whose combined support still amounted to 13 million votes (or one-third of the electorate) in the Reichstag elections of November 1932. Ideological and tactical differences between them, however, had prevented any effective joint action against the Nazi seizure of power, and the period between February and December 1933 saw a mass wave of arrests and 'preventative detentions', which largely destroyed both organisations. By the end of 1933 most of the top Communist and Social Democrat functionaries were dead, on the run, in concentration camps or living in exile, and those who still lived in freedom in Germany were reluctant to engage in reckless acts of heroism, which – as they had now learned through brutal experience – would result only in pointless sacrifice of life and liberty. Instead they tended to meet in small groups for orientation, mutual support and political education, often using the camouflage of gardening clubs or hiking associations. This form of small-scale organisation also had the advantage of minimising the danger of betrayal through informers. At first, few socialists and communists believed that the Nazi regime would remain in power for long, certainly not longer than a few years; later they resigned themselves to sitting out the war until the moment when Hitler was defeated or overthrown, at which point they could emerge from the shadows in order to make their own contribution to the democratic reconstruction of Germany.

Source 3.3: Extracts from an article by Martin Broszat, published in 1991

Official Communist documents and the records of the Gestapo portray this Communist underground as an ideologically firm and well-organized resistance. A different image of these groups emerges, however, when one focuses instead upon their sociological composition and behavioral and psychological tendencies. This approach reveals a Communist underground whose activism was largely spontaneous and implemented by radical youth groups ...

Varying degrees of willingness to commit illegal acts ... reflected differences in ideology and class. The Communists tended to support a more radical political creed and the Social Democrats a more pragmatic one. Members of the Communist underground were usually young and often socially disenfranchised – facts that may explain some of their readiness to participate in risky activities. The majority of the Social Democrats, by contrast, were skilled workers or artisans, who generally enjoyed the respect of their non-Socialist, middle-class neighbors in the small towns or urban districts in which they lived. Most of them, firmly bound in their Socialist convictions, proved to be as immune to Nazi ideology and propaganda as the Communists but refrained from dangerous undertakings and illegal forms of opposition. They withdrew instead into an attitude of silent, passive resistance designed to see them through the Nazi era. Although some acts of illegal resistance expressed a youthful adventurousness, the more cautious attitude of the great majority of Social Democrats was in general a testament to this movement's essential commitment to political reason and responsibility. Working within this framework, many Social Democrats engaged in impressive, though largely silent, acts of passive resistance. On the whole their campaign displayed more consistency than that of the Communist underground, which was often erratic and was also undermined by the many members who became traitors.

Source 3.4: Extracts from Joachim Fest's *Plotting Hitler's Death: The German Resistance to Hitler 1933–1945*, published in English in 1996

The venerable Social Democratic Party met an equally pathetic end … The SPD leadership had no ready response either to Hitler's accession to power or, once he was in office, to his tactics. It was especially in the tactical arena that it utterly failed to match him. …

The Communist Party, too, disappeared with barely a whimper, in an atmosphere of quiet terror, flight, and quick reversals of old allegiance. Right up to the brink of Hitler's 'new age' it had stood its ground as a powerful foe not only of the Nazis but of the entire established order … But the Communist opponent, like other opponents, failed to materialize. … Seemingly unimpressed by either the persecution and flight of its leading members or the mass desertions among the rank and file, which began immediately upon Hitler's appointment as chancellor, the Communist Party persisted in its dogmatic belief that its most dangerous enemy was the Social Democrats. …

The Communists paid dearly for their blindness. The party evaporated without any sign of defiance, act of resistance, or even parting message to its militants. Its officials were arrested and its subsidiary organizations crushed. Those members who escaped became fugitives. Some took to plotting in nameless conspiracies that were usually quite local in nature. It is true that many Communists sacrificed their lives resisting the Nazis long before military, church, or conservative circles got into the act. But the Communist Party itself was responsible for the isolation in which its members found themselves and from which they never escaped. … Over the years, Communist resistance cells occasionally approached other resistance groups, Social Democrats in particular, with offers to join forces, but the distrust sown between 1930 and 1934 never dissipated and these feelers were generally ignored. …

The crushing of left-wing parties and the trade unions left the working class without an organizational framework. Individuals who resolved to continue the struggle found themselves alone or in league with just a few close friends. Many working-class leaders were imprisoned. Others withdrew into their private lives and a few went underground. But most left Germany to live in exile, continuing to send messages home, encouraging and advising those who remained behind. It soon became clear, however, that very few of the former rank and file were still listening.

Questions

1. Compare the views expressed in Sources 3.1 and 3.3 about the *organisation and aims* of Communist resistance to the Nazi regime.
2. Compare the views expressed in Sources 3.1, 3.2 and 3.4 about the *effectiveness* of Communist resistance to the Nazi regime.
3. Using Sources 3.1 to 3.4 – and your own knowledge – consider whether the left-wing resistance was the most widespread to the Nazi regime between 1933 and 1945.

7

THE NAZI ECONOMY

BACKGROUND

Hitler came to power after the worst of the Depression. Chancellor Brüning (1930–2) had introduced a series of deflationary measures which were intended to promote early recovery even at the expense of accelerating short-term economic decline. There is evidence that his policies were beginning to work: unemployment was already on the downturn and Hitler was able to claim the credit for the recovery.

The period 1933–6 was dominated by the Economics Minister, Hjalmar Schacht, whose New Plan of 1934 was intended to promote Germany's exports, reduce imports, strengthen the currency and establish a series of bilateral trade agreements with those less developed countries which were rich in raw materials. For a while, therefore, there was economic equilibrium. Between 1935 and 1936, however, an economic crisis forced Hitler to make a decision about future priorities. He therefore introduced in 1936 the Four Year Plan, the intention of which was to develop substitutes for essential raw materials which Germany lacked and to move to a war footing. The result was a rapid increase in the rate of rearmament. Military expenditure increased from 1.9 billion marks in 1933 to 5.8 billion at the start of the Four Year Plan, rising to 18.4 billion in 1938 and 32.3 billion in 1939. Accompanying rearmament was a series of measures to create a more disciplined workforce. In place of the trade unions, the workforce had to accept membership of organisations such as Strength through Joy (KdF) and Beauty of Labour (SDA), while at the same time coming to terms with falling living standards.

Three key issues arise from this outline. The first is the running of the economy in the first six years of the Third Reich; this is covered in Analysis 1 which examines the wide range of historians' views. Second, Analysis 2 deals with Hitler's overall economic strategy as connected with his schemes for territorial expansion and the achievement of *Lebensraum.* The ways in which this affected the German people is the theme of Analysis 3.

ANALYSIS 1: HOW HAVE HISTORIANS ASSESSED NAZI ECONOMIC POLICY BETWEEN 1933 AND 1939?

Three basic assumptions were made by the earlier historians of the Nazi economy. First, it represented a major departure from the economic policies of the Weimar Republic. Second, it came under a system of totalitarian control, which meant that priorities could be more definitively established and more effectively imposed on the population: without democratic constraints, the Nazi regime could therefore take shortcuts to speed up the process of economic recovery. Third, by 1939 this had been largely successful: through a new set of policies, ruthlessly enforced, the regime had reduced unemployment to insignificant levels, greatly increased the national income and, at the same time, rearmed in preparation for war. Innovation, control and success: these have remained the three main areas of debate among historians, each assumption being in turn dismantled then partially restored. The debate on this, the formative period of Nazi economic policy, also throws more light on the longer-term objectives, dealt with in Analysis 2, and the social impact on the German people (Analysis 3).

Innovation?

The first debate, therefore, is whether Nazi economic policies after 1933 were innovative, or whether they were based – at least initially – on those of the Weimar period. The original argument, most common during the 1950s, was that the policies of the Third Reich were a new departure. The Nazis imposed a controlled economy which contrasted with the western capitalist influences experienced by the Weimar Republic, especially during the period when the latter had been dependent on loans from the United States. These, of course, had been ended by the Wall Street Crash and the Great Depression, with the consequences of reduced production and rising unemployment. The government controls exerted by Schacht's New Plan and intensified by the Four Year Plan were a move away from earlier economic principles and resulted in new jobs being created by central planning for industrial output, public works and rearmament. The result was a huge contrast with the period before 1933. Whereas Weimar Germany had been the first industrial state to enter the Depression, Nazi Germany was the first to emerge from it – certainly in terms of production and re-employment. Whatever the cost in terms of lost freedom and subsequent aggression, this was an achievement in its own right.

Although some historians still see a major break between the economic policies of the regimes before and after 1933, the broad consensus is that there were similarities that were not originally recognised or acknowledged. James, for example, maintains that 'there existed substantial continuities between the course taken by Weimar's presidential governments and that of the National–Nazi coalition under Hitler's chancellorship'.[1] There are two particular examples of the connections which operated at least until 1936. The first was the influence exerted by the policies of Heinrich Brüning, Chancellor between 1930 and 1932; he had reduced the budget deficit by cutting government expenditure on welfare and on salaries and pensions for public employees. He had also introduced currency reform, trade restrictions and measures to promote self-sufficiency. These provided the basis for the measures introduced by Schacht in the New Plan of 1934. Second, it has been argued that Brüning's measures, considered so harsh in 1932, had begun to achieve the results intended in 1933, although it was Schacht who was given the credit. At the very least, the cycle of depression had reached its lowest level under Brüning and his successors, Papen and Schleicher, so that when Hitler was appointed Chancellor in January 1933 the upturn was imminent – irrespective of any contributions he might have made to this. The dual nature of the continuity between 1932 and 1936 has been expressed by Frei:

> It is indisputable that, at the beginning, the Nazis benefited from being able to fall back on the investment plans of preceding governments, and even more from a change in economic trends which had become apparent since 1932.[2]

Hence Hitler's early measures have been seen as a continuation of the policies and instruments started by the Brüning government. But it is important also to acknowledge that, by 1936, the Nazis were moving on and away from the Brüning base: some historians see this as the end of the economic conservative–Nazi connection a few years after the abandonment of the National–Nazi political coalition in 1933. A more distinctively Nazi policy developed in three ways. First, the regime exerted ever increasing controls over the labour movement, wages and living conditions. Brüning had attempted to do this through fiscal constraint and the calculated use of unemployment. Once the cycle of Depression passed its lowest level, Hitler moved to a more direct political involvement which was an integral part of his overall concept of the *Volksgemeinschaft* and reinforced it with all the social and racial propaganda at his disposal. Second, the Nazis accentuated Germany's separation from the other economies. For Brüning this had been part of the process of removing the alleged stranglehold of reparations and developing German self-sufficiency. For Hitler autarky was a prelude to achieving German domination of other economies, not the reestablishment of favourable trading terms with them. Third, the whole emphasis on economic planning after 1936 was contained within the Four Year Plan. This contained two main objectives: German armed forces were to be 'operational within four years' and the economy 'must be fit for war within four years'.[3] The Four Year Plan would, however, have been difficult to implement without the consolidation already achieved by the New Plan; the period of conservative influence had clearly been necessary before the transition, with its new administrative structures, could take place.

Control?

This brings us to the second key issue: how efficient was the management of the Nazi economy? Those who argued that Nazi economic policy was innovatory also tended to hold the view that it was carefully controlled at the centre and efficiently organised to maximise the results needed over a short period. The resources were carefully targeted at the priority – rearmament. A careful and stringent basis had been laid by Schacht, after which the Four Year Plan introduced a new layer of administration under the direction of Goering. This was part of the process by which Germany, like the Soviet Union, was being transformed into a totalitarian state with all the ruthless efficiency that this implied.

The opposite approach is that Nazi economic management was actually remarkably inefficient. This is related to the arguments over 'monocracy' and 'polycracy': both assumed that the administration was chaotic but were divided as to whether this was deliberate on the part of Hitler or due to unintentional defects within the system. In political terms, this was dealt with in the context of 'intentionalism' and 'structuralism' in Chapter 3, Analysis 2. In the case of the economy, the 'monocratic' approach emphasises that Hitler remained in control of a situation that was not entirely to his liking. By 1939 the economy had delivered less than he had hoped for in terms of military power; nevertheless, he dealt with the shortfall logically and adopted a *Blitzkrieg* strategy in which a series of short wars would enable Germany to accomplish conquests without inflicting financial hardship on the population. This argument is considered in Analysis 2 below. The 'polycratic' version, by contrast stresses that the administrative problems relating to the economy were innate rather than intentional. The new institutions established by the Four Year Plan were not under the Führer's control. Instead, he was subject to constraints entirely beyond his powers and had to come to terms with a variety of clashing interests. The different groups may have tried to serve the Führer, but they constantly transgressed on each other's territory and interfered with each other's decision making. In the words of Kitchen, 'Economic mobilisation was hampered . . . by the administrative chaos and ill-defined areas of competence so typical of Nazi Germany'.[4] The basis of the argument is that the multi-layering of agencies and a lack of clear delineation produced an underlying conflict which inevitably reduced administrative efficiency within the economy. Two developments were particularly detrimental. From 1935 the newly-appointed civilian official, the Plenipotentiary for the War Economy, came increasingly to conflict with the War Ministry, especially over the priority of armaments. Then, in 1936, a massive new Office of the Four Year Plan was set up to accelerate the pace of rearmament. Although intended to collaborate with existing institutions, there was much rivalry with the Ministry of Economics, as well as with the War Ministry and the Plenipotentiary for Economics (the renamed version of the Plenipotentiary for the War Economy). There were also conflicts between the personnel serving these roles: between Walter Funk (who was both Minister of Economics and Plenipotentiary) and Schacht, whom Funk eventually replaced as President of the Reich Bank. Funk, in turn, was subordinate to Goering and was notoriously unable to control Hitler's wilder economic fantasies. Further attempts at change in 1939 did not solve the problem. The creation of a new Ministerial Council for the Defence of the Reich, also under Goering only made the administration more complex, increasing the number of competing sub-agencies. Even the most efficient of the subsequent new appointments, General Thomas, failed to restore effective overall control

Some historians have partially reversed such criticisms. Overy, for example, believes that 'the degree of planlessness and polycratic confusion in the economic policy of the Third Reich has been much exaggerated', especially when it is measured against some non-existent 'ideal of rational, totalitarian economics'.[5] Hayes goes further, emphasising that the competition within the economic administration was not entirely negative in its results. Indeed, the 'genius of the Nazi regime' lay in its 'installation of a road race of organizations' backed by 'the threat in cases of recalcitrance to entrust doing the dirty work to another'. Hence there was always an organisation to carry out policies and decisions, even if it took time for this to emerge. In any case, where there *were* faults, it is misguided to blame the system itself. Rather, responsibility should rest with the authors of the policy. Hence 'the key Nazi failings were ones of conception, not coordination'.[6] Most recently, Tooze has labelled the 'polycracy' argument as a 'grotesque exaggeration', maintaining that the economic administration was surprisingly well run.[7]

Success?

The third debate concerns the practical results of the economic policies and their administration by the outbreak of war in 1939. One of the earliest views on this was best expressed by the Cambridge economist, Guillebaud:

> When it is remembered that in March 1938 Germany was in a state of full employment, that there was an extreme scarcity of labour, and that many of the most important industries were working to capacity, with heavy overtime, this relative stabilization of wages and prices must be regarded as a very remarkable achievement. It is certainly unique in economic history down to the present time.[8]

It has even been argued that Nazi Germany, while showing repression and dictatorship in the political and policing spheres, provided a good example of Keynesian policy in action – by being one of the best instances in Europe of the state intervening at a crucial time in order to revive those economic forces which had stagnated. The result was a surprisingly rapid increase in industrial production and a rapid fall in unemployment. Keynes, not entirely happy with being associated with Nazi measures, drew the conclusion that if regimes like those of Hitler and Stalin were not to triumph economically, the western democracies would themselves have to involve themselves more wholeheartedly in the process of economic management. The assumption that Nazi policy did much to stimulate recovery and growth from a disastrously low situation was also reflected by historians in the late 1940s and 1950s. According to Jarman, for example,

> as each year passed the German factories grew busier: the great blast furnaces in the Ruhr and the Saar poured out their glowing, molten lava at night as well as day, and the railways rattled and rumbled with the passage of their freights. A mighty nation was at work.[9]

There are at least some figures to support such views. Unemployment had fallen from 5.6 million in 1932 to 119,000 by 1939, external debt was down from 20,000 million Reichsmarks in 1932 to 9,000 million in 1938, interest rates had been reduced from 6 per cent to 3 per cent over the same period and national income had risen from 43,000 million marks to 80,000 million.

Yet there is also a case for arguing that, far from being healthy, the German economy was in crisis by 1939. The rapid fall in unemployment had, in fact, created severe shortages in labour, especially in heavy industry and engineering. The standard of living was at best stagnating as any increase in wages was more than offset by substantially longer working hours. Exports were in decline as Germany deliberately cut itself off from the liberalising trading policies being adopted by other advanced economies. And there was growing tension between the requirements of rearmament and meeting consumer needs. By 1939 rearmament had distorted the shape of the economy and had grown more rapidly than expected because of the annexations of Austria, the Sudetenland and Bohemia. In the process, the consumer-based economy had been severely curtailed, with implications examined in Analyses 2 and 3 below. The most recent critic of the state of the German economy, Buccheim, argues that 'the growth achieved up to 1938/9 was of a very special nature. It deformed the structure of the German economy and already carried in itself the seed of eventual decline'.[10] Indeed, 'Nazi economic policy appears to have been directed against the development of a normal growth pattern'.[11]

Perhaps, however, this line of reasoning has been taken too far. Four historians question the more negative views of the state of the economy after five years of Nazi management. Overy maintains that it was 'certainly not facing a conventional economic crisis in 1938–9',[12] while, according to Hayes, 'To say that economic "crisis" afflicted the Reich in 1939 appears somewhat exaggerated'.[13] It is true that the gloomiest assessments tend to overlook the absence of crippling levels of unemployment, falling prices, agricultural crisis and general slump – all of which had clouded the scene in 1932. Nor, it has been argued, was the competition between the government agencies running out of control: there was no criticism even from Schacht, despite his dislike for Goering and the new officials installed at the time of the Four Year Plan. As for the problems the government did face, these were being dealt with by new strategies. Arrangements were being implemented for the import of foreign workers to reduce labour shortages, while trade imbalances had been partially offset by agreements with Balkan states, whereby German manufactured articles were exported in exchange for raw materials. As to the 'distorting' effect of rearmament, again this has been exaggerated. Klein has argued that 'Germany's rearmament was on a much smaller scale than was generally assumed' and 'did not involve a large drain of resources from the civilian economy'.[14] Between 1933 and 1938, rearmament took up less than 10 per cent of GNP, rising in 1938 to 15 per cent.[15] According to Klein, Hitler feared that greater expenditure would lead to inflation, undermine economic recovery and impoverish the German people through 'a sharp curtailment of some types of civilian goods production, notably consumer durables and residential construction'.[16] Finally, a new twist has been given by Tooze. Germany, he maintains, was a relatively poor state, and not the powerful industrial economy usually claimed. Within the limits he faced, therefore, Hitler had accomplished much by 1939.[17] This, according to James, looks like a partial return to earlier views that 'Hitler was directing a powerful and efficient machine toward complete mobilization for war'.[18]

The economy is probably the most genuinely controversial aspect of Nazi Germany. It is true that other areas – race, government and terror – all have extensive debates. But these have been contained with the confined vision of a regime pursuing – successfully or unsuccessfully – detestable policies. In the case of the economy, some of the debates remain within these confines, especially when economic policies are considered in relation to territorial expansion, *Lebensraum* and war (see Analysis 2 below). Others, however, extend to comparisons with regimes considered less objectionable, conceding that there might be instances of benefit as well as exploitation – this is more apparent in Analysis 3.

Questions

1. Could more have been achieved for Germany's economy by 1939?
2. How much do historians actually disagree over what *had* been achieved by 1939?

ANALYSIS 2: HOW DID HITLER'S ECONOMIC POLICIES RELATE TO HIS SCHEME FOR TERRITORIAL EXPANSION?

Hitler was not an economic theorist. Unlike Marxism, the ideology of Nazism had no underlying economic component: there was no equivalent to the notion of political change occurring through the dialectical conflict between classes exerting their economic interest. Nazism was fundamentally racist and *völkisch* in its conception, and economic factors were always subordinate. It would therefore be inappropriate to seek in it any autonomous economic strategy.

Nevertheless Hitler did have ideas which influenced his economic policy. These can be extracted from *Mein Kampf* and the *Zweites Buch.*

Four main priorities can be deduced. First, Hitler aimed to create an autarkic system which would enable Germany to sustain a broader hegemony within Europe. He intended, second, to target, above all, the lands to the east. Third, since this inevitably involved expansion – and therefore conflict – the economic infrastructure would have to accommodate a considerable increase in military expenditure. But, fourth, he needed the support of the German people and could not therefore risk severely depressing their living standards in any quest for military supremacy. Some historians have added a fifth priority: Hitler's desire to compete with the United States. According to Tooze, the threat of US economic strength was even more of a preoccupation to Hitler than the danger of Bolshevism and the Soviet Union.[19]

Hitler's underlying economic approach emerged during the course of the 1920s. During this period there were two possible approaches to the establishment of future Nazi economic policy. One was socialism, which was strongest in the early 1920s. As we have seen in Chapter 1, this was championed by Gregor Strasser against the strong opposition of Hitler, who preferred the alternative to which he was becoming personally committed. This was a distinctively nationalist approach, based on the logical connection between territorial expansion and self-sufficiency: *Lebensraum* and autarky, the twin pillars of Hitler's strategy, were developed in the second volume of *Mein Kampf*, published in 1925, and his *Zweites Buch*, written in 1928 but never published. In the former he argued that Germany should abandon its former pursuit of economic power through colonies or attempts to dominate western Europe and, instead, should be 'turning our eyes towards the land in the east. We are finally putting a stop to the colonial and trade policy of the pre-war period and passing over to the territorial policy of the future'.[20] This would have the additional advantage of avoiding a conflict with Britain, whose real interests lay outside Europe. Indeed, Britain might even come to see Germany as an ally in a longer-term but inevitable competition with the United States.[21] Large peasant communities would eventually be established in the future in Poland and Russia on land carved out of these countries by the German army. German hegemony would also ensure self-sufficiency in all raw materials and food as well as guaranteed outlets for manufactured goods. Such goals would, of course, involve conflict, another key ingredient of Hitler's thinking. After all, Hitler said in a speech in 1923: 'It has ever been the right of the stronger . . . to see his will prevail.' Indeed, 'All of nature is one great struggle between strength and weakness, an eternal victory of the strong over the weak . . . The nation which would violate this elementary law would rot away'.[22]

These ideas have sometimes been dismissed as the vague fantasies of an immature fringe politician. This is a mistake, on two counts. First, there were many on the conservative right who took them seriously in the late 1920s and early 1930s because *Lebensraum* fitted closely into the pan-German concepts apparent in the Second Reich. Hitler therefore found ready converts among the so-called respectable sectors of big business, the armaments industry and the military high command. Many non-Nazis, in other words, recognised the flow of the argument and were certainly willing to take it seriously. Second, the eventual shaping of German hegemony in Europe bears a close resemblance to the original prototype, even if it was to be implemented by the SS rather than through Hitler's State channels. *Mein Kampf* need not be considered the 'blueprint' for Hitler's future projects, as suggested by Trevor-Roper, but it is surely more than the daydreaming attributed to it by A.J.P. Taylor.

How did these components fit together? Broadly, the 1920s saw the emergence of Hitler's policy on *Lebensraum*, which was to provide the infrastructure for all of Hitler's ideas about the ultimate purpose of economic change. Then, after 1933, Hitler had the opportunity to implement these ideas. This is where explanations can be advanced which are so different as to be almost the reverse of each other.

Argument 1

One line of argument would stress that the implementation of economic policy became essentially pragmatic. Hitler had to modify his theories on the domestic front, just as he did in his foreign policy, until he could be certain of his power base. The initial policies of Schacht, Hitler's Economics Minister, were therefore based on immediate requirements such as job-creation to reduce unemployment and wage controls to prevent the threat of inflation. Above all, Schacht followed the sensible course of establishing trade agreements with the Balkan states: these provided for the import of essential raw materials in exchange for credits on German industrial goods. Hitler tolerated Schacht until 1936, by which time he had come to place more emphasis on rearmament than Schacht thought wise. By now, Hitler reasoned, recovery from the depression had been sufficiently rapid to allow an acceleration of the rearmament policy: this was to be the key factor in the Four Year Plan (1936–40). In 1937 Hitler made clear his decision to prepare for war at the meeting with his chiefs of staff recorded in the Hossbach Memorandum. Hence Goering, at the Four Year Plan Office, was instructed to place the German economy on a war footing by promoting self-sufficiency and developing substitutes for any essential materials which Germany had to import.

It was once argued that the Four Year Plan had succeeded in its objective of preparing Germany for war within four years: indeed, Hitler was able to launch his conflict a year early and concentrate a massive onslaught on Poland before switching his attention to northern and western Europe in 1940. All of Hitler's preparations had made possible the *Blitzkrieg* strategy – an overwhelming strike on an unwary enemy using the large stockpiles of aircraft, tanks and armoured vehicles. This was to be the first stage in his ultimate ambition to dominate Europe. The German economy had been carefully and successfully prepared for this eventuality.

Or had it? Some historians have argued that *Blitzkrieg* was a reflection of the limitations rather than the strength of Germany's rearmament – that it was a concession to economic realities rather than the pursuit of a policy geared to total mobilisation and total war. Klein maintains that Hitler still needed the support of the German consumer and therefore had 'a disinclination to ask for civilian sacrifices'.[23] This meant that he had to settle for a compromise – for an economy which would permit a limited degree of rearmament while, at the same time, allowing a reasonable level of consumer affluence. According to Sauer, this balance meant the creation of a 'plunder economy'. The only way in which Germany could grow from limited mobilisation was by steadily expanding its economic base through a series of rapid and specifically targeted conquests. Hence Hitler 'committed himself to starting a war in the near future'.[24] The method used, *Blitzkrieg*, was as much an economic strategy as a military device. And it seemed to work. By 1941 *Blitzkrieg* seemed to have produced the required impetus for the achievement of the early stages of *Lebensraum.* Germany had gained military and economic control over Czechoslovakia, Poland, the Ukraine and a sizeable area of European Russia, as well as direct influence over Hungary, Romania and Bulgaria. With these victories, the economic dimension of *Lebensraum* became clearer. According to Hiden and Farquharson:

> the economic reorganization of Europe continued also to reflect the durability of National Socialist attempts to bring into being a viable alternative both to centralized state planning, as under Marxism, and to the liberal capitalist order which they had seen collapse in 1929.[25]

The former was repugnant on ideological grounds – especially since Nazism had abandoned the socialist elements of its early policy. The capitalist system was based on the sort of liberal principles which were incompatible with Nazi occupational policies. Hence the Nazis in implementing *Lebensraum* developed a policy of internal economic empire akin to the earlier European policy of mercantilism.

Then came total war, which wrecked the new economic order. Total war is often projected as the logical final step: the total mobilisation of the economy to enable it to achieve the final stage. Actually, it was a response to failure to achieve a further rapid victory through *Blitzkrieg.* It was an admission that the previous delicate balance between consumer and military needs could no longer be maintained. Germany's economic deficiencies under the pressure of war has been emphasised by Klein, who argues that the real nature of inefficiency became more apparent in wartime than in the period before 1939. 'Contrary to the impression that most of us have had, the Germans did a far from distinguished job in managing their wartime economy.'[26] The impact of 'total war' reversed the relative efficiency of *Blitzkrieg.* Even Speer's improvements in the economy in 1943 and 1944 were impressive only 'by comparison with the previous state of affairs'. Many of his so-called revolutionary measures 'were revolutionary only to Germany'.[27] It seemed that the German economy proved less adaptable to total war than those of its three main rivals. It was massively outproduced in terms of war material by the United States and Soviet Union, while even Britain, with a smaller, economic base, managed to maintain a larger per capita output of aircraft and artillery. It could, therefore, be argued that 'total war' was a desperate attempt to cling on to what *Blitzkrieg* had already achieved rather than its logical completion.

Argument 2

This is one view of the relationship between *Blitzkrieg* and total war. It is, however, possible to put forward an entirely different scenario. From the start, Hitler moved systematically towards equipping Germany with an economic base capable of achieving *Lebensraum.* According to Berghahn,

> the rearmament programme which was begun in 1933 amounted . . . to nothing less than a deliberate unhinging of the national economy with the intention of recovering the financial losses by exploiting other national economies of Europe within the confines of German-dominated empire conquered by force.[28]

It is true that some of Schacht's policies were a continuation of the deflationary approach of Brüning. They were, however, tolerated by Hitler who saw them as essential for the establishment of the infrastructure of autarky. Hence the trading networks with the Balkans would become the first step in the establishment of German hegemony; the public works schemes, especially for the *Autobahns,* would help create a military infrastructure; and the controls on wages would provide a disciplined workforce which would become increasingly receptive to intensive mobilisation. Hitler was therefore using Schacht's New Plan as the first stage in the move towards total war.

But the process was not to be so easy. Hitler's hand was forced by a major economic crisis between 1935 and 1936 in the form of a food shortage affecting the whole of the German workforce. He took what he considered to be the only way out: to impose further constraints on the workforce while, at the same time, accelerating rearmament to achieve *Lebensraum* and autarky. The whole purpose of the Four Year Plan was therefore to prepare for war; this became clear in the Hossbach Memorandum, which anticipated that:

> Our relative strength would decrease in relation to the rearmament which would by then have been carried out by the rest of the world. If we did not act by 1943–45, any year would, owing to a lack of reserves, produce the food crisis, to cope with which the necessary foreign exchange was not available.[29]

It seems, therefore, logical that Hitler was gearing the German economy to the 'total war' which would be necessary in order to achieve the *Lebensraum* that would be its long-term economic salvation.

There were, however, to be complications. The outbreak of war with Britain and France in 1939 was premature, which meant that the economy could support only *Blitzkrieg* military strategies. *Blitzkrieg* was therefore an *emergency* response – or, in the words of Overy, 'total war by default'.[30] It was not until 1941 that the economy of Germany had been sufficiently enlarged to move to a full-scale mobilisation of resources – the whole point of total war. But total war now went on to produce defeat rather than victory. This was because of the original mistiming of *Blitzkrieg* (which had prevented a proper build-up of resources) and the subsequent involvement of the United States (which meant the dissipation of those resources in a conflict on two fronts). Hence the total-war economy failed not because it was the reversal of a successful phase of *Blitzkrieg,* but because it was rendered incomplete by *Blitzkrieg* as an unnecessary diversion. Overy's view is therefore the reverse of that of Sauer and Klein. He argues that:

> If war had been postponed until 1943–5 as Hitler had hoped, then Germany would have been much better prepared, and would also have had rockets, inter-continental bombers, perhaps even atomic weapons. Though Britain and France did not know it, declaring war in 1939 prevented Germany from becoming the super-power Hitler wanted.[31]

There are therefore two contrasting approaches to the development of a German economy that would achieve Hitler's aims of territorial expansion and the eventual achievement of an enlarged Germany and *Lebensraum* in the east. By the first argument, preparations were made during the 1930s for limited levels of rearmament which would protect the standard of living of the German people while, at the same time, these would provide the capacity for a series of swift victories that would gradually expand Germany's economic base. Although this worked well during the first two years of conflict after 1939, Hitler's involvement against the Soviet Union and the United States – in addition to Britain – greatly increased the pressure on Germany and necessitated the very 'total war' economy that Hitler had initially tried to avoid. Although Speer effected the transition, Germany was still overwhelmed by the weight of the opposition. The alternative argument reverses the relative connection between *Blitzkrieg* and 'total war'. The levels of rearmament started during the 1930s envisaged a steady build-up towards a full-scale or 'total' war at the outset. There was no question as to priorities – the achievement of *Lebensraum* was to be paramount and the German consumer would have to wait. But war broke out earlier than expected, which meant that *Blitzkrieg* had to be employed as an alternative to 'total war'; ultimately it was to prove a disastrous diversion. Although these interpretations look at the issue of the economy and territorial expansion from opposite directions, they do have one thing in common: they both acknowledge that Nazi Germany had too limited an overall capacity to fight the type of war it ultimately envisaged. This is considered in further detail in Chapter 10.

Questions

1. What was the relationship between 'autarky' and '*Lebensraum*' in Nazi economic theory?
2. In economic terms, was 'total war' the logical outcome – or the reversal – of '*Blitzkrieg*'?

ANALYSIS 3: DO THE STATISTICS SHOW THAT THE GERMAN PEOPLE WERE BETTER OFF AS A RESULT OF HITLER'S ECONOMIC POLICIES?

In 1938 the Cambridge economist, Guillebaud, wrote after a visit to Germany: 'No-one who is acquainted with German conditions would suggest that the standard of living is a high one, but the important thing is that it has been rising in recent years.'[32] At a superficial level this statement can be supported by statistics of the period. More detailed analysis, however, shows a different picture: that, in relative terms, the standard of living was at best static and, by some criteria, actually deteriorating.

There seemed to be much to support the view that Germany was experiencing a return to prosperity after the trauma of the Depression. For one thing, unemployment was in rapid decline. The figure had stood at 4.8 million in 1933, dropping thereafter to 2.7 million in 1934, 2.2 million in 1935, 1.6 million in 1936, 0.9 million in 1937, 0.4 million in 1938 and a mere 0.1 million by 1939.[33] This was far more rapid than the reduction of unemployment in comparable economies such as the United States and France, while Britain still had 1.8 million on the dole in 1938. Corresponding with the decline in unemployment was an increase in wages. Falling to a low in 1933 of 70 per cent of their 1928 level, these had recovered to 75 per cent by 1934, 80 per cent by 1936 and 85 per cent by 1938.

Thus by a double criterion more and more people became better and better off during the six years after 1933. They were also part of a general increase in prosperity represented by a steady growth of Germany's national income from 44 billion marks in 1933 to 80 billion in 1938. This was particularly impressive since the 1938 figure was actually greater than the 72 billion of 1928, despite the fall in the value of the mark in the meantime. The workforce benefited at certain key outlets within the economy as the production of some consumer goods seemed to take off. Germans, for example, became the world's largest per-capita owners of radio sets, while progress was also made in developing the comparatively cheap Volkswagen car. More fundamentally, between 1932 and 1938 food consumption increased by a sixth, clothing by a quarter and furniture and household goods by a sixth. Housing units were constructed at the rate of 300,000 per annum compared with 200,000 per annum during the Weimar period.[34] Added to these benefits was the vast range of activities provided in Strength through Joy (KdF): these included concerts, operas, theatre, cabaret, films, guided tours, sporting events and gymnastics, cruises and hikes. Meanwhile, Beauty of Labour (SDA) did much to improve working conditions, reduce problems such as noise levels and increase cooperation and solidarity in the workplace. Certainly the workforce as a whole was far better off than that in the Soviet Union. It was not, by and large, in constant dread of being denounced to the Gestapo or being forced to reach unrealistic targets by being driven to breaking point. Overall, it is easy to see why contemporaries should have seen Nazi Germany as a country undergoing a transformation in its economy to the ultimate benefit of its people.

There are, however, fundamental problems with this line of reasoning. Its underlying assumption is that any improvements after 1933 were due directly and solely to Hitler's policies. But this is flawed, on two counts. First, as explained in Analysis 1, there is more continuity between the early policies of the Third Reich and the later policies of the Weimar Republic than is often realised. In economic terms, the dividing line is really in 1929. There was far more difference between the policies of Müller and Brüning than between those of Brüning and Hitler. Second, the policy of Brüning created a dynamic which was of double benefit to Hitler. In ruthlessly taking control of the economy, Brüning intended to deal forcefully with the problems as quickly as possible in order to enable Germany to come through the other side of the economic crisis more quickly than any of the other leading industrial powers. This benefited Hitler's reputation by creating a huge peak of unemployment which Hitler could not help but alleviate. And, by the time that Hitler had come to power, the worse was over as Brüning's policies were beginning to have an admittedly belated impact. In other words, Hitler inherited a disastrous situation which was just about on the mend.

Even so, the improvement which did occur was not fully transmitted to the workforce, since it was not consumer-based. The focus of the economy was switched, especially from 1936, to rearmament and an expansion in the size of the armed forces. Declining unemployment was, it could be said, artificially induced. This was also apparent in the calculated use of the unemployed on public works schemes such as the construction of *Autobahnen* and in the introduction of a six-month compulsory labour service. Such expedients are rarely possible within a democracy since they remove the element of choice from unemployment. It might be argued that the unemployed have no choice, but it is important for the government of a democratic regime to assume that they do, so that it will place solutions on persuasion rather than coercion. This was certainly the case with Roosevelt's New Deal. On the other hand, a totalitarian regime can dispense altogether with the very notion of choice and, through coercive measures, generate an immediate impact on unemployment levels. As Germany accelerated the pace of rearmament through the Four Year Plan, unemployment levels were bound to drop.

The counterpart to forced employment was a disciplined workforce held to lower wage levels. Pay may have increased relative to the year 1933 but there was no return to 1928: indeed the percentages for 1933 and 1939 were 77 per cent and 89 per cent respectively.[35] This was hardly a massive upswing. Besides, the wage earner was actually worse off in terms of the cost of living. This had increased from 71 per cent of the 1928 level in 1932 to 90 per cent in 1939. In real terms, therefore, those in employment had been marginally better off in 1933 than they were in 1939. The workforce received an ever-declining proportion of the national income as wages. In 1933, for example, wages amounted to 63 per cent of the national income, while by 1938 they had dropped steadily each year to 57 per cent. It is also significant that these wages were earned through a working week which had been extended on average by over seven hours.

Most of the wages went on food, clothing and housing. Although consumption of these did increase during the 1930s, it remained lower than the levels of 1928 in real terms – that is once the increase in population over the ten-year period is taken into account.[36] Direct comparisons between 1932 and 1938 show that food consumption was not appreciably higher and in some cases food was sometimes of poorer quality. The consumption of vegetables declined by 10 per cent, and, although sugar increased by 10 per cent between 1932 and 1938, by the latter date it was still only half the average in the United Kingdom and the United States. Meat consumption grew by one-eighth but was only 76 per cent of the equivalent level in the United Kingdom – as indeed was butter. Goering made a public issue out of this with his insistence that Germans should place 'guns before butter'. This meant that heavy industry and rearmament had to come before even the most basic consumer requirements: autarky therefore had a considerable impact on the quality of the diet of ordinary German people. Housing, too, had severe shortcomings. Although the Nazi average annual house-building levels were 150 per cent higher than those of Weimar, these need to be adjusted to take account of the faster rate of population growth during the pre-war period in Nazi Germany. Housing shortages actually increased, while inadequate materials and constraints placed by other industrial priorities meant a reduction in the quality of new units. For example, the standard area for a couple in Germany was 26 square metres, compared with 40 in the Weimar period and 50 specified in the 1936 Housing Act in Britain.

There was also reduced attention to other consumer needs. It is true that between 1933 and 1938 the level of consumer goods rose by 69 per cent. But, over the same period, industrial goods increased by 389 per cent. In other words, workers were producing proportionately more in terms of heavy industrial goods and armaments than they were consumables. It can also be deduced from import and export figures that the general flow of trade was not in the consumers' interest. Imports in 1932 totalled 4.6 billion marks, compared with 5.7 billion marks for exports. The corresponding figures for 1930 had been 12.4 billion and 12.0 billion. The consumer suffered in two ways – the imposition of tight import controls by Schacht and the huge drop in consumer goods from abroad.[37] Even the much-vaunted increase in car ownership was limited. Although it trebled during the 1930s, this was from a low base in 1932; in any case, by 1939 it was still 50 per cent lower than British ownership had been in 1935. 'Thus,' says Grunberger, 'Germany was not moving appreciably closer to a consumer society.'[38]

As to the new employee organisations, these may have had certain benefits and attractions, but they were very much in line with the aims of a totalitarian regime. The workforce was strictly regulated even down to its use of free time. This was done partly to break any desire to revive consumer habits, which would draw off resources from rearmament, and partly to keep open the channels of propaganda and indoctrination. The KdF and SdA were therefore no substitute for the trade unionism which had been banned by Hitler in 1933. Free collective bargaining, which had been such a prominent feature of the Weimar Republic, had been replaced by the creation of corporate identity and interest. This meant a decline in voluntary initiative in work: the introduction of the Workbook in 1935 restricted the freedom of workers to choose a job and provided an instrument for state control over allocation of labour. In effect, Nazi Germany experienced the application of wartime labour controls even before war broke out. It is true that it lacked the crude terror of the Soviet system, but it was no less pervasive in its destruction of individual values. Exploitation was as much a feature of the Nazi economy as of its Soviet counterpart – even if in Germany the stick was disguised as the carrot.

Finally, the figures do not show the disadvantages suffered by one particular section of the population – those who lived on and worked the land. Although they were idealised in Nazi propaganda, the small landowners – mainly peasants – actually experienced fewer benefits than did their counterparts in urban industry. They were badly affected by numerous government regulations, including state pricing and the restrictions imposed by the Reich Entailed Farm Law of 1933. Mechanisation, too, fell far behind the comparable developments in industry. Government assistance here was entirely inadequate: the Hitler Youth Land Service and Harvest Help were no substitute for the increased mechanisation which industrial demands and rearmament prevented from happening. Agricultural workers were even worse off, many experiencing poverty and dreadful housing conditions. Despite restrictions on movement, they left the land at the rate of 2.5 per cent per annum, a total of 1.4 million heading for better prospects in the cities.

In reality, therefore, the German workforce was putting in longer hours for a fractional notional increase in wages. In real terms wages were actually in decline compared to the increase in the standard of living.

The input that workers had into the economy was substantial but largely one-way: it fed into rearmament but received few consumables in exchange. Returning to the opening quotation, therefore, it now seems that the standard of living was falling, not rising.

Questions

1. Was the Cambridge economist quoted at the beginning of Analysis 3 correct in his assessment?
2. Was the German workforce exploited by the Nazi regime?

SOURCES

1: THE FOUR YEAR PLAN

Source 1.1: Extracts from Hitler's announcement of the Four Year Plan (1936)

Politics are the conduct and the course of the historical struggle of nations for life. The aim of these struggles is survival … No nation will be able to avoid or abstain from this historical conflict …

Germany's economic situation is … in the briefest outline as follows:

1. We are overpopulated and cannot feed ourselves from our own resources …
6. The final solution lies in extending our living space, that is to say, extending the sources of raw materials and foodstuffs of our people. It is the task of the political leadership one day to solve this problem …

I thus set the following tasks:

I. The German armed forces must be operational within four years.
II. The German economy must be fit for war within four years.

Source 1.2: Schacht's comment, written in his autobiography in 1949, on the management of the Four Year Plan by Goering

Goering set out, with all the folly and incompetence of the amateur, to carry out the programme of economic self-sufficiency, or autarky, envisaged in the Four Year Plan. Hitler had made him chief of the Four

Year Plan operations in order to extend his own influence over economic policy, which he did not find difficult, since he was now, of course, in a position to place really large contracts. … On December 17th 1936, Goering informed a meeting of big industrialists that it was no longer a question of producing economically, but simply of producing. And as far as getting hold of foreign exchange was concerned it was quite immaterial whether the provisions of the law were complied with or not. … Goering's policy of recklessly exploiting Germany's economic substance necessarily brought me into more and more open conflict with him, and for his part he exploited his powers, with Hitler and the Party behind him, to counter my activity as Minister of Economics to an ever-increasing extent.

Source 1.3: From a speech given by Goering to German industrialists, 17 December 1936

The context to which we look forward calls for enormous efficiency. No end to rearmament is in sight. All that matters is victory or defeat. If we conquer, the business world will be fully indemnified. We must not reckon profit and loss according to the book, but only according to political needs. There must be no calculations of cost. I require you to do all you can and to prove that part of the national fortune is in your hands. Whether new investment can be written off in every case is a matter of indifference. We are playing for the highest stakes. What can be more profitable than rearmament orders?

Source 1.4: From an analysis in a report produced by *Sopade* (the Social Democratic Party in Exile)

The Nazis try to persuade the nation that the problem of economic constraints is nothing but a foreign exchange problem, whereas in reality it is a problem of the capacity of the economy and of the nation's willingness to make sacrifices. This problem has two aspects: on the one hand, the problem of economic resources, of the maximum level of production and the minimum level of consumption; and, on the other hand, the problem of money, of the financial constraints. What the superficial observer normally notices, however, is the constricting effect of the foreign exchange shortage with which Germany continually has to cope …

If, in contrast to the foreign trade of America and Britain and that of other industrial countries, German foreign trade cannot recover, the cause lies primarily in the enormous demands placed on the German economy by rearmament ... If production geared to rearmament and the autarky programme is set against the production for export and consumption (including production geared to the expansion of the consumer goods industries), it is clear that the one can grow only at the expense of the other ...

The shortage of foreign exchange is, therefore, in reality only a reflection of the overloading of Germany's economic strength through rearmament and the autarky programme.

Questions

1. How much light does Source 1.3 throw on Source 1.4?
*2. What are the comparative advantages and disadvantages of Sources 1.2 and 1.4 to the historian studying the Four Year Plan?
3. 'The Four Year Plan was designed to break normal economic relations with other states and to create an economy geared to plunder.' Do these sources, and your own knowledge, support this view?

WORKED ANSWER

*2 *[This questions requires comments on the nature and content of the two sources, written within the context of an overall comparison between the two.]*

A number of advantages and disadvantages emerge from a comparison of Sources 1.2 and 1.4. First, in terms of personal involvement and immediate knowledge, Source 1.4 seems to have the main advantage, since Schacht was Reich Finance Minister between 1933 and 1937. The Social Democratic Party, by contrast, had never had any role in the German economy after 1933 and could be seen to have lost all contact while in exile. Second, in terms of detachment, however, Source 1.2 has an obvious disadvantage: Schacht bitterly resented his replacement by Goering in 1937 and his description of the latter's 'folly and incompetence' was clearly personally motivated. Source 1.4 keeps personalities out of the picture, concentrating on gathering information for use in an assessment of how to oppose the regime. Third, the date of publication is significant. Source 1.2, published in 1949, has the advantage of longer-term perspective but the disadvantage of Schacht's obvious desire to distance himself from the policies of a defeated and discredited regime. Source 1.4 has a more immediate view, which is not informed about the future. Finally, there is a clear contrast in terms of content. The focus of Source 1.2 is stronger on the implementation of the

Plan than on its principles, while Source 1.4 shows the reverse. In this respect, the two Sources are most useful when taken in conjunction.

2: HISTORIANS ON GERMANY'S ECONOMIC PERFORMANCE 1933–9

Source 2.1: Extracts from an article by C. Buccheim, 'The Nazi Boom: An Economic Cul-de-Sac', published in 2001

The growth achieved up to 1938/9 was of a very special nature. It deformed the structure of the German economy and already carried in itself the seed of eventual decline …

The economic situation in the Third Reich can be interpreted as having been characterized by the overall aim of the regime – to reserve as big a share of the social product as possible for the purposes of rearmament and autarky. In doing this the government was greatly helped by the Great Depression. For in that crisis consumption as well as investment and exports fell considerably …

Nothing could be less apt than characterizing the economic policy of the period as Keynesian. According to Keynes, government expenditure has to replace private expenditure only so long as private forces are too weak to produce an upswing. But if they get stronger, the government voluntarily steps into the background as an agent of growth. Whereas Keynesian policy wants to stimulate multiplier effects through additional state demand, National-Socialist economic policy suppressed them as much as possible, in order to leave room for further increases of state demand. By doing so, the German economy in fact became more and more dependent for its growth on the continuous enlargement of state demand …

Instead of being specially conducive to growth, as the boom after 1932 might suggest at first sight, Nazi economic policy was in reality inimical to it.

Source 2.2: An explanation by Peter Hayes of the state of the Nazi economy, from an article published in 1993

On the economy by 1939: To say that economic 'crisis' afflicted the Reich in 1939 appears somewhat exaggerated. … The German economy was not unmanageable in 1939, not threatened by bankruptcy, inflation, and proletarian dissatisfaction, and not falling between the two stools of guns and butter, but more or less on course and only somewhat behind the schedule Hitler had laid down in 1936 and then amended at the Hossbach Conference in November 1937.

On polycracy: The genius of the Nazi regime lay in its installation of a 'road race of organizations' backed by 'the threat in cases of recalcitrance to entrust doing the dirty work to another'. By mobilizing individual initiative in this manner, the Nazi economy, despite all the confusion and contentiousness it contained, performed so formidably from 1933 to 1944. Thus, if polycracy characterized the execution of German economic policy, it did so to productive as well as destructive effect. Moreover, polycracy did not determine the fate of that policy.

... In these words lies the resolution of the debate between monocrats and polycrats and the basis for an appropriate assessment of the importance of administrative shortcomings and economic mismanagement in the Third Reich. Hitler, not someone else, overreached, and he did so in response to fundamental and almost intractable material deficiencies, not in passive acceptance of such epiphenomena as courses of action presented him by the nature of the power structure over which he presided. That his actions had such devastating effects resulted, not least, from the way his Darwinian economic system tapped and channeled the energy and ingenuity of his *Volk*. Thus, an emphasis on the confused and competitive nature of policy in Nazi Germany can tell us much about *how* it wrought what it did and then failed, but not about *why*.

Source 2.3: From R.J. Overy, '"Domestic Crisis" and War in 1939', an article published in 1999

But the truth is that there was no such crisis in 1939 for the Nazis to perceive. There is no evidence at government and ministerial level of a 'crisis' in the summer of 1939. There were no suggestions that the economy was in severe difficulties, 'out of control', in either the Finance Ministry, the Foreign Office, the Economics Ministry, the Four Year Plan Office, the armed forces' economic office, or the Labour Front. Not even Schacht, least likely to disguise the amateur economics of his Nazi successors, suggested that a serious crisis existed in 1939, however much he disapproved of the way in which the German finances were being run. 'Crisis' is an inappropriate characterization of the German economy in the months before the war.

Source 2.4: From M. Kitchen, *Nazi Germany at War*, published in 1995

Economic mobilisation was hampered not only by the need to take public opinion into account, but also by the administrative chaos and ill-defined areas of competence so typical of Nazi Germany. The Reich

Defence Law of 21 May 1935 created the post of a civilian 'General Plenipotentiary for the War Economy' whose tasks were not clearly delineated and who was bound to conflict with the War Ministry which was responsible for armaments. In the following year the massive bureaucracy of the Four Year Plan, designed to force the pace of rearmament, provided a third powerful organisation which worked closely with the Ministry of Economics and which was potentially a further rival to the War Minister and the Plenipotentiary for Economics, as he was renamed in 1938. This organisational confusion was only partly overcome by the fact that Walter Funk was both Minister of Economics and Plenipotentiary and in 1939 replaced Schacht as President of the Reich Bank. Funk was behoven to Göring, one of whose functions was to direct the Four Year Plan and who was thus the key figure in the war economy. But Göring was idle, Funk insignificant and the rivalries between the civilian organisations and the military, between the three services and amongst the civilian organisations were never overcome by forceful leadership. As one industrialist said, 'business is not in the least bit concerned whether it is ruled by a tin helmet or a top hat, but it is about time that it was decided which headgear will be worn'.

Questions

1. Compare the arguments of:
   a Buccheim (Source 2.1), Hayes (Source 2.2) and Overy (Source 2.3) on the *condition* of the German economy by 1939.
   b Hayes (Source 2.2), Overy (Source 2.3) and Kitchen (Source 2.4) on the *management* of the German economy by 1939.
2. Using Sources 2.1 to 2.4, and your own knowledge, comment on the view that Germany was ready for war in 1939.

8

OUTSIDE THE *VOLKSGEMEINSCHAFT*

BACKGROUND

The Nazi regime was totally committed to the pursuit of a racial policy of Aryanism, or the projection of the German people as the master race. This involved the concept of Social Darwinism, or the survival of the fittest – within the People's Community or *Volksgemeinschaft*. Analysis 1 shows the origins of racial theories and the impact of the regime's actions on those who were, for some reason, considered unworthy of inclusion in, or a threat to, the *Volksgemeinschaft*. Those who were 'alien to the community' (*gemeinschaftsfremd*) included people with hereditary or transmissible 'impairments'; those – such as vagrants, alcoholics or homosexuals – with unacceptable lifestyles; and members of 'inferior' races, including gypsies (more accurately called Sinti and Roma), Negroes, Slavs and – above all – Jews. Measures included disabling legislation, deprivation of civil rights, sterilisation, confinement to concentration camps and, under the radicalising impact of war, 'euthanasia' and extermination.

The most extreme manifestation of Nazi racial policies was the Holocaust, in which over six million Jews and several hundred thousand gypsies were killed from 1941 onwards by SS squads (*Einsatzgruppen*) and units of the *Wehrmacht* or, following the Wannsee Conference of January 1942, in gas chambers at Auschwitz, Treblinka, Maidenek, Sobibor and Chelmo. Analysis 2 considers different interpretations about the origins of the Holocaust, about the extent to which the German people were involved, and the type of mentality needed to take part in acts of genocide. Despite the difficulty of maintaining a balance between historical objectivity on the one hand and an awareness of the scale of suffering on the other, more books have recently been published on the Holocaust than on all other aspects of the Third Reich.

ANALYSIS 1: WHAT ROLE, AND WITH WHAT EFFECTS, DID THE CONCEPT OF RACE PLAY IN THE NAZI SYSTEM?

Race is usually seen as the most illogical component of the entire Nazi system, the one which made it a totalitarian regime capable of committing acts of great evil. This is, of course, the truth – but not the whole truth. Race was also the fundamental rationale for all social developments within Nazi Germany: indeed, race and society were inseparable. The foundation of the Nazi race doctrine was the concept of genetic drive. This was rooted in nineteenth-century ideas of fringe theorists such as Gobineau, Houston and H.S. Chamberlain. Collectively known as Social Darwinists, they transferred the scientific concept of the survival of the fittest from the animal to the human world. The biologist Haeckel argued that 'the theory of selection teaches us that organic progress is an inevitable consequence of the struggle for existence'.[1] He asked in his *The Riddle of Life* (1904) 'What profit does humanity derive from the thousands of cripples who are born every year, from the deaf and dumb, from cretins, from those with incurable hereditary defects etc. who are kept alive artificially and then raised to adulthood?'[2] Thus there were already strong beliefs in racial 'purity' and warnings against 'contamination'.

Hitler took this a stage further and based his whole ideology on the premise of struggle, which he saw as 'the father of all things'. From this emerged the right of the strong to triumph over the weak. Indeed, this was essential, since the strong created, while the weak are undermined and destroyed. He emphasised that 'All the human culture, all the results of art, science and technology that we see before us today, are almost exclusively the creative product of the Aryan'.[3] Conversely, 'All the great cultures of the past were destroyed only because the originally creative race died from blood poisoning'. The solution was obvious: 'Therefore, he who would live, let him fight, and he who would not fight in this world of struggle is not deserving of life.'[4] He amplified this in a speech made in 1929: 'If Germany was to get a million children a year and was to remove 700,000 to 800,000 of the weakest people then the final result might even be an increase in strength.'[5] Such views provided the justification for both exclusion and elimination.

The implications of this theoretical framework were huge. Race, linked to struggle, provided a new approach to the organic development of the Nazi society and state. In this respect Nazism was as utopian and revolutionary as Communism, since it aimed at nothing less than total transformation. Between 1933 and 1945 the enforcement of Nazi racial doctrine had three dimensions: it provided Germany with its purpose, its cohesion – and its victims.

The ultimate purpose of the Nazi system was to transcend the existing limits of the State. Here we can see a contrast with fascist Italy. Mussolini saw the highest political form as the nation state, which he sought to extend into a revived form of the Roman Empire. This expansion of the *etatist* core into a larger *imperium* was both historical and traditional in its concept. In the case of Nazi Germany, *etatism* was not the main priority: this was the *Volksgemeinschaft*, or the 'people's community', which was to be the higher form of the State. Similarly, the focus of German expansion was not the establishment of a traditional empire, but rather to provide 'our nation with sufficient living space. Such living space can only be in the east'.[6] Unlike Mussolini, Hitler's emphasis was not imperial, but *volkisch. Etatism*, for Italy the main aim, was, for Nazi Germany, merely the first step to Aryanism and *Lebensraum.* The driving force for this was the concept of the master race.

Racial theory also aimed at creating a new form of social cohesion – by replacing class divisions with racial unity and racial supremacy. The *Volksgemeinschaft* would reconcile what Peukert calls a 'society of fractured traditions, social classes and environments'.[7] In place of embittered Germans from competing economic groups, there would emerge healthy, vigorous, and productive Aryans, united in their loyalty to a regime which had only Aryan interests in mind. The new stereotype proved attractive to most of the population and therefore ensured their allegiance to a regime which appeared to value them so highly. This, of course, was part of the overall formula. For, in return for their new unity of purpose and elevated status, the people were to be 'primed for self-sacrifice'.[8] Hence the racial policies were closely connected not only with the propaganda and indoctrination trends within Germany's schools (see Chapter 4) but also with the new work ethic implicit in organisations like the Reich Labour Service (RAD), SdA and KdF.

To be fully effective the *Volksgemeinschaft* needed to have its 'impurities' removed. The victims were all those who, for genetic reasons, did not fit into the stereotype of Aryanism. These were considered 'alien to the community' (*gemeinschaftsfremd*) and had therefore become race enemies in the broader sense. There were three broad types. First, there were threats from 'biologically impaired' individuals. Some of these might have been Aryan by origin but, for a specific reason, now threatened to 'pollute' the community through diseases or defects which were transmissible to future generations. Second, individuals or groups following certain lifestyles threatened to undermine the social integrity or economic performance of the *Volksgemeinschaft*; these included vagrants, alcoholics and homosexuals. Third, groups classified by membership of an 'inferior' race had to be prevented from 'contaminating' the *Volksgemeinschaft* by being deprived of certain forms of contact with it. Among these targets were Sinti and Roma, Negroes and Slavs. The last of these became far more important with the expansion of the Reich into eastern Europe in 1939 and again in 1941. The most important racial 'threat' of all came from the Jews. It was possible to fall victim to Nazi racial policy through belonging to any of these three categories – or even to more than one. Indeed, Hitler emphasised that there was a 'Jewish conspiracy' to coordinate all three. The Third Reich systematically targeted all groups with a combination of legislation promulgated either by the government or issued by the Reichstag, and executive action by the SS–Gestapo complex. The latter became increasingly important with the ever-growing involvement of Himmler himself. Already one of the key executive agencies before 1939, during the war the SS became the main functionary in all cases. (See Chapter 10, Analysis 2.) Such action was underpinned by a huge amount of 'research' into all aspects of racial 'purity' – coordinated by the German Society for Racial Hygiene and the Kaiser Wilhelm Institute for Anthropology, Heredity and Eugenics – and conducted by the likes of Wilhelm Abel, Robert Ritter and Josef Mengele.

The first group mentioned – those suffering from hereditary ailments – came within the scope of the Law for the Prevention of the Hereditarily Diseased Progeny, issued in July 1933. This covered manic depression, schizophrenia, Huntington's chorea, hereditary blindness and deafness, epilepsy, 'congenital feeble-mindedness' and 'serious physical deformities'. Victims could be compulsorily sterilised after secret decisions made by Hereditary Health Courts. Between 1934 and 1939 this affected up to 0.5 per cent of the entire population. From 1939 the scope was extended through the introduction of the euthanasia program organised by Philipp Bouhler, Head of the Chancellery of the Führer: between 1939 and 1941 about 72,000 people were killed through gassing, lethal injections or starvation. Despite attempts to keep the process secret, sufficient details emerged to start an opposition campaign from members of the Catholic Church, especially the Bishop of Münster, Galen. (See Chapter 6, Analysis 2.) The German population at large showed less concern, many having been indoctrinated at school through classes in eugenics or persuaded of the rightness of 'euthanasia' through feature films such as *I Accuse* (1941). Although the regime called a temporary halt to the 'euthanasia' programme in the context of hospitals and asylums, those considered a physical threat to the *Volksgemeinschaft* were within a year being eliminated in larger numbers through the extermination camps.

The second category of 'threat' had already been defined in 1930 by Hans Frank as 'criminal character substances', further extended to include people categorised as 'asocials'. Campaigns started with the Law Against Dangerous Habitual Criminals (November 1933), which targeted 'disorderly wanderers'. The main objections to this category were that it sought to escape from legitimate authority and productive labour while, at the same time, fostering criminal behaviour. By 1937 an official circular even included persons 'against whom it can be proved that on two occasions they turned down jobs offered to them without reasonable grounds'.[9] In the same year the age limit for prosecution was reduced by the Law on the Punishment of Juvenile Offenders. Most arrests were made outside the scope of the criminal law, based on Himmler's decree on crime prevention of December 1937. A further target within the 'asocial' group was homosexuals, seen as a danger to the *Volksgemeinschaft* because they incurred a loss of potential children, indulged in 'unnatural behaviour', and constituted a 'danger to public morality'.[10] Persecution began in May 1933 when Nazi students destroyed the Institute for Sexual Science. This was followed by the increased involvement of the SS under Himmler, with the formation in 1936 of the Reich Central Office for the Combating of Homosexuality. During the war many male homosexuals were interned in concentration camps, executed or castrated. Action was also taken against lesbians for their 'subversion' of the 'natural' gender role, seen as a threat to birth rate. After 1939, therefore, there were substantial numbers of outcasts in the concentration camps, each wearing triangles to identify the particular reasons for their exclusion from the *Volksgemeinschaft* – black for 'asocials' and pink for homosexuals. These were in addition to the red markings already assigned to left-wing political prisoners such as Communists and Social Democrats.

One of the stigmatised racial groups, the Sinti and Roma, had originated from the Punjab area of northern India and had settled in Germany in the late fifteenth century. The Nazi 'case' against them was they were originally Aryans but had become 'polluted' during their westward migration by mixing with 'inferior races' in eastern Europe. They were considered a serious threat to Germans partly because of this miscegenation and partly because of their frequent contacts with Germans through their itinerant lifestyle. This dual 'problem' was emphasised by the establishment in 1936 of a Reich Central Office for the Fight Against the Gypsy Nuisance. Large numbers were forcibly rounded up, especially when the number of foreign visitors increased for the Berlin Olympics. Then, from 1939, Heydrich's 'Final Solution' to the 'Gypsy Question' was initially to concentrate Roma and Sinti groups in designated sites. During the war years Eichmann recommended another approach by placing the 'Final Solution' to the 'Gypsy Question' alongside that to the 'Jewish Question'. This was implemented in the extermination camps, most of the Roma and Sinti being sent to the 'BII' section at Auschwitz. Other ethnic minorities within Germany were Kashubians, Poles and black people. The last of these were the product partly of Germany's nineteenth-century colonial empire and partly of the occupation of parts of the Rhineland and Ruhr by the French, whose troops included men from Senegal, Morocco and Madagascar. These were a particular cause of resentment. Hitler saw a deliberate plot in the 'black curse'; in *Mein Kampf* he wrote that the Jews 'brought the negroes to the Rhineland' to destroy the white race through 'bastardisation'.[11] Such views also showed the inward-looking nature of the *Volksgemeinschaft*, ignoring the athletic achievements of black people in the sporting world and branding their cultural contributions as 'degenerate'.

The largest single group of racial victims was the Jews. Their persecution transcended all other exclusions while, at the same time sharpened the focus on them all. It also provided the regime with its dynamic and with the primitive elements of vicious hatred that were at the very core of Nazi ideology. In part, German anti-Semitism was the culmination of centuries of discrimination throughout Europe: this had reared its head again after 1880, with violence in Vienna and Berlin, blatant discrimination in the French army and a series of pogroms in Tsarist Russia. H.S. Chamberlain justified such events within the context of tradition. He wrote in 1901: 'The entrance of the Jew into European History had meant the entrance of an alien element – alien to that which Europe had already achieved, alien to all it was still destined to achieve.'[12] Anti-Semitism could therefore be seen as a tidal force: its high-water mark at the turn of the nineteenth century brought Hitler in with its flotsam.

Hitler's own views on Jews were the main driving force behind the whole Nazi ideology and movement; anti-Semitic policies were therefore a sublimation of his personal obsession. *Mein Kampf* and his speeches are full of the most inflammatory references. In the former he created the stereotype of the Jew as a parasite and pollutant: 'Culturally he contaminates art, literature and the theatre, makes a mockery of national feeling, overthrows all concepts of beauty, and instead drags men down into the sphere of his own base nature.'[13] At the same time, there was also a deliberately pragmatic use of the techniques of scape-goating: the paradox was that anti-Semitism as an irrational force could be used rationally to strengthen the *Volksgemeinschaft.* There would be numerous occasions on which the regime called for sacrifice. This would elicit two sentiments: a positive effort and negative feelings of resentment at the sacrifice required. The former would be used by the regime, but the latter would be deflected away from the regime – against a minority group picked out by the Führer from the taint of many centuries.

Official policy towards the Jews unfolded in four broad stages. From March 1933 the government groped its way towards a set of regulations, trying to impose some sort of order after the chaos caused by the initial ransacking of Jewish properties and the SA boycott. Pseudo-legal measures removed Jewish civil servants in April 1933 and dismissed Jews from public employment the following month. The two key measures, however, were introduced in November 1935 under the collective name of the Nuremberg Laws. The Law for the Protection of German Blood and Honour prevented mixed marriages, while the Reich Citizenship Law removed basic civil rights from all Jews, effectively expelling them from the *Volksgemeinschaft.* Legislation was combined with indoctrination and propaganda, anti-Semitism acting as the negative pole of race 'education' in schools. Jews were also subjected to the extreme slurs of Streicher's newspaper *Der Stürmer*, which alleged the ritual killing of Christian children. At this stage, however, there was still some form of constraint: the Minister of the Interior, Frick, issued a memorandum instructing authorities not to exceed their authority in relation to the Jews. During the second stage such moderation disappeared as the government gave ground to the SS as the chief enforcer of policy. Himmler and Heydrich became more directly involved, supplementing government legislation with their own edicts and making full use of the growing network of concentration camps for any infractions. In November 1938 Goebbels tried to take back some of the initiative by orchestrating the violence of *Kristallnacht*, which saw the destruction of most of Germany's synagogues and 7,000 Jewish businesses – a strange reversal of government attempts to control the violence of 1933. A few days later the government confirmed its redirection of Jewish policy by the Decree for the Exclusion of Jews from German Economic Life. The third stage, which was launched by Germany's invasion of Poland, saw the SS regain the ascendancy, this time with full government approval. Between 1939 and 1941 Germany's Jews were brought under the same restrictions as those of conquered Poland by being forced to identify themselves with the Star of David and by being confined to ghettoes. These were preparatory to the fourth phase, which followed the invasion of the Soviet Union. The Holocaust itself is dealt with in Analysis 2.

In summary, Nazi race policy did three things. First, it converted traditional *etatism* into a more radical Aryanism, the ultimate thrust of which was *Lebensraum*. Second, it substituted for the older class divisions of German society the new unity of the *Volksgemeinschaft*. And, third, this unity was maintained at the expense of minorities which had no place within it. Some, the 'community aliens', were removed with as little fuss as possible. Others, especially the Jews, were deliberately set up as targets for any resentment which might be felt by members of the *Volksgemeinschaft* at the extent of the sacrifice demanded of them. Anti-Semitism was the obvious vehicle for this, since it had deep historic roots and seemed to fit into the Führer's messianic claims. Hitler remained convinced of the rightness of his cause to the very end. In his *Political Testament*, he wrote, a few days before his suicide, 'Above all, I charge the leadership of the nation, as well as its followers, to a rigorous adherence to our racial laws and to a merciless resistance against the poisoner of all peoples – international Jewry'.[14]

Questions

1. Was 'race' fundamental to Nazi theory?
2. What was the connection between 'race' and the *Volksgemeinschaft*?
3. Was there a difference between anti-Semitism and the hatred of '*gemeinschaftsfremd*'?

ANALYSIS 2: HOW WAS THE HOLOCAUST POSSIBLE?

No historical topic is immune to controversy. Even the Holocaust, perhaps the most cataclysmic event in history, has produced polarised views. One of these can be dismissed quickly. Irving's view that there was no gas-chamber based extermination has been discredited by the vast majority of historians who accept that the evidence for the Holocaust is overwhelming. There are, however, three genuine controversies. First, was it the logical outcome of Hitler's hatred of the Jews, implemented when circumstances were propitious? Or is there more in the argument that the Holocaust was the result not of careful planning but rather of the failure of alternative strategies? The second debate concerns the extent of complicity: how far was the German population aware of and involved in the Holocaust? And, third, how was it possible for individuals to come to terms with the evil intrinsic to their actions?

The debate on origins

The first debate concerns the nature of the events leading to the implementation of the Holocaust. Briefly, these occurred during the context of the war against Russia, which started in June 1941, although their antecedents were in the filling of ghettoes after the conquest of Poland in 1939. The mass killings were undertaken initially by mobile units of the SS (the *Einsatzgruppen*) and police detachments of the *Wehrmacht*. The decision to introduce gas chambers was conformed at the Wannsee Conference in January 1942, and the necessary equipment was built into extermination camps established at Auschwitz-Birkenau, Maidenek, Sobibor, Treblinka, Belzec and Chelmo. Jews were transported to these by rail from all parts of Nazi-occupied Europe, with the cooperation of authorities at every level in the bureaucracy. The process was under the control of the SS and implemented by Himmler, Heydrich (until his assassination in 1942) and Eichmann. But it remains open to discussion as to whether the instructions for the genocide came directly from Hitler himself and whether it emerged as a planned and orderly scheme.

One school of thought, often called the 'intentionalists', attributes the policy of genocide to the Führer state as a function of a personalised totalitarian regime. Historians who follow this line include Fleming, Jäckel and Hillgruber. Although no document has ever been found linking this order directly to Hitler, it makes no logical sense to deny his ultimate authorship. According to Fleming, for example, the line leading from the early manifestations of Hitler's anti-Semitism 'to the liquidation orders that Hitler personally issued during the war' is a 'direct one'. (See Source 2.1 below.) Dawidowicz, too, maintains that there was a gradual escalation of persecution from the nineteenth century, through to Hitler's ideas in the 1920s, then to implementation in the 1930s, and ultimately to extermination in the 1940s. This approach has been reaffirmed by more recent historians. Dülffer argued in 1992 that the Holocaust was 'inconceivable without Hitler's firm will and dictatorial authority'.[15] In 1996 Goldhagen presented a forcefully argued case that there were clear precursors for the Holocaust in Hitler's ideas and speeches: these are set out in Source 2.2 below. Goldhagen concludes that the genocide was the result not of structural factors but of Hitler's aim to 'eliminate all Jewish power'.[16]

There is, alternatively, a 'functionalist' or 'structuralist' argument that the extermination was a process which was arrived at as a logical sequence of administrative actions rather than as a preconceived plan. This view was pioneered by Hilberg as early as 1961.[17] It was subsequently continued – and refined – by Mommsen and Broszat. The basis of their argument is that the 'Final Solution' was not the outcome originally intended but rather that arrived at because of the failure of all other possibilities. It was also the result of growing incompetence, not increased efficiency. The original intention had been to resettle Jews, first in Madagascar, then in Siberia. The former had been made impractical by the outbreak of war, which had focused Germany's priorities on Europe itself. The latter was impeded by the nature of the war against Russia. Proposals to transport all Jews over the Urals were set in motion but were then blocked by the revival of Russian resistance to the German advance. This meant an accumulation of peoples in eastern Europe with no obvious long-term destination in view. The result was the search for a swift solution, first through the SS *Einsatzgruppen* killings, then through the use of extermination camps. The actual process involved decisions taken by bureaucrats at different levels rather than through a single centralised order. Mommsen, for example, maintains that:

> The Holocaust was not based upon a programme that had been developed over a long period. It was founded upon improvised measures that were rooted in earlier stages of planning and also escalated them. Once it had been set in motion, the extermination of those people who were declared unfit for work developed a dynamic of its own.[18]

Further extracts from Mommsen and Broszat are in Sources 2.3 and 2.4.

This debate fits into the broader one of the nature of the Nazi state. It is no coincidence that the 'intentionalists' also argue that the structure of dictatorship in Germany depended on the personality of Hitler himself and that he deliberately exploited any weaknesses and contradictions within it to his own advantage; this has already been discussed in Chapter 3. He would therefore have chosen the time, the method and the institutions for the implementation of a scheme of extermination which had always existed in his mind. The 'functionalists', by contrast, see consistency in the weakness of Hitler's response to institutional chaos and the disorganised way in which the Holocaust was finally implemented. This makes it possible to conclude that the Holocaust was the administrative response to the failure of earlier policies. As we have seen in Chapter 3, 'intentionalism' and 'structuralism' are not necessarily mutually exclusive. A possible synthesis may be that, while he was out of power, Hitler initially thought in terms of genocide – but then moderated this in order to broaden his support once he was in power. This explains why he limited early measures to the Nuremberg Laws and ordered the removal of discriminatory public notices at the time of the 1936 Berlin Olympics. It is true that there was a violent acceleration on

Kristallnacht (1938). Nevertheless, there was no inexorable move towards extermination. Furthermore, during the first two years of the war, Hitler hoped for a possible peace with Britain and did not at this stage wish to antagonise the United States. The reaction of public opinion in these countries to genocide would have been one of horror, compared to the apparent indifference which had previously prevailed over earlier anti-Semitic policies.[19]

But the onset of 'total war' (see Chapter 10) changed the whole situation for several reasons. First, in invading the Soviet Union, Hitler was signalling that he considered that Britain was no longer capable of exerting any real threat: that Britain was now marginalised and therefore irrelevant. Germany could now focus on the racial struggle which Hitler had always foreseen. The defeat of the Soviet Union could now be accompanied by the removal of Jewry – by whatever method. This point is stressed by Browning, who considers himself a 'moderate functionalist'. (See Source 3.2.) But, with the failure to inflict permanent defeat on Russia in 1941, the struggle for racial conquest became one for racial survival – in which Hitler's ideas of extermination, already strongly hinted at, were crucial. The pursuit of total war against the Soviet Union required the complete removal of the perceived racial enemy within. (See Chapter 10, Analysis 2.) The belief that this internal enemy had always had strong connections with Soviet Marxism made the 'Final Solution' the more obvious. So far the impetus for genocide must be considered Hitler's. But the means by which this would be carried out resided with the SS, which alone could provide the degree of organisation and commitment that was needed. This anticipates one of the debates considered in Chapter 10: whether during the war the Nazi State had finally been superseded by the SS State.

The debate on 'complicity'

The controversy over the origins of the Holocaust also raises that over the 'complicity' of the German people.

The original interpretation placed the responsibility firmly on Hitler and his immediate henchmen, largely within the SS. In support of this, it can be argued that much of the population were held in the grip of a dictatorship which had two key advantages. One was its absolute control over information, the other the capacity to terrorise. It is highly significant that both processes were under the control of one institution – the SS. Himmler gave explicit instructions for secrecy: he said of the extermination to an assembly of SS officials in Posen in 1943, 'Among ourselves, we can talk openly about it, though we can never speak a word of it in public'. He added, 'That is a page of glory in our history that never has been and never can be written'. (See Source 1.5.) There was therefore a huge barrier of credibility: the idea of genocide was to most people unimaginable. And, if it was denied by the regime, why should rumours to the contrary be believed? Besides, if rumourmongers were disposed of by the SS, this did not necessarily mean that the rumours were true: the use of terror had long been institutionalised for any form of dissent. How, therefore, could the majority of German people reasonably have been expected to know what was going on? It was one thing for officials in key positions to deny knowledge of what was happening around them – but there is perhaps more credibility to similar claims made by ordinary civilians.

A more recent argument strongly contests these points, spreading more widely both involvement and responsibility. Dülffer's view is typical. He argues that, although the Holocaust was above all due to Hitler, nevertheless 'to recognize this is not to exculpate the hundreds of thousands of others who were involved in carrying out the Final Solution'.[20] Goldhagen goes further – much further. Hitler's ideal, he maintains, was 'broadly shared in Germany'.[21] This can be seen in several ways. The bureaucracy was involved on a huge scale (and with numerous participants) and there was massive collaboration between the SS, the civil service and business corporations. This deprived Jews of their rights and assets, isolated them, deported them and killed them. The army, too, was heavily implicated. In many cases the *Wehrmacht* actively cooperated with the SS. The true extent of knowledge about and acceptance of the Holocaust will probably never now be known. But it is undoubtedly much wider than was once believed. The motive was anti-Semitism on a massive scale, which affected the entire German population. This was 'the central causal agent of the Holocaust' which 'moved many thousands of "ordinary" Germans' and 'would have moved millions more, had they been appropriately positioned' to 'slaughter Jews'. (See Source 3.1.)

Has the pendulum swung too far in the opposite direction? Goldhagen's blanket condemnations have come in for some criticism, especially from Rosenfeld, who maintains that the method of extermination was intended to 'minimise contact between victim and perpetrator'; as such, the gas chambers 'should not have been necessary for a people thirsting to kill Jews *en masse*'.[22] Browning, too, stops short of associating the Holocaust with the eliminationist anti-Semitism of the German people. While acknowledging that anti-Semitism undoubtedly existed, he emphasises the pull of allegiance felt by most Germans to their country in circumstances which became more and more extreme. (See Source 3.2.) This type of reasoning goes beyond the original exculpation of ordinary Germans on the grounds that they were terrorised by the institutions of a totalitarian state. Instead, it acknowledges German complicity. At the same time, it avoids the blanket generalisation that the German people were willing participants, driven by their historic anti-Semitism. Instead, it sees the sweeping away of earlier restraints by the military and ideological threat posed by the Soviet Union. This is a different type of accusation – unwilling complicity through an acknowledgement that 'national survival' was a cause that was 'higher' than the survival of the Jewish people and an acceptance that extermination might for this reason be justified. An underlying anti-Semitism therefore made it possible to accept an extreme version of 'my country – right or wrong'.

A final consideration is the involvement of other peoples in the Holocaust. Here, too, views have been modified. The traditional argument is that the Nazis imposed the Holocaust on the countries conquered by or allied to Germany, and that the indigenous population suffered as well. Although some collaborationist regimes assisted with the organisation of the Holocaust beyond the borders of the Reich, the impetus came entirely from Germany, either as the occupying power or, as in the case of Hungary and Romania, under the direct threat of invasion. Recent research has, however, emphasised the importance of indigenous variants of anti-Semitism, especially in those countries which experienced dictatorship in the inter-war period. This meant that there was an element of complicity with Nazi policies, even if this varied from country to country. Poland was the worst affected by Nazi brutality: its statehood was obliterated and the Poles despised as an 'inferior race'. Yet even here there were spontaneous outbreaks of civilian violence against Jews and collaboration with the Nazi authorities from the Polish or Blue Police. Poles were therefore both 'victimizers and victims'.[23] Under the Szálasi regime, from October 1944, Hungarian officials collaborated on a large scale with Eichmann's deportation of Hungarian Jews to the death camps in Poland. Another independent regime, Antonescu's Romania also applied Nazi measures against its own Jewish population. Without losing sight of the primary initiative of Germans in the Holocaust, it could therefore be argued that there were also 'willing executioners' elsewhere.

The debate on motivation

Useful as they are, the debates on 'intention' and 'complicity' have sometimes been accused of drawing attention away from the sheer horror and inhumanity of the Holocaust. Certainly the human dimension needs to be considered – in terms of the suffering of the victims and the mentality of the perpetrators. Although his interpretations have been open to criticism in terms of balance, Goldhagen has performed an important service in reminding us of the collective scale of evil in the actions of the enforcers, whether SS officers, soldiers or bureaucrats. Yet the question remains as to how so many people could have allowed themselves to be involved – individually and collectively – in acts of such monstrous evil. Many explanations have been given for the distortion of normal human feelings that must have been involved.

The most basic self-defence was a 'lack of awareness' of the full implications of actions contributing to the Holocaust. This applied especially to bureaucrats and organisers who were one step removed from the actual process of killing; it has also been used as an argument to deny the complicity of the broader German population. It could not, of course, apply to the executioners in the *Einsatzgruppen* or the police units, nor to the SS guards at the death camps. For them the defence was 'obedience to orders' defined by others, and the fulfilment of the 'duty' which was part of the job; after all, a soldier could not select the 'front' on which he fought. Such an argument could, of course, go right up the chain of command. Eichmann, for example, said after organising the Wannsee Conference: 'I felt something of the satisfaction of Pilate, because I felt entirely innocent of any guilt.'[24] Indeed, he could have been speaking for many others when he said at his trial in Jerusalem in 1961: 'I never did anything, great or small, without obtaining in advance express instructions from Adolf Hitler or any of my superiors.' But, although doubtless genuine in many cases, for most these were excuses or 'legal defences', especially at the Nuremberg tribunal in 1946. They do not fully explain why civilians, military men and SS officials participated so readily in mass murder.

Another possibility might be a taste for sadistic behaviour and wanton cruelty. Goldhagen makes constant reference to 'brutality', 'torture' and sadistic 'games', all carried out with 'evident gusto'. He adds:

> Small wonder that to the eyes of the victims – but not in the self-serving testimony of the perpetrators – these ordinary Germans appeared not as mere murderers, certainly not as reluctant killers dragged to their task against their inner opposition to genocide, but as 'two-legged beasts' filled with 'bloodthirstiness'.[25]

Here evil would have shown through as an active force, released by psychopathic behaviour. The main example would be the influence of Streicher, who derived sexual gratification from the persecution and torture of helpless people. There is no doubt that many thousands of similar characters were attracted to membership of the SS by similar prospects. Of course, nothing could be further from the official view of the SS that those involved in genocide remained 'decent' human beings while carrying out difficult tasks on behalf of the *Volk*. (See Sources 1.5 and 1.7.) Hannah Arendt, too, maintains that the process of extermination was dealt with 'neither by fanatics nor by natural murderers nor by sadists'.[26] Far from being sadistic, Himmler, the *Reichsführer* SS, was actually squeamish about the details of mass murder and issued official instructions that SS officials were not to torment the inmates of the camps. In 1943 an SS officer was even sentenced to death for succumbing to the temptation to 'commit atrocities unworthy of a German or an SS commander'.[27] There must, therefore, be an explanation which goes beyond the assumption that all members of the SS were psychopaths.

Perhaps those who implemented the Holocaust had experienced a total change of 'conscience'. There are two possibilities here. One is the disintegration of previous norms. According to Götz Aly, 'Far beyond the level reached in the first six years of Nazi dictatorship, the war promoted a non-public atmosphere, atomizing individuals and destroying any ties they still had with religious and legal traditions'.[28] The other possibility is that the moral-based conscience had been replaced by a new racial one. Claudia Koonz argues that 'Because they believed that concepts of virtue and vice had evolved according to the needs of particular ethnic communities, they denied the existence of universal moral values and instead promoted moral maxims they saw as appropriate to their . . . community'. Those with this new 'morality' would conceive the Holocaust not in 'savage hatreds' but 'lofty ideals'.[29] This line of reasoning would explain the quotation attributed by Prosecutor Hausner to Eichmann at the latter's trial: 'I will leap into my grave laughing because the feeling that I have five million human beings on my conscience is for me a source of extraordinary satisfaction.'

Underpinning these changes to the moral consciousness would have been the constant and cumulative impact of indoctrination. Again, this would have worked in two ways. First, it desensitised, dulling the capacity of the conscience to 'prick'. People were reassured by the views of those in authority. Koonz maintains that 'Like citizens in other modern societies, residents of the Reich believed the facts conveyed by experts, documentary films, popular science, educational materials, and exhibitions'.[30] Popular desensitisation to anti-Semitic actions occurred through gradations; first came the acceptance of new legislation, then – with *Kristallnacht* – a resignation to worse to come. Alternatively, of course, indoctrination had the capacity to fanaticise, creating a conscience as a driving force for certain directed attitudes and actions. Extreme anti-Semitic attitudes were created by Streicher's *Der Stürmer* and the SS publication, *Das Schwarze Korps*, both of which incited revulsion against the victims of their hatred. Bartov emphasises the enormous power of Nazi indoctrination, initially during the 1930s, then as part of training – not only in the SS, but also in the *Wehrmacht*. It was, he argues, sufficient to turn ordinary workers into fanatical soldiers capable of killing civilians to order; far from being forced, their participation was willing and enthusiastic. Indoctrination was also regularly reinforced. Himmler's instructions were that the police battalions should receive weekly ideological instruction for 'shaping the political consciousness of the martial combatant'.[31]

Some authorities have stressed that 'modernisation' facilitated the participation in the Holocaust. According to Mommsen, modernity produced 'a purely technocratic and bureaucratic mentality'. This helped to distance the participant from the result of his or her actions, whether this applied to the bureaucrat organising the transport that would lead to the certain deaths of thousands or to the impersonal use of gas rather than the multiple individual shootings initially carried out by the *Einsatzgruppen* and the police battalions. By contrast, 'modernity' offered others the opportunity for personal advancement. Men like Heydrich and Hans Frank took full advantage of the short cuts to unprecedented levels of power over others. Housden rejects the notion of Frank thinking of himself as 'a cog in a much wider machine'. Instead, 'He was thrilled and seduced into expecting much more than this for himself. He wanted more in terms of intellectual prestige, national respect, financial wealth, historical importance, even sexual delight'.[32] The comfort of anonymity within a larger process or the thrill of controlling that process – modernisation offered both possibilities.

The willingness to commit appalling crimes was caused by a combination of all these factors, although in different proportions in accordance with the nature of each personality involved. Some participants were more heavily indoctrinated than others; some were driven by sadism; others responded to the call of 'duty'; others, again, had been desensitised by indoctrination – perhaps reinforced at the moment of action by alcohol. All responded to orders – with or without the foundation of a new 'conscience'. Yet one problem remains. The vast majority of those involved in acts of genocide had normal family lives themselves and convinced themselves that they were no different to organisers or workers in an animal abattoir – carrying out a task which was unpleasant but necessary for the community. How could one side of the human conscience remain intact while the other became so perverted? Hoess, for example, always maintained that he was doing to the best of his ability the job allocated to him as Commandant of Auschwitz and that, at the same time, he remained 'completely normal': 'Even while I was carrying out the task of extermination I led a normal family life. I never grew indifferent to human suffering.'[33]

Despite the criticism it has recently received from many historians, there may still be much to say for Arendt's view that evil was essentially 'banal'. Among the sadists handling the extermination programme were 'normal' family men, who presided over them and tried to do their duty like 'decent' German citizens. The extermination programme was seen as an arduous duty to be carried out. It actually involved the denial of the preferences of the participant, not their sublimation. But this was the clue. Denial of preference was initially directed by external discipline. External discipline led to internal self-discipline as the participant adapted to a new routine. Routine brought familiarity with the task which, in turn, reduced the chance of rejecting it. Yet in all this, some absolute values could remain. These were parallel to and yet entirely cut off from the genocidal tasks being carried out. Hence men like Hoess, who remained a practising Catholic, literally led double lives, neither of which intruded on the other. In its ordinariness evil can therefore affect any group of people at any time. This is a far more frightening concept than a system dominated by psychopaths. Yet, for all that, evil can operate as banality only in the most extraordinary situations. This brings us full circle back to trying to understand the nature of the ideology and regime which managed to capture a cultured and civilised people.

Questions

1. Was the Holocaust 'deliberate'?
2. 'The Holocaust was a "Nazi" crime in which all "Germany" shared.' Discuss.

SOURCES

1: THE NATURE OF ANTI-SEMITISM

Source 1.1: From an article written by Goebbels, 30 July 1928

'Isn't the Jew a human being too?' Of course he is: none of us ever doubted it. All we doubt is that he is a decent human being.

Source 1.2: From Hitler's speech to the Reichstag, 30 January 1939

In the course of my life I have very often been a prophet and have usually been ridiculed for it ... Today I will once more be a prophet: if the international Jewish financiers in and outside Europe should succeed in plunging the nations once more into a world war, then the result will not be the Bolshevizing of the earth and thus the victory of Jewry, but the annihilation of the Jewish race in Europe!

Source 1.3: From an article by Goebbels, 16 November 1941

So, superfluous though it might be, let me say once more:

1. The Jews are our destruction. They provoked and brought about this war. What they mean to achieve by it is to destroy the German state and nation. This plan must be frustrated ...
3. Every German soldier's death in this war is the Jews' responsibility. They have it on their conscience: hence they must pay for it ...
9. A decent enemy, after his defeat, deserves our generosity. But the Jew is no decent enemy. He only pretends to be one.
10. The Jews are to be blamed for this war. The treatment we give them does them no wrong. They have more than deserved it.

Source 1.4: From the diary of a Polish visitor to the Warsaw ghetto, Stanislav Rozycki, 1941

The majority are nightmare figures, ghosts of former beings, miserable destitute, pathetic remnants of former humanity ...

On the streets children are crying in vain, children who are dying of hunger. They howl, beg, sing, moan, shiver with cold, without underwear, without clothing, without shoes, in rags, sacks, flannel which are bound in strips round the emaciated skeletons, children swollen with hunger, disfigured, half conscious, already completely grown up at the age of five, gloomy and weary of life. They are like old people and are only conscious of one thing: 'I'm cold.' 'I'm hungry.' ...

I no longer look at people: when I hear groaning and sobbing I go over to the other side of the road: when I see something wrapped in rags shivering with cold, stretched out on the ground. I turn away and do not want to look. I can't. It's become too much for me. And yet only an hour has passed.

Source 1.5: From Himmler's speech to SS officers in Posen, 4 October 1943

I also want to talk to you quite frankly about a very grave matter. We can talk about it quite frankly among ourselves and yet we will never speak of it publicly. Just as we did not hesitate on 30 June 1934 to do our duty as we were bidden, and to stand comrades who had lapsed up against the wall and shoot them, so we have never spoken about it and will never speak of it.

I am referring to the Jewish evacuation programme, the extermination of the Jewish people. It is one of those things which are easy to talk about. 'The Jewish people will be exterminated' says every party comrade. It's clear, it's in our programme. Elimination of the Jews, extermination and we'll do it. ... To have stuck it out and – apart from a few exceptions due to human weakness – to have remained decent, that is what has made us tough. This is a glorious page in our history and one that has never been written and can never be written.

Source 1.6: From evidence provided at a postwar trial of former SS guards at Sobibor

The Jewish workers were at the complete mercy of the German camp guards who were the lords of the camp. Most of them had a very limited education, were completely under the influence of the major Nazi figures and their anti-Semitic ideology and in most cases their moral sense had been totally blunted by their activity in the euthanasia centres. Their relations with the prisoners who – as they knew – were nothing but work slaves, who were living on borrowed time, but who were often far more highly educated than themselves, generated among a number of them a sense of superiority and primitive cravings for power and domination.

Source 1.7: Rudolf Hoess giving evidence at his trial after the war

I am completely normal. Even while I was carrying out the task of extermination I led a normal family life. I never grew indifferent to human suffering. I have always seen and felt for it. ... From our entire training the thought of refusing an order just didn't enter one's head, regardless of what kind of order it was.

QUESTIONS

1. Is Source 1.2 conclusive evidence that Hitler always intended an extermination programme?
2. How much do Sources 1.5, 1.6 and 1.7 show of the mentality of the SS officials?
*3. 'In its anti-Semitic policies the Nazi leadership destroyed all notions of "decency"'. Comment on this in the light of these sources and your own knowledge.

WORKED ANSWER

*3 *[The wording of this question should not be seen as licence to express emotive viewpoints; despite the horrific nature of the subject, the approach must remain firmly historical and rooted in the evidence.]*

It is clear from the sources that Nazi concepts of 'decency' were highly selective, compared with the more universal values prevalent in an open society. 'Decency' was taken automatically to exclude the Jews, as Goebbels stated in Source 1.1. Indeed, Sources 1.2 and 1.3 point to the alleged danger posed by Jews to German society: 'The Jews are our destruction'. Hence, they could not be construed as 'a decent enemy' and, as such, were worthy of no normal consideration. The logic of this was that Germans could take radical measures against the Jews while, in the words of Himmler, ensuring that they 'remained decent' (Source 1.5). This was taken even further by Hoess, who could claim to be 'completely normal' and, even while 'carrying out the task of extermination', to have led 'a normal family life' (Source 1.7). The reason for this capacity to lead two lives is hinted at in Source 1.7: the 'influence of the major Nazi figures and their anti-Semitic ideology'. This was in overall contrast to a civilian who had not been exposed to this and reacted in the more normal way shown in Source 1.4: 'I turn away and do not want to look. I can't. It's become too much for me.'

There is plenty of additional evidence to support the existence of these double standards and the delusion that the persecutors were able to retain their decency. Acts of violent anti-Semitism, such as *Kristallnacht* (1938) had been justified as 'righteous indignation' against Jewish exploitation, while the ethic of devotion to duty – even the unpleasant one of extermination – had already been rehearsed in the euthanasia programme for the mentally ill, referred to in Source 1.6. It is also known that Himmler issued regulations for the punishment of SS officials who sullied this duty by acts of sadism. Such was the twist in logic that evil acts were sanitised and made to appear commonplace, as shown by Arendt's description of 'the banality of evil'.

2: HISTORIANS ON THE ORIGINS OF THE HOLOCAUST

Source 2.1: From G. Fleming's *Hitler and the Final Solution* (University of California Press, 1984)

We shall begin by focusing on the earliest attestable symptoms in the biographical record of Hitler's personal anti-Semitism, his congenital hatred for the Jews. For the line that leads from these early manifestations to the liquidation orders that Hitler personally issued during the war – the actual target of this investigation – is a direct one.

Source 2.2: An extract from D.J. Goldhagen, *Hitler's Willing Executioners*, published in 1996

1. Hitler expressed his obsessive eliminationist racial antisemitism from his earliest days in public life. Indeed, his first published political writing was devoted to antisemitism, as was his final testament to the German people. Eliminationist antisemitism was the linchpin of his worldview, as stated in *Mein Kampf* and repeatedly elsewhere. It was the single most consistent and passionately held aspect of Hitler's political thought and expression.
2. Upon assuming office, Hitler and his regime, in keeping with Hitler's prior pronouncements, turned the eliminationist antisemitism into unprecedented radical measures and pursued them with unceasing vigor.
3. Before the outbreak of the war, Hitler announced, and then during the war repeated many times, his prophecy, indeed his promise: the war would provide him with the opportunity to exterminate European Jewry.
4. When the moment was ripe, when the opportunity appeared, Hitler carried out his intention and succeeded in slaying approximately six million Jews.

Source 2.3: Views of the German historian M. Broszat, published in 1994

It thus seems that the liquidation of the Jews began not solely as the result of an ostensible will for extermination but also as a 'way out' of a blind alley into which the Nazis had manoeuvred themselves. The practice of liquidation, once initiated and established, gained prominence and evolved in the end into a comprehensive 'programme' …

It appears to me that no comprehensive order for the extermination existed and that the 'programme' for the extermination of the Jews developed through individual actions and gradually attained its institutional and factual character by the spring of 1942 after the construction of the extermination camps in Poland.

Source 2.4: Extracts from an article by H. Mommsen, 'The Realization of the Unthinkable', published in 1986

The Holocaust was not based upon a programme that had been developed over a long period. It was founded upon improvised measures that were rooted in earlier stages of planning and also escalated them. Once it had been set in motion, the extermination of those people who were deemed unfit for work developed a dynamic of its own. The bureaucratic machinery created by Eichmann and Heydrich functioned more or less automatically … There was no need for external ideological impulses to keep the process of extermination going …

The widespread assumption that the systematic policy of genocide rested on a clear directive from Hitler is based on a misunderstanding of the decision-making process in the Führer's headquarters. If such an order had been given, even if only orally, then those in high office around Hitler must have known about it; they had no motive to deny the existence of such a directive in their personal records and testimonies after 1945 …

In fact, the idea that Hitler set the genocide policy in motion by means of a direct instruction can be completely rejected …

The absence of any direct order for extermination also explains how almost all those in an influential position were able to suppress their awareness of the fact of genocide. Albert Speer provides the most striking example of this tendency. Hitler's dominant position at the centre of all the National Socialist elites reinforced such behaviour, because his conduct was exactly the same as theirs: he took care not to allow conversation to turn to events in the concentration camps. This gave rise to the widespread impression that Heinrich Himmler was the driving force. In terms of ideological motivation this was not the case, for Hitler was always the advocate of radicalization.

QUESTIONS

1. Compare the treatment in Sources 2.1 to 2.4 of Hitler's direct responsibility for launching the Holocaust.
2. 'The genesis of the Holocaust was long-term and deliberate.' Using Sources 2.1 to 2.4, and your own knowledge, explain whether you agree with this view.

3: HISTORIANS ON GERMAN 'COMPLICITY' IN THE HOLOCAUST

Source 3.1: Extracts from D.J. Goldhagen, *Hitler's Willing Executioners*, published in 1996

Germans' anti-Semitic beliefs about Jews were the central causal agent of the Holocaust … not only of Hitler's decision to annihilate European Jewry … but also of the perpetrators' willingness to kill and to brutalize Jews … Anti-Semitism moved many thousands of 'ordinary' Germans – and would have moved millions more, had they been appropriately positioned – to slaughter Jews. Not economic hardship, not the coercive means of a totalitarian state, not social psychological pressure, not invariable psychological propensities, but ideas about Jews that were pervasive in Germany, and had been for decades, induced ordinary Germans to kill unarmed, defenseless Jewish men, women, and children by the thousands, systematically and without pity …

The beliefs that were already the common property of the German people upon Hitler's assumption of power and which led the German people to assent and contribute to the eliminationist measures of the 1930s were the beliefs that prepared not just the Germans who by circumstances, chance, or choice ended up as perpetrators but also the vast majority of the German people to understand, assent to, and, when possible, do their part to further the extermination, root and branch, of the Jewish people. The inescapable truth is that, regarding Jews, German political culture had evolved to the point where an enormous number of ordinary, representative Germans became – and most of the rest of their fellow Germans were fit to be – Hitler's willing executioners.

Source 3.2: Extracts from C.R. Browning, *The Origins of the Final Solution*, published in 2004

... How in three brief years had 'ordinary' Germans been transformed from 'onlookers' squeamish and disapproving of vandalism, arson, and assault into 'willing executioners' who could perpetrate mass murder with unfettered violence?

Change in time and place was vitally important. After September 1939 Germany was at war, which in turn created a vast German empire in eastern Europe. Even though the initial popular reaction to the outbreak of war was one of apprehension rather than enthusiasm, almost no one in Germany was prepared to engage in dissident, critical, or nonconformist behavior in this regard. It would be no exaggeration to state that the single greatest consensus in the political culture of German society (and scarcely unique to Germany) was the obligation to do one's duty and support one's country in time of war. This consensus was not invented by the Nazis, but it served them well. War in general meant the suspension of critical stance, the temporary erasure of the distinction between loyalty to country and loyalty to regime, the acceptance of demands for sacrifice and toughness, the predisposition to see the world as divided between friends and enemies, and the expectation that terrible things will inevitably happen paradoxically combined with the tendency to dismiss reports of such as exaggerated enemy propaganda ...

German anti-Semitism was not static but intensified with the changing historical context ... [But] as of 1938, aside from a minority of party activists, most Germans were not yet ready or willing to visit physical violence upon their Jewish neighbors but neither were they interested in coming to their defense.

With the outbreak of war and the commencement of racial empire building, first in Poland but above all on Soviet territory, that situation changed. Two vicious circles were set in motion. For the decision makers at the top, each victory and territorial expansion was a setback in solving their self-imposed Jewish problem, as the number of Jews within the German sphere swelled inexorably. For the occupiers in the east, each measure taken brought a solution no closer but instead contributed to 'untenable circumstances' (or at best a precarious stabilization) that dehumanized the Jews yet further and at the same time disposed the German occupiers to expect and advocate yet more radical measures. The solution to the Jewish problem through the eventual disappearance of the Jews – sometime, somehow – was taken for granted.

Within the context of the murderous 'war of destruction' against the Soviet Union, the leap from disappearance of the Jews 'sometime, somehow' to 'mass murder now' was taken in the summer of 1941. Once underway on Soviet territory, this ultimate or Final Solution beckoned to the Nazi regime as a solution for the rest of Europe's Jews as well. Already in the midst of committing mass murder against millions of Jews and non-Jews on Soviet territory, 'ordinary' Germans would not shrink from implementing Hitler's Final Solution for the Jews of Europe as well.

Questions

1. Compare the arguments used by Goldhagen and Browning on the way in which anti-Semitism influenced the German population.
2. Which of Sources 3.1 and 3.2 offers the more convincing argument about German complicity in the Holocaust?

9

FOREIGN POLICY

BACKGROUND

On coming to power in January 1933, Hitler had of necessity to pursue a cautious policy abroad while consolidating his position at home. His first move, however, was to take Germany out of the League of Nations Disarmament Conference, arguing that the proposals would have stripped Germany of the means of self-defence. He followed this by withdrawal from the League itself, an action heavily endorsed by a plebiscite within Germany. In 1934 Hitler sought to allay suspicion that he was preparing a general offensive by drawing up a Non-Aggression Pact with Poland.

Meanwhile, between 1933 and 1935, Hitler had begun to undermine the armaments limitation clauses of the Treaty of Versailles. By 1934 he had broken the limits imposed on the armed forces and in March 1935 he announced the creation of an air force and the introduction of conscription. Britain, France and Italy showed initial concern about these developments and, in April, came together in the Stresa Front. This, however, rapidly disintegrated. Italy became involved in a campaign in Abyssinia from October. In response to this, Britain and France imposed sanctions on Italy. Britain also sought to draw up its own armaments settlement with Germany in the form of the Anglo-German Naval Agreement of June 1935. Hitler used this apparent softening of the potential opposition against him to remilitarise the Rhineland in March 1936, again in direct defiance of a key clause of the Treaty of Versailles. In the same year he provided German assistance to Franco and the Nationalist side in the

Spanish Civil War, and in November drew up the Rome–Berlin Axis with Italy and the Anti-Comintern Pact with Japan. In October he announced the Four Year Plan which was designed to accelerate rearmament and place the German economy on a war footing (see Chapter 7).

In 1937 Hitler stepped up the pace: the Hossbach Memorandum of November records a meeting between Hitler and his chiefs of staff in which Hitler stated that Germany must be prepared for war with the western powers, especially France, by 1942–3 at the latest. In 1938 he took advantage of the Anglo-French policy of appeasement by annexing Austria in the *Anschluss* (March) and, in September, by forcing Chamberlain, the British Prime Minister, to agree to the German annexation of the Sudetenland from Czechoslovakia. In March 1939 Hitler proceeded to occupy the rest of Bohemia, at which point Britain and France extended guarantees to Poland and Romania. In August 1939, Hitler proceeded to form a Non-Aggression Pact with the Soviet Union. This contained a secret additional protocol to divide Poland between the two signatories. In his quest to enforce the territorial terms, Hitler invaded Poland on 1 September. This provoked Britain and France into declaring war on Germany on 3 September.

ANALYSIS 1: HOW 'INTENTIONAL' WAS HITLER'S FOREIGN POLICY?

As in the domestic sphere, German foreign policy from 1933 has come within the scope of a broad debate between historians, especially whether Hitler had clear long-term intentions; whether he acted under the influence of an underlying continuity with the policies of his predecessors; and whether he acted on his own initiative or under the influence of domestic groups or interests.

In addition to his speeches and conversations, Hitler's own statement of his objectives in foreign policy can be found in the two books he wrote before coming to power. *Mein Kampf* dealt with the essentials of his racial doctrine and accepted the inevitability of struggle and war as part of the human condition. He was also explicit about territorial expansion: 'The acquisition of land and soil' should be 'the objective of our foreign policy'. This should not settle for the 'restoration of the frontiers of 1914', which would be 'a political absurdity'. Instead, it meant expansion. But it was the *Zweites Buch* that provided what has sometimes been described as a 'programme'. Written in 1928, this constructed a foreign policy programme of five stages. The first was the removal of the restrictions of Versailles, including the demilitarisation of the Rhineland. The second stage was the end of the French system of alliances in eastern

Europe and the establishment of Germany's control over Austria, Czechoslovakia and Poland. The third would be the defeat of France. The fourth would then be the invasion of Russia, and the fifth a contest for world supremacy possibly against Britain and the United States.[1]

Hitler's long-term intentions?

Did these ideas amount to a programme of intent? Some historians, like Trevor-Roper, have argued that Hitler had plans which were 'unmistakably stated in *Mein Kampf* and that all the evidence of the 1930s shows that Hitler intended to carry them out'. Indeed, *Mein Kampf* was 'a complete blueprint of his intended achievements'. He added that, although they were 'spread over a period of 22 years' and 'issued in very different circumstances', all of Hitler's utterances – written or oral – 'show an absolute consistency of philosophy and purpose'. Hence 'it seems odd to me that distinguished historians should insist that Hitler had no such consistent war aims'.[2] He is not alone in this. Jäckel, too, believes that there is 'ample documentary evidence to prove that he always kept this programme in mind'.[3] Certainly there appears to be a close parallel between Hitler's stated priorities and what actually happened. The disarmament provisions of the Treaty of Versailles were reversed between 1934 and 1935 and the Rhineland remilitarised in 1936; Austria was taken over in 1938, as was the Sudetenland of Czechoslovakia, with Bohemia following in March 1939 and Poland in September; France was invaded in 1940; Operation Barbarossa was launched in 1941; and Hitler declared war on the United States in 1941. Since this seems to replicate the programme in the *Zweites Buch* with some precision, the case for premeditation must be a strong one.

For other historians there is similarly no controversy as to *whether* Hitler had consistent long-term aims, whatever the short-term strategies he used to attain them. To them the key issue is rather the *extent* of Hitler's ambitions. Some, like Jäckel, argue that he confined himself mainly to 'continental' ambitions and, above all, the achievement of *Lebensraum* in the east at the expense of Poland and Russia. Two points particularly favour this view. One is that it was more suited to Germany's limited size and resources; after all, past problems – resulting in defeat by 1918 – had arisen when previous German governments had switched from a continental to a world role. Second, Hitler's two ideological enemies – the Bolsheviks and the Jews – were most apparent in continental Europe, especially in the block of territory from the Vistula to the Urals. The achievement of *Lebensraum* would eliminate both simultaneously. Certainly there is little reference in *Mein Kampf* to anything resembling a world role. A number of historians, however, have rejected this line. The most influential of the 'globalists' are Hillgruber and Hildebrand, who maintain that the achievement of the 'continental empire' was the first step in the *Stufenplan*, or the accomplishment of world conquest by stages. Hildebrand, for example, considers that Hitler had a definite programme which comprised three phases: the conquest of western and eastern Europe, taking advantage of an agreement with Britain; a war between German dominated Europe and the United States; and, finally, German racial supremacy over the world. Again, there are considerations which might support this. Hitler's perception of the United States clearly changed between the publication of *Mein Kampf* and the writing of the *Zweites Buch*. For one thing, he became more conscious of the United States as the world's major economic power, which gave it considerable military potential; this threat would have to be dealt with after the completion of Nazi continental hegemony. Hitler considered that the agreement with Britain (referred to in the *Zweites Buch* as 'Germany's natural friend') made this a feasible long-term objective.

Yet Hitler seemed to switch these objectives in a way which suggests that he experienced a partial change of mind at certain key points in his career. 'Continentalist' aspirations were always there, but 'globalism' seemed to strengthen in the late 1920s, before weakening in the 1930s and reappearing after 1941. A key influence in this change was the impact of the Great Depression which, in Hitler's mind, showed the United States as a 'degenerate' power, weakened by its 'racial mixing' as well as by economic collapse. It was therefore weak enough not to pose an immediate threat and could therefore wait its turn. More urgent in the late 1930s was the achievement of the 'continental' vision – to which the greatest obstacles were Britain, France and Russia. The early phase of war between 1939 and 1941 had little perception of global conquest. This reappeared in December 1941 with Germany's declaration of war on the United States. This seems a departure from the stages of any '*Stufenplan*' – after all, the first phase of 'continental' conquests had not yet been completed. The reason for this was that, since Britain had refused to cooperate with this first phase, Hitler had to go to war with a coalition of 'world' powers before he had attained final control over the 'continent'. Whether this was a switch in offensive strategy or a defensive reaction to changed military circumstances is another matter. (See Chapter 10, Analysis 1.)

So far the arguments have all been in favour of Hitler having had long-term plans, even if temporarily altered by short-term expediency; but there are those who regard it as inappropriate to deal in 'programmes' or fixed objectives in any sense. Again, however, there are different approaches. Some see Hitler's foreign policy as influenced more by the structure of his domestic power base. A conventional Marxist approach would emphasise, above all, the primacy of class-based factors which had been responsible for the rise of Nazism as a particularly virulent form of fascism. In the domestic context Hitler was the pawn of big business; in foreign policy, therefore, he was driven by the demands and needs of the great industrialists and of the armaments interest. A non-Marxist alternative to this is that Hitler's initiatives in foreign policy were typical of the confusion inherent in the polycratic state. (See Chapter 3, Analysis 2.)

A third possibility was put forward by A.J.P. Taylor. In his *Origins of the Second World War*, Taylor argued that Hitler was above all an opportunist. 'Hitler did not make plans – for world conquest or for anything else. He assumed that others would provide opportunities and that he would seize them'.[4] Hitler's projects for expansion and conquest were 'in large part day-dreaming, unrelated to what followed in real life'. Hence 'Hitler was gambling on some twist of fortune which would present him with success in foreign affairs, just as a miracle had made him Chancellor in 1933'. The implication of this line of reasoning is that the sequence of events was entirely fortuitous and controlled by external factors rather than by Hitler himself. This is examined further in Analysis 2.

Continuity with past foreign policy?

Some historians claim, above all, the uniqueness of Hitler's foreign policy and dissociate it from any substantial connection with that practised in the past – whether in 1871 or 1914 or 1933. According to Trevor-Roper, 'Hitler's war aims are written large and clear in the documents of his reign. They are quite different from the war aims of the men who, in 1933, admitted him to power and who, after 1933, served him in power'.[5] On the other hand, German historians have established a considerable degree of continuity between the objectives of Hitler on the one hand and those of the Wilhelmine era and the Weimar Republic on the other. Fischer, for one, maintains that Germany was on an expansionist path well before the Nazi era and that Hitler enlarged this into a concept of *Lebensraum*.[6] Hillgruber goes back to 1871: he maintains that there was a direct connection between the policies of the Second Reich and those of the Third, constituting a 'road from Bismarck to Hitler'.

There is certainly much evidence for the 'continuity' argument from the Second Reich, especially in the later period 1890–1918. The creation of a *Grossdeutschland*, through union with Austria and control over Bohemia, had been the vision of Austrian members of the Pan-German League before 1914: Hitler was not the only Austrian who wanted to see the end of the Habsburg monarchy and the building of an enlarged German Reich on its ruins. There was more official support for a 'continentalist' vision. Germany's aims during the First World War were extensive, comprising economic control over Belgium, Holland and France in the west; domination of Poland and the Baltic coastline in the east, as well as over Serbia, Bulgaria and Romania in the Balkans; unification with Austria and the establishment of a Greater Germany; rule over a dismantled Russia; and hegemony over the eastern Mediterranean and Turkey. In March 1918 the German government implemented at least some of this through the Treaty of Brest-Litovsk, which dismantled part of European Russia with the creation of independent states in Finland, Ukraine, Poland and the Baltic States, all of which were intended for German control. Hitler is known to have been much in favour of the settlement at the time. As for a 'global vision', there had been a clear aim to introduce a phase of *Weltpolitik* and to challenge Britain for naval and colonial supremacy; 1890–1914 had, after all, been the period of the Pan-German League, the Navy League, the 'risk strategy' of Admiral Tirpitz, the race to build Dreadnoughts and the race for colonies in Africa and the Pacific. Even during the 1920s, some of the support for Hitler came from those who had once been involved in such organisations and activities.

If the Second Reich provided Hitler with at least some of his long-term objectives, the Weimar Republic helped shape his early approach. The policy of Gustav Stresemann, Foreign Minister between 1923 and 1929, had focused on the revision of the Treaty of Versailles and, in the longer term, on redrawing Germany's frontiers in the east; he even had ambitions to unite Germany with Austria. Meanwhile, the *Reichswehr*, under von Seeckt, had already begun to evade the military restrictions imposed on Germany in 1919 by secret rearmament and military training in Russia. Hitler continued and accelerated the process between 1933 and 1936 – until, by 1937, he was sufficiently confident to revive the more expansionist aims of the Second Reich.

Yet the connection between Hitler's policies and those of his predecessors should not be overstated. If there were obvious similarities, even precedents, there were also fundamental differences. For example, no German government had seriously considered the disintegration of Austria-Hungary – its closest ally since the Dual Alliance of 1879. Indeed, Bismarck had been strongly against the formation of any *Grossdeutschland*, believing that this would only serve to dilute the influence of Prussia. If *Anschluss* entered any official plans, it was towards the end of the First World War and as a means of preventing the collapse of Germany's coalition partner. As for any 'continental objectives', these were given a powerful racial emphasis by Hitler. This may have been apparent in the ideas of some of the pre-1914 *Lebensraum* fringe groups, but they were never part of any government or military policy – during the period of either the Second Reich or the Weimar Republic; no such considerations featured in the diplomatic machinations of Bülow, Bethmann-Hollweg or Stresemann. Under Hitler, race shifted from the fringe to the core and redefined official policy towards the Slavs of eastern Europe so fundamentally as to allow unprecedented measures for evacuation after 1939 and extermination from 1941. The push for *Lebensraum* became a new dynamic very different to the military objectives of the Wilhelmine period. Even the pursuit of 'world objectives' had a new emphasis. Wilhelmine *Weltpolitik* was primarily a challenge to Britain to concede Germany a 'place in the sun' as a colonial and naval power as well as the supreme military influence on the continent. Hitler's *Stufenplan* was intended to lead to something very different – Germany's racial domination on a global scale.

The primacy of Hitler's involvement in foreign policy?

So far we have looked at two controversies: whether Hitler had long-term intentions and whether he was influenced by policies from the past. These, in turn, are associated with the extent to which Hitler actually defined the shape taken by German action after 1933. Was he in control of the major initiatives in foreign policy? Or was he affected by domestic pressures and groups?

In two ways he can be seen as the key influence. First, he defined Germany's general approach to specific countries. Poland and Russia were seen as Germany's targets for future *Lebensraum*, although short-term strategy meant that they could be played off against each other between 1933 and 1939. In his *Zweites Buch*, Hitler cast France as Germany's 'natural enemy' since she could be expected to resist any attempts by Hitler to change the existing balance of power in Europe. Italy, by contrast, was Germany's 'natural ally' and needed to be carefully managed over Germany's plans for Austria. Britain, he hoped, would cooperate with the achievement of Germany's interests and, as with Italy, would need to be dealt with circumspectly. Second, when it came to the actual decision-making between 1933 and 1939, Hitler was clearly in control of the process. Once fully established in power, he challenged traditionalist opinions in the Foreign Ministry to draw up his Non-Aggression Pact with Poland in 1934; he was personally responsible for both the Anglo-German Naval Agreement of 1935 and the remilitarisation of the Rhineland in 1936; and he pushed the Sudeten issue to the point of war in 1938, eventually manipulating both Chamberlain and Daladier into making the concessions he had demanded. Although the details were delegated to Ribbentrop, Hitler was also instrumental in the 1939 Pact of Steel with Italy and the Non-Aggression Pact with the Soviet Union. Above all, it was Hitler who took the decision to invade Bohemia and to ignore the Anglo-French guarantee to Poland. As Kershaw states, 'Evidence of a "weak dictator" is, therefore, difficult to come by in terms of Hitler's actions in the foreign policy arena'.[7] Even though most of the officials and diplomats were retained on his coming to power, Hitler took the early decision to downgrade the role of Foreign Minister, taking over many of its functions himself or delegating them to party functionaries and advisers. Of these the most important was Ribbentrop, who was responsible to Hitler personally. In some cases – such as the Sudeten Crisis of 1938 – the Foreign Ministry was not even kept informed of the latest developments.

In some ways, however, Hitler was affected by the impact of domestic factors. Mommsen, for example, sees Hitler's foreign policy as a manifestation of the chaotic polycratic structure and as 'domestic policy projected outwards'. Hitler contrived to 'conceal the increasing loss of reality only by maintaining political dynamism through incessant action'. In this way he acted irrationally and undermined 'political stabilization'.[8] Although most historians consider this approach too radical (it is certainly a contrast to Kershaw's view given above), there is a case for the influence of economic issues. Recent historians have argued strongly that there is a direct correlation between Germany's economic problems and performance and the pursuit of an expansionist policy in Europe. Sauer, for example, maintains that *Blitzkrieg* was an economic as well as a military strategy. (See Chapter 7, Analysis 2.) It was developed to enable Germany to increase rearmament without causing the German consumer excessive suffering and thereby depriving the regime of its support.[9] The practical effect was the deliberate dismantling of neighbouring states in order to strengthen the German economic base. Kershaw sees the relationship between the economy and militarism as more problematic. Hitler's Four Year Plan and his Hossbach Memorandum were a response to the economic crisis of 1935–6 and locked Germany into a course of rearmament – and war.[10] The process was less deliberate than Sauer maintains – but no less inexorable. It could also be argued that Hitler accelerated the pace of his foreign policy in order to divert German public opinion from domestic problems, especially economic. This was a well-worn device, used both in the Second Reich and in Mussolini's Italy.

Overall, Hitler was influenced by internal trends and pressures but, at the same time, he controlled the outlet points at which these pressures emerged. It was therefore Hitler who decided how internal trends should be translated into external action. Returning to the first debate, this is far more than mere pragmatism, or opportunist reaction. But it is not quite as much as master-planning or blueprinting.

Questions

1. Was Hitler's foreign policy 'planned' or 'improvised'?
2. How much of Hitler's foreign policy was 'new'?
3. Was Hitler fully in control of Germany's foreign policy?

ANALYSIS 2: 1939: HITLER'S WAR?

According to the 1946 Nuremberg Judgement, the Second World War was the outcome of Nazi policy and of Hitler's determination 'not to depart from the course he had set for himself'.[11] This raises three major issues. First, was the Nuremberg Judgement correct in apportioning to Hitler the prime responsibility for the outbreak of war? Second, if it was, can other leaders and powers be held in any way responsible for not having stopped Hitler by following a more robust resistance to Hitler's demands? And third, had such a course itself resulted in an earlier war, in 1938, might this not have been preferable to that in 1939?

The responsibility of Hitler?

Hitler's own attitude to war was uncompromising. He saw it as the highest form of struggle, which was at the core of his racial policy. 'War,' he said, 'is the most natural, the most ordinary thing. War is a constant; war is everywhere. There is no beginning, there is no conclusion of peace. War is life. All struggle is war. War is the primal condition.' Most historians accept Hitler's statements as a true reflection of his ultimate intentions. Some go as far as to associate them directly with the outbreak of war in 1939, thereby fully justifying the wording of the Nuremberg Judgement. According to Trevor-Roper, 'The Second World War was Hitler's personal war in many senses. He intended it, he prepared for it, he chose the moment for launching it'.[12] Hitler's was therefore unquestionably the main responsibility. His aims were 'quite different from the war aims of the men who, in 1933, admitted him to power and who, after 1933, served him in power'. (See Source 2.1.) This argument, first advanced in 1961, has been reactivated in similar terms more recently by Spielvogel, who also places the blame on 'the man who believed that struggle was the very essence of life itself and that only force ruled'. Western appeasement may have been 'foolish' and Soviet cooperation with the Nazis 'criminal' but the Second World War was 'rooted in the ideology of Hitler and the National Socialists'.[13] Between Trevor-Roper and Spielvogel is a direct link provided by others, such as Hildebrand and Weinberg, who adopt a similar, if more ambivalent, emphasis.

There is, however, a minority argument which switches the emphasis from the overriding force of an underlying ideology to short-term and largely undirected expediency. A.J.P. Taylor's case, originally made in 1961, is that Hitler was the supreme opportunist, taking advantage of mistakes made by other leaders. Far from preparing for a new world order, he was actually in line with the policies of his predecessors in trying to secure a revision of the Treaty of Versailles: he refers to the conflict in 1939 as 'the second World war, or rather of the war between the three Western Powers over the settlement of Versailles; a war which had been implicit since the moment when the first war ended'. (See Source 2.2.) Hitler did not plan war; he simply took advantage of the apparent hesitancy of the other powers – until he finally misread their change of mind. There may well be some evidence for this. Hitler was given his opportunity to remilitarise the Rhineland in 1936 by the diversion of Britain and France against Italian aggression in Abyssinia the year before. He was able to take Austria with so little effort in 1938 because Mussolini, who had originally opposed German schemes there, was now concentrating on an expanded overseas empire. The Sudetenland went Hitler's way because of the ardent desire of Chamberlain to avoid a European conflagration which the lessons of the Spanish Civil War seemed to suggest might happen all too easily. The outbreak of war in 1939 was not the deliberate upgrading of policy but rather Hitler's misreading of the Anglo-French guarantee made to Poland in March. More contentious, however, is Taylor's assertion that, in foreign policy, Hitler should not be seen in a different light to the other national leaders in the 1930s. Although in domestic affairs he 'bears the greatest responsibility for acts of immeasurable evil', in foreign policy by contrast, his aims 'were little different to those of his contemporaries'. In a characteristically mischievous twist, Taylor adds that 'In international affairs there was nothing wrong with Hitler except that he was a German'.[14] (See Source 2.2.)

Taylor's greatest critic was Trevor-Roper; indeed, the two dominated the television screens in the early 1960s to an extent that no historians have managed since – though many have tried. Trevor-Roper's accusation was that Taylor had trivialised Hitler's writings by refusing to take any of them at face value or to accept that Hitler meant what he had said. Taylor's analysis of Hitler as a typical opportunist of the 1930s also seems out of line with the much greater emphasis given to the racial motives behind all of Hitler's actions, both domestic and foreign, by historians such as Burleigh and Wippermann[15] and the vast majority of the latest writings on the Holocaust.[16] It is, therefore, hardly surprising that Kaiser should be of the view that Taylor's arguments 'have not held up'. (See Source 2.3.) Nevertheless, one aspect has prevented Taylor from sinking without trace: he was able to put a particularly strong case for Hitler manipulating a faulty international situation – often without clear intentions; this is an approach which is used by Kaiser himself. (Source 2.3.) There is also a parallel with those historians who maintain that Hitler manoeuvred within the parameters of a flawed and chaotic *internal* political structure. 'Taylorism' may have been discredited – but it is far from dead.

The responsibility of other powers?

An alternative approach is to place substantial responsibility on other powers for the outbreak of war. After all, they pursued policies which failed to restrain Hitler and increased Germany's advantages, and then signalled a major change of approach which Hitler did not believe. Britain and France, for example, bowed to Hitler's unilateral decision to remilitarise the Rhineland in 1936 and incorporate Austria into the Reich in 1938, and agreed to pressurise Czechoslovakia into handing over the Sudetenland (1938). Then, following Hitler's annexation of the rest of Bohemia in March 1939, they drew the line against further acquisitions by extending guarantees to Poland, Romania and Greece. Finally, when Hitler went ahead with his invasion of Poland in September 1939, both Britain and France declared war on Germany. The whole process has been compared by Liddell Hart with stoking up a boiler until the pressure rises to danger level – and then closing the safety valve. The other powers therefore failed to pursue consistent policies to Hitler, allowing him to become more radical and disinclined to believe them when they signalled a change in their intention.

This approach involves a series of criticisms of the policy of appeasement. Britain's role has been especially contentious. Chamberlain's policy over Czechoslovakia was seen by a minority at the time as both dishonourable and ineffectual. Churchill told him after the Munich agreement: 'You were given the choice between war and dishonour. You chose dishonour and you will have war.'[17] The main indictments at the time were that Chamberlain was prepared to abandon one of the few remaining democracies in Europe and that he even put pressure on France not to invoke the 1935 pact with Russia and call upon Russia to take part in the defence of Czechoslovakia (something that Litvinov had indicated a willingness to do). Churchill called it 'a mad lack of foresight on our part, at a time of great danger, to put obstacles on the road of the general association of the huge Russian mass with the resistance to a Nazi act of aggression'.[18] Similar criticisms were made in *Guilty Men* published in Britain in 1940, shortly after Chamberlain's resignation. But Chamberlain has been defended by a number of historians, such as Dilks, on the grounds that: he was warned by the chiefs of staff that Britain was not ready for war in 1938; levels of aircraft production were much lower than those in Germany; and public opinion and the Dominions were unprepared. In 1939, by contrast, Chamberlain was able to change his approach and issue guarantees to Hitler's next intended victim because British rearmament was well under way and the British people were more united and resolute. Other historians, including Aster, have rebutted this revisionist approach. Britain was blind to the nature of Hitler's policies and it is time 'to be done with the appeasement debate – for it is over'.[19]

France, too, comes out of the crisis in 1938 with little credit. In her case there was a strange anomaly. After her experiences in the First World War, France had built up a network of alliances and agreements with eastern European countries – first Poland, then Czechoslovakia, then Soviet Union; she had constructed the Maginot Line and built up her armed forces, especially tanks. But then successive French governments failed to take action over Hitler's remilitarisation of the Rhineland in 1936 or to call upon the Soviet Union to assist with the defence of Czechoslovakia in 1938. Stackelberg makes the telling point that: 'A firm Western pledge of support for Czechoslovakia might have deterred Hitler from attack in the foreseeable future.' This was the more likely 'as the Soviet Union seemed ready to honour its treaty obligations to Czechoslovakia if France did so.' Above all, 'Hitler was pragmatic enough to want to avoid a repetition of the two-front war that had fatally over-extended German forces in the Great War'.[20] Explanations for such lack of action range from semi-deterministic interpretations of French inter-war decadence and capitulation, to a collective pacifism in the face of a renewed threat from Germany and economic crises as a result of the Depression. Adamthwaite is more specific, blaming the lack of 'decisive leadership' and of 'revised grand strategy'. He adds: 'If rulers and ruled had possessed the courage to say *merde* to Hitler before 1939 the story would have had a different ending.'[21] An alternative view – that Daladier's government was placed under heavy pressure by

Chamberlain – is rejected by Adamthwaite on the grounds that the French wanted themselves to follow appeasement partly to satisfy public opinion and partly to disengage from obligations in eastern Europe; British pressure was therefore an advantage. Weinberg maintains that 'French contingency planning for any aggressive move by Germany was of an essentially defensive nature' and that France was 'withdrawing into a shell'.[22] It could, of course, have been argued that war was unthinkable to the west before appeasement had run its full course. Both Britain and France had to try everything to maintain peace, even to the extent of trusting Hitler's promises for the future. Yet this added immeasurably to Hitler's confidence to turn next on Poland – in the expectation that he would meet the same irresolution.

Two other powers contributed to the diplomatic environment which was so favourable to Hitler during the 1930s – the United States and the Soviet Union. The former was too preoccupied with the impact of the Depression and the pursuit of a policy of isolationism to bring any influence to bear on the deteriorating situation in Europe. This was important because, as Weinberg argues, 'the absence of any active American role and the general expectation that that absence would continue could only encourage German adventures and discourage any thoughts of resistance'.[23] The case of the Soviet Union is more complex, partly because its own leader, Stalin, was just as unscrupulous and opportunist as Hitler, and partly because Soviet policy towards Hitler was as inconsistent as that of Britain and France. It is true that the Soviet government tried to persuade France to invoke the 1935 pact for the defence of Czechoslovakia. When Daladier's government failed to do this, the Soviet Union pulled away from any obligations and eventually sought an agreement with Germany in the form of the Nazi–Soviet Non-Aggression Pact in August 1939. This, of course, gave Hitler the backing he needed to defy the guarantees of Britain and France and invade Poland in September. The official Soviet version of this was that the Soviet Union had no choice: abandoned by Britain and France, it needed time to rearm against Germany. But this ignores the tortuous path pursued by Stalin's policy since 1931. At first he had been favourable to Germany, hoping that the latter would start a war between the western powers; then, from 1935, he had come to realise the more general danger posed by Germany and had switched to attempts to contain Hitler through multilateral action; when his failed, he proceeded to his own bilateral arrangements which were not dissimilar to his original ones with Germany.

It was doubly fortunate to Hitler that western and Soviet determination to control him did not coincide. When Britain and France were engaged in appeasement in 1938, the Soviet Union was prepared to resist Hitler. By the time that Britain and France had come round to resisting Hitler, the Soviet Union was slipping into appeasement of its own. There is no question that such mistiming was a vital factor in encouraging Hitler to intensify his claims in the increasing certainty that he would not have to engage all the powers simultaneously.

A missed opportunity?

If Britain and France succeeded in delaying the outbreak of war until 1939 – before accepting the inevitable – was this actually the best outcome? It is arguable that a war fought in 1938 would have been far more damaging to Germany. In not drawing the line earlier, therefore, the western powers missed the opportunity not only to resist further demands from Hitler but also to inflict a defeat on him should he have continued with his course.

The key point here is that Czechoslovakia was more defendable in 1938 than was Poland a year later. As the one remaining democracy in a sea of dictatorship, it had taken measures to strengthen its military position by constructing the strongest set of fortifications in Europe along its frontier with Germany, and increasing its army to 35 divisions and its air force to 1,500 fighters and bombers. Although Hitler was confident that Germany's resources were sufficient to defeat Czechoslovakia, could he have been quite so sanguine about the type of general war that might have occurred in September 1938? At that stage Germany was less prepared and the combination against him was – relatively speaking – stronger than in September 1939. For one thing, Germany was outflanked by the Franco–Soviet Pact of 1935, which Litvinov was prepared to activate on Czechoslovakia's behalf. By not calling upon Russia, Britain and France effectively dismantled what could have become an alliance against Germany. During the following ten months their position weakened considerably. The Soviet Union was lost as a potential ally as Stalin promised neutrality through the Non-Aggression Pact with Hitler. Instead, Britain and France set up a network of guarantees with Poland, Romania and Greece. These they were hardly in a position to implement, whereas a similar undertaking to Czechoslovakia would have had the means ready for immediate enforcement.

There would, of course, have been logistical problems had hostilities broken out in 1938. Since there was no direct frontier between Czechoslovakia and the Soviet Union, the latter would have needed the cooperation of Romania and Poland to send troops or aircraft. Poland would probably have refused, not wanting to risk the territory it had gained in the Russo–Polish War (1920–1); it might even have opted to convert its 1934 Non-Aggression Pact with Germany into a military alliance. Yet Poland's strength, as it turned out a year later, was in its cavalry. This was easily swept aside by German tanks in September 1939 and would have suffered the same fate against Russia – which had stockpiled more tanks by that date than the rest of Europe put together. In 1938, too, the Four Year Plan was in its early stages and Hitler's forces and tanks were still outnumbered in the west by the French; by 1939 the gap had closed and the promise of 19 British divisions were no compensation for the loss of the Czech forces to the south and of the Soviet military threat to the east. Even the style of warfare could well have differed. In 1939 Hitler was able to use *Blitzkrieg* strategies first against Poland, then against northern Europe and France. These separate and intensive offensives would not have been possible against three fronts and the potential coalition of 1938. A weaker Germany might have had to resort to a more defensive strategy which, in turn, could have prevented the catastrophic collapse of France. The Maginot Line was, after all, intended for use in conjunction with a military ally in eastern Europe; this France had in 1938, whereas in 1939 she had more of a dependant.

All this is, of course, hypothetical. But some historians have recently interested themselves more in 'counterfactual' history. This is one case, surely, in which there was a genuinely alternative scenario. Although it did not occur, it can still be used to illustrate the chaotic weakness of the European diplomatic structure and the advantages that Hitler was able to extract from it – even though his diplomatic options could actually have been much more restricted. It was the uncertainty of the other powers which enabled him to probe for weaknesses which need not necessarily have been there.

Overall, there is no serious question as to ultimate responsibility for the outbreak of war in terms of motive or dynamics. The debate on Hitler as a typical diplomat of the time seems to have dissipated. But it can still be argued strongly that the way in which Hitler was handled produced a war in 1939 which unnecessarily favoured Germany.

Questions

1. How does the meaning of 'responsibility for the outbreak of war' differ when applied to Germany on the one hand and to Britain and France on the other?
2. Is there any longer a case for seeing Hitler as a supreme opportunist rather than as a fundamental ideologue?

SOURCES

1: THE AIMS OF HITLER'S FOREIGN POLICY

Source 1.1 Extracts from *Mein Kampf* (1925)

The foreign policy of a folkish state must first of all bear in mind the obligation to secure the existence of the race incorporated in this state. This must be done by establishing a healthy and natural relationship between the number and growth of the population, on the one hand, and the extent and quality of its soil on the other. ... Only a sufficiently large space on this earth can ensure the independent existence of a nation. ...

Germany today is not a world power. ... The National Socialist movement must seek to eliminate the present disastrous imbalance between our population and the area of our national territory, regarding the latter as the source of our food and the basis of our political power. And it ought to strive to eliminate the contrast between our past history and the hopelessness of our present political impotence ...

The demand for the restoration of the frontiers of 1914 is a political absurdity of such proportions and implications as to make it appear a crime. Apart from anything else, the Reich's frontiers in 1914 were anything but logical. In reality they were neither final in the sense of embracing all ethnic Germans, nor sensible with regard to geomilitary considerations. ... We are putting an end to the perpetual German march towards the south and west of Europe and turning our eyes towards the land in the east. We are finally putting a stop to the colonial and trade policy of the pre-war period and passing over to the territorial policy of the future ...

However, when we speak of new land in Europe today we must principally bear in mind Russia and the border states subject to her. Destiny itself seems to wish to point the way for us here. ... The colossal empire in the East is ripe for dissolution. ... If we look round for European allies from this point of view, only two states remain: England and Italy ...

Source 1.2: Extracts from Hitler's *Zweites Buch* (unpublished until 1962)

On France: In any conflict involving Germany, regardless on what grounds, regardless for what reasons, France will always be our adversary ... [France was] in a position to be able to threaten almost the whole of Germany with aircraft even an hour after the outbreak of a conflict.

On Britain: England actually concerned herself very little with European conditions as long as no threatening world competitor arose from them, so that she always viewed the threat as lying in a development which must one day cut across her dominion over the seas and colonies ... If England remains true to her great world-political aims, her potential opponents will be France and Russia in Europe [since they challenged Britain's imperial position], and in other parts of the world especially the American Union in the future.

On future territorial expansion: For this earth is not allotted to anyone nor is it presented to anyone as a gift. It is awarded by providence to people who in their hearts have the courage to conquer it, the strength to preserve it, and the industry to put it to the plough. ... The present distribution of possessions has not been designed by a higher power but by man himself. ... No. The primary right of this world is the right to life, so far as one possesses the strength for this. Hence on the basis of this right a vigorous nation will always find ways of adapting its territory to its population size.

Source 1.3: From the Hossbach Memorandum, a record made by Colonel Hossbach of a confidential meeting between Hitler and the chiefs of German staff, 5 November 1937

The Führer then continued:

The aim of German policy was to make secure and to preserve the racial community and to enlarge it. It was therefore a question of space.

The German community comprised over 85 million people and, by reason of their number and the narrow limits of habitable space in Europe, it constituted a tightly packed racial core such as was not to be found in any other country and such as implied the right to a greater living space than in the case of other peoples ... and in the continuance of these political conditions lay the greatest danger to the preservation of the German race at its present peak.

Source 1.4: Extracts from a reported conversation between Hitler and Lord Halifax, 19 November 1937

Hitler: There were two possibilities in the shaping of relations between the peoples: the interplay of free forces, which was often synonymous with great and grave encroachments upon the life of the peoples and which could bring in its train a serious convulsion which would shake the civilisation we had built up with so much trouble. The second possibility lay in setting up in place of the play of free forces the rule of 'higher reason'. ... In the year 1919 a great chance to apply this method had been missed. At that time a solution of unreasonableness had been preferred: as a consequence Germany had been forced back on the path of the free play of forces, because this was the only possible way to make sure of the simplest rights of mankind ...

Halifax: On the English side, it was not necessarily thought that the status quo must be maintained under all circumstances. ... It was recognised that one might have to contemplate an adjustment to new conditions, a correction of former mistakes and the recognition of changed circumstances when such need arose. In doing so England made her influence felt only in one way – to secure that these alterations should not be made in a manner corresponding to the unreasonable solution mentioned by the Chancellor, the play of free forces, which in the end meant war. He must emphasise once more in the name of H.M. Government that possibility of change of the existing situation was not excluded, but that changes should only take place upon the basis of reasonable agreements reasonably reached.

Questions

1. Compare and contrast the aims expressed by Hitler in Sources 1.1 and 1.2.
2. What are the main differences between the arguments and language used by Hitler in Sources 1.3 and 1.4? How would you explain these differences?
3. What does Source 1.4 show about the attitude of the British government towards Hitler's foreign policy objectives?
4. What light does Source 1.2 throw on Hitler's attitude to Halifax in Source 1.4?

2: HISTORIANS ON THE OUTBREAK OF WAR

Source 2.1: Extracts from H. Trevor-Roper, 'Hitler's War Aims', an article published in 1960

Hitler's war aims are written large and clear in the documents of his reign. They are quite different from the war aims of the men who, in 1933, admitted him to power and who, after 1933, served him in power ...

These four sources ... are, first, *Mein Kampf*, Hitler's personal credo, written in prison in 1924 after the total collapse of his first bid for power; secondly, Hermann Rauschning's *Gespräche mit Hitler*, which were first published in 1939 and are the record of Hitler's private political conversations at the time of his second and successful bid, that is, in 1932–4; thirdly, the official record of Hitler's *Tischgespräche* at the time of his apparently universal military triumph in 1941–2; and, finally, the similar record, discovered last year and still unpublished in Germany, of his *Tischgespräche* at the time when he first acknowledged final defeat, in February 1945. These four documents are like four windows, opened, by different hands, into the inmost recesses of Hitler's mind at four crucial moments of his career: the moments of political defeat, political triumph, military triumph, military defeat …

Now the interesting thing about all these documents is that though spread over a period of 22 years, and issued in these very different circumstances, they all show an absolute consistency of philosophy and purpose. This consistency, this purpose has often been denied. It was denied at the time by those, in Germany and abroad, who wished to disbelieve it: whether, like some western statesmen, they feared to contemplate this hideous new power or, like some German statesmen, they hoped to harness it to their own more limited aims; and it has been denied since, by historians who are so revolted by Hitler's personal character, by the vulgarity and cruelty of his mind, that they refuse to allow him such virtues as mental power and consistency. But in fact I believe that all these denials are wrong.

Source 2.2: Extracts from A.J.P. Taylor, *The Origins of the Second World War*, published in 1961

Little can be discovered so long as we go on attributing everything that happened to Hitler. He supplied a powerful dynamic element, but it was fuel to an existing engine. He was in part the creation of Versailles, in part the creation of ideas that were common in contemporary Europe. Most of all, he was the creation of German history … Hitler bears the greatest responsibility for acts of immeasurable evil: for the destruction of German democracy; for the concentration camps; and, worst of all, for the extermination of peoples during the second World war … His foreign policy was a different matter. He aimed to make Germany the dominant Power in Europe and maybe, more remotely, in the world. Other Powers have pursued similar aims, and still do. Other Powers treat smaller countries as their satellites. Other Powers seek to defend their vital interests by force of arms. In international affairs there was nothing wrong with Hitler except that he was a German …

Hitler's exposition was in large part day-dreaming, unrelated to what followed in real life. Even if seriously meant, it was not a call to action, at any rate not to the action of a great war; it was a demonstration that a great war would not be necessary ... Hitler did not make plans – for world conquest or for anything else. He assumed that others would provide opportunities, and that he would seize them ...

Such were the origins of the second World war, or rather of the war between the three Western Powers over the settlement of Versailles; a war which had been implicit since the moment when the first war ended. Men will long debate whether this renewed war could have been averted by greater firmness or by greater conciliation; and no answer will be found to these hypothetical speculations. Maybe either would have succeeded, if consistently followed; the mixture of the two, practised by the British government, was the most likely to fail.

Source 2.3: Extracts from 'Hitler and the Coming of the War', an article by D. Kaiser, published in 1992

Thirty years after the publication of A.J.P. Taylor's controversial work, *The Origins of the Second World War,* the essential goals of Hitler's foreign policy are not a source of much dispute. Taylor's most contentious statements – that Hitler did not intend war to break out in September 1939, that he lacked a real plan for the conquest of Europe or the world, and that other governments had played a critical role in unleashing German expansion – have not held up. Recent treatments agree that Hitler *did* have a comprehensive plan for German expansion dating from before his accession to power and did intend a war in September 1939 ...

Hitler's tactics in foreign policy closely resembled his domestic political strategy before and after his seizure of power. Both relied upon dramatic measures and announcements, decisive displays of force and a knack for seizing and keeping the initiative. Both also took advantage of the structural weaknesses within contemporary domestic and international politics and of the confusion, disunity and paralysis that characterized the opposition to him. Hitler, in short, succeeded largely because he knew how to take advantage of the opportunities offered by the existing situation. And to a large extent, both his domestic and foreign opportunities resulted from the cataclysm of the First World War. At home, the collapse of imperial Germany, the Treaty of Versailles, the reparations question and the depression prevented the Weimar Republic from establishing itself upon a secure footing. Abroad – as A.J.P. Taylor argued in one of his more brilliant insights – the simultaneous defeat of Germany and Russia, combined with the collapse of Austria-Hungary, left behind a new territorial structure in central and eastern Europe that was likely to unravel as soon as the first few threads were pulled away.

Source 2.4: Extracts from 'Hitler's War? The Origins of the Second World War in Europe', an article by P. Bell, published in 1992

The principal origins of the war thus emerge with considerable clarity. There was a powerful German drive for expansion, arising partly from ambitions present well before 1914, partly from Nazi ideology, and partly from economic motives – all shaped by Hitler's powerful personality. This drive was continuous, and did not halt even in 1940 when Germany was in control of the whole of central and western Europe. It was not checked from outside at an early stage, because of the constraints and inhibitions which guided the policies of Britain and France and caused them for a long time to try to reach an accommodation with Germany by methods of concession and negotiation. But this never meant peace at any price, so that a conflict was certain at some time. Germany's opponents had opportunities to fight an earlier war and to deter Germany by means of an alliance, but did not take them. However, these opportunities were neither as simple nor as painless as they have been made to appear, and it is easy to see why they were passed over. For Britain and France to be convinced that they would have to fight another European war, the necessity had to be overwhelming. It was only the persistence of German expansion which created that necessity.

Questions

1. Why did Trevor-Roper not mention Hitler's *Zweites Buch* in Source 2.1? How significant is this omission for his argument?
2. Using Source 2.3, and your own knowledge, do you agree with Kaiser's view that 'Taylor's most contentious statements . . . have not held up'?
3. How convincing and complete is Bell's argument in Source 2.4 as an overall summary of the causes of the outbreak of the Second World War? Use Sources 2.1 to 2.3 and your own knowledge.

10

GERMANY AT WAR

BACKGROUND

The first stage of the war proved a spectacular success for Germany. Poland fell within weeks and the western half was absorbed into the Reich. In April 1940 Hitler conquered Denmark and Norway, before moving on to the Netherlands and Belgium in May, while France was defeated in June. All this was a spectacular success for the military strategy *of Blitzkrieg.* The subsequent attempt to prepare an invasion across the Channel was frustrated by the Battle of Britain. By June 1941 Hitler had lost interest in Operation Sealion and concentrated instead on Operation Barbarossa against Russia. This opened up a new phase, generally referred to as one of 'total war'. Despite initial German victories, the Soviet Union recovered in 1942 and stemmed the German advance – especially at Stalingrad (1943). At the same time, the tide was also turning in North Africa, to which Hitler had been forced to send German troops to reverse the disastrous defeats suffered there by the Italians at the hands of the British. Total war assumed a global aspect when, in December 1941, Germany's ally, Japan, attacked Pearl Harbor. Hitler declared war on the United States in support of Japan, only to find that President Roosevelt made the decision to give priority to the war in Europe. In 1944 Hitler was therefore confronted by the advancing Russians from the east and the Anglo-American forces from the south and west, while German cities were pounded by heavy bombing. Out-produced and outnumbered by the Allies, Germany surrendered on 7 May 1945, following Hitler's suicide on 30 April.

This chapter deals with two issues arising from these events. Analysis 1 covers the role played by Hitler himself in the various stages of the war, especially the extent to which he was responsible for the key decisions contributing to Germany's initial victories and ultimate defeat. Analysis 2 considers the impact of the war on the Nazi regime and, in the process, draws together the main themes already covered in Chapters 4 to 8.

ANALYSIS 1: DID HITLER CONTROL THE DEVELOPMENT OF THE SECOND WORLD WAR?

The controversy about the development of Hitler's foreign policy up to the outbreak of war in 1939 has its parallel in his involvement in the war itself. Did he control its various stages, converting initial victory to eventual defeat through the defects of his obsessive personal leadership? Or were his decisions largely shaped by factors beyond his control? The answer to these questions depends very much on the type of war actually fought. By and large, it could be argued that Hitler dominated the phase generally described as *Blitzkrieg*, while the total war which followed he found increasingly problematic. Yet – perversely – Hitler's dominance increased after 1941 in a way which imposed a stranglehold on appropriate military strategy. His attempts to regain control, after losing the initiative, brought the Reich to total destruction.

There is considerable evidence that Hitler dominated the successful *Blitzkrieg* phase of the war, especially between 1939 and 1940. This involved the core areas of Europe and saw a deliberate expansion of Germany's frontiers at the expense of weaker opponents like Poland. According to some historians,[1] this fitted well with the economic objectives of the Nazi regime, which were to achieve conquest without too high a cost to the German consumer. The Non-Aggression Pact with the Soviet Union (August 1939) was intended to facilitate the process and to avoid any possibility of a long and drawn-out war at this stage. Once Poland had been destroyed, Hitler also set the agenda for the conflict in western Europe. Britain and France had taken no direct military action between September 1938 and the spring of 1939 and it was on Hitler's initiative that the war spread to Denmark, Norway, the Netherlands, Belgium and France. In the case of France, the initiative seems to have been entirely a personal one, since the German High Command warned against the invasion in June 1940. The result was, however, a spectacular victory for the German *Panzer* divisions who bypassed the Maginot Line and the French defences on the Belgian frontier with a rapid advance through the Ardennes. To an extent,

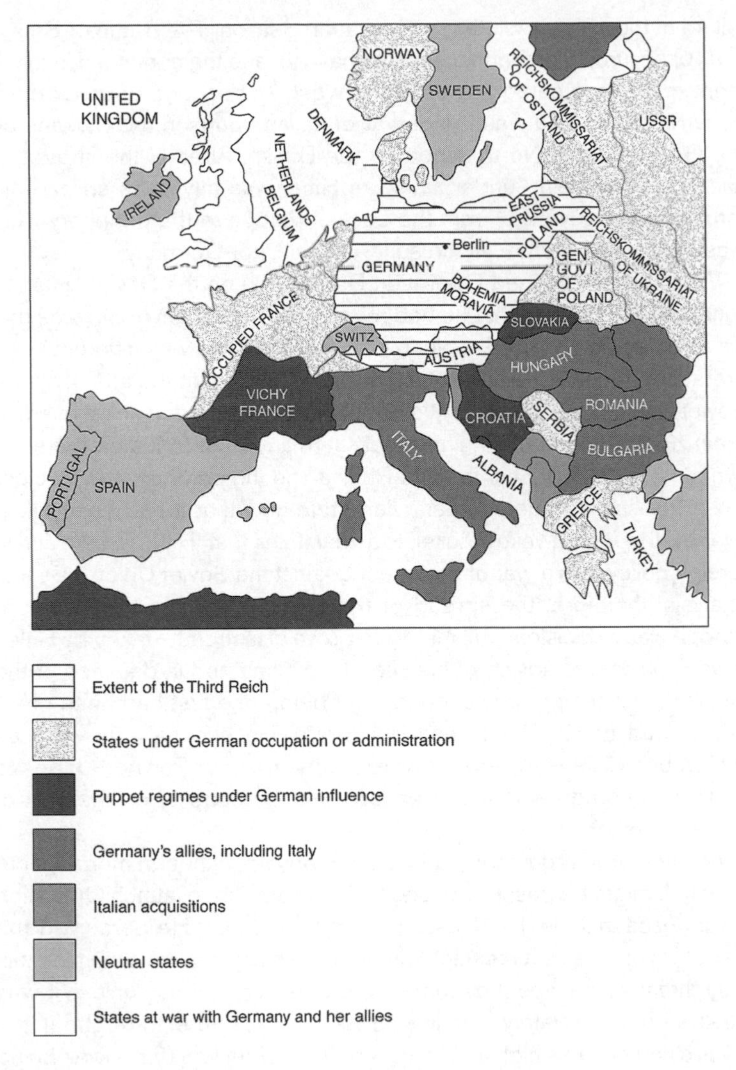

Figure 4 Europe under Nazi influence by 1942

therefore, we can refer to the early stage of the conflict as 'Hitler's war'. It seems to accord with long-term objectives to achieve *Lebensraum,* to defeat the country most likely to prevent this – France – and to implement the timetable implicit in the Hossbach Memorandum.

Yet even at this early stage Hitler was confronted by two factors beyond his immediate control. One was his inability to detach Britain from the conflict by means of a negotiated settlement, followed by the failure of the military solution – Operation Sealion. The Battle of Britain (1940) ensured that Germany would have to face the continued involvement of an undefeated power in the west. The second unpredictable occurrence in 1940 was the defeat of Italian troops in the Balkans by the Greeks and in North Africa by the British. Already the impact of *Blitzkrieg* was being undermined as Hitler was having to spread his forces more thinly away from the core of Europe to the periphery. This was the type of warfare which suited Britain, not Germany.

When Hitler launched Operation Barbarossa on the Soviet Union in June 1941, it seemed that he had recaptured the initiative. But was this his own decision? It is possible to present this in two very different interpretations. On the one hand, it is normally argued that the attack on the Soviet Union was the culmination of everything he had ever believed. In *Mein Kampf* he had maintained that Germany must focus on the east: 'we must principally bear in mind Russia and the border states subject to her'. Russia had become an alien state now that it had been taken over by 'the Jewish yoke'. Jäckel, too, maintains that 'Hitler's main aim in foreign policy was a war of conquest against the Soviet Union'.[2] By this analysis, therefore, the spread of the war into the plains of eastern Europe was a decision – ultimately to prove disastrous – taken by Hitler. It was against the advice of his High Command and in defiance of the logic of not opening up a second front before the first had been properly closed down. But it was deliberate. He had said as early as 9 October 1939 – a mere six weeks after invading Poland – that 'No treaty and no agreement can ensure lasting neutrality on the part of Soviet Russia'.[3]

An alternative argument could be put forward, although more speculatively. It might be possible to see Hitler's decision to launch Operation Barbarossa in June 1941 as a pre-emptive strike. He perceived the Soviet Union less as a race and ideological enemy than as a looming military threat which would become more and more serious unless it was dealt with immediately. Stalin's military expenditure throughout the 1930s had been as high as Hitler's and the Soviet workforce was being prepared for total war in a way which the German workforce was not. By June 1941 the Red Army stood at 5.4 million. It also had more tanks than all the other countries of the world together.[4] Aircraft production far outran that of Germany and new industrial complexes were springing up in the east, out of the range of German bombers. It must have seemed to Hitler that the gap was growing rapidly between the military strengths of the two powers. Bearing in mind the strategy announced in the Hossbach Memorandum to deal with the west sooner rather than later, might the same not apply to the Soviet Union? After all, Hitler's hands were free: France had been smashed and Britain, although undefeated, was unable to bring the war to the continent. The most appropriate time for another strike was 1941, particularly since the Red Army had recently lost many of its most able officers as a result of Stalin's purges. Indeed, it is possible that Stalin was preparing action of his own against Germany for the near or intermediate future.

A similar dichotomy exists over the declaration of war on the United States. According to Hillgruber, Hitler's policy was 'designed to span the globe: ideologically, too, the doctrines of universal anti-Semitism and Social Darwinism, fundamental to his programme, were intended to embrace the whole of mankind'.[5] Hildebrand and Hauner also see this stage as the pursuit of global domination. On the other hand, where was the sense of *voluntarily* extending the conflict from the continent to the periphery? Germany was already hard pressed in North Africa and would be further weakened by maritime involvements. In any case, Hitler had once claimed in his *Zweites Buch* that the major mistake of the Second Reich was to challenge for imperial and maritime supremacy before imposing control over the continent. The answer must, therefore, be that circumstances pushed Hitler into a course of action which he would have preferred to avoid. The Japanese attack on Pearl Harbor involved the United States in a conflict which was bound to link up in an alliance with Britain. Hitler was therefore bolstering up Japan in the belief that the United States would be kept preoccupied by the Japanese in the Pacific until Germany had won the war in Europe. Roosevelt's decision to give priority to the defeat of Germany shows that Hitler's logic was flawed – but also that this made very little difference to the outcome. Hitler had very little control over the arrival of war between Germany and the United States.

It seems therefore that, although he did have long-term objectives, Hitler tended to defer them when the time was unfavourable and to adopt them when obliged by circumstances to do so. This means that he was less in control of the situation than is often thought. This brings a 'structuralist' emphasis even to what is generally seen as the biggest personal decision – and error – of Hitler's entire career. Hence he hated the Soviet Union and hoped eventually to destroy it. But the decision was taken under pressure. He also considered it likely that Germany would have to contest global supremacy with the United States, but he declared war only after the United States was brought in as a result of the Japanese connection.

How could Hitler have countenanced such a spread in the conflict, given the enormous disparity of resources between Germany and the Anglo-Soviet–American combination? Again, there are two possibilities. One is that Hitler had become blind to all military reason and oblivious to advice. The popular perception of Hitler is that he succumbed to megalomania from 1941 onwards and personally dragged Germany to defeat and destruction in the mistaken belief that he could bring ultimate and total victory. This would be an argument based on 'intentionalism' gone wrong: Hitler created his own pressures. The alternative is that Hitler was under *external* pressures and that he tried to respond to them in ways that had worked before. Hence the solution was to use *Blitzkrieg* against larger opponents. It failed because it was never intended for use in this way.

By 1942 the whole character of the war had changed. Thereafter Germany's role in it was more and more affected by Hitler's deliberate decisions and input. According to Hildebrand, the regime's original 'politico-military needs' and its 'racial and ideological aims' diverged when Hitler 'embarked on his war for *Lebensraum* in Russia' and 'the aims and assumptions of doctrinaire ideology came more and more to predominate'.[6] This deliberate emphasis, it could be argued, determined the scope and priorities of the war in several crucial ways. In each, it was clear that Hitler remained in control of the decisions taken, even though he was losing control over their military outcomes. In the first place, vital military resources were, from 1942 onwards, diverted from the military campaigns on the eastern front to the implantation of a policy of extermination in the 'racial war'. Second, his fixation with this priority meant that he refused to give any ground strategically. As early as the winter of 1941, Hitler ordered his crumbling army outside Moscow to hold positions at all costs 'without regard to the consequences'.[7] Similar orders in 1943 resulted in the destruction of the German armies at Stalingrad. Third, as the remainder of the *Wehrmacht* was being forced by the Red Army out of eastern Europe, Hitler switched the emphasis to 'defensive' struggle against Bolshevism. But his orders transcended all normal principles of military defence, taking on more the character of self-destruction.

This brings us to the final issue. Germany was crushed in a way that is unusual for a defeated country in warfare. Its cities were shattered by saturation bombing and both military and civilian deaths mounted steadily. Yet by far the greatest destruction and bloodshed occurred late in 1944 and in 1945 – at the very time that the outcome of the war had become inevitable. Hitler appeared determined to condemn his own people to annihilation. Refusing to listen to any of the – admittedly belated – advice of those around him, he ordered a scorched earth policy. By the notorious Nero Order of 19 March 1945, he demanded the obliteration of 'all military, communications, industrial and logistics installations as well as material assets within the Reich territory which the enemy can use for continuing his struggle either immediately or in the foreseeable future'.[8] When Speer tried to persuade him to change his mind, Hitler reminded him that 'If the war is lost, the *Volk* will also be lost'. It was therefore unnecessary 'to bother about the basic requirements which the German *Volk* needs to ensure even its most primitive survival'.[9] When faced with inevitable defeat, most countries begin to moderate their more extreme policies and to seek some form of 'exit strategy'. Nazi Germany, by contrast, radicalised itself still further. The problem was the absence of any collective evaluation of appropriate military strategy or diplomacy for reasons suggested in Analysis 2. By the last two years of the war, the *Wehrmacht* had been nazified far beyond the levels already undertaken in 1938, and the decision-making process had been centred more completely on Hitler himself – at the very time that he no longer had any options to take.

Questions

1. 'Hitler lost control over the course of the war. That is why he lost the war.' Discuss.
2. What questions remain to be answered about the way in which '*Blitzkrieg*' developed into 'total war'?

ANALYSIS 2: HOW DID THE EXPERIENCE OF WAR RADICALISE THE NAZI REGIME?

Involvement in the Second World War radicalised every aspect of the Nazi regime. This process occurred in two broad phases. Between 1939 and 1941 the population was brought under military control and, since the regime was under fewer constraints to take account of public opinion, there were more opportunities to introduce major changes to policy, organisation and structure; these all took place within an environment of successful military campaigning. Then, from late 1941, came a second wave of radicalisation as the war for *Lebensraum* in eastern Europe shifted military priorities and placed greater demands on the economy and on the *Volksgemeinschaft*. Horowitz goes so far as to say that the Nazi onslaught on Russia from June 1941 to May 1942 meant that the 'war aims of the Nazis shifted from victory over the Allied powers to victory over the Jews'.[10] It could, however, be asked whether radicalisation involved an alteration in the direction originally taken by the pre-war regime, or whether the war merely caused an acceleration. In the process of becoming more extreme, therefore, was the regime actually *changing*? And if it did change, were the stability and equilibrium which had just about been achieved by 1939 irrevocably destroyed? These issues will be considered in the following paragraphs, within the overall context of radicalisation.

The war certainly had a major impact on the political structure of the regime. The administration expanded rapidly after 1939, and again from 1941, to take in the conquered territories in eastern Europe. In 1939 the Reich absorbed from Poland the areas known as West Prussia, Southern Silesia and Posen, while imposing direct rule on the rest through the General Government of Occupied Polish Territories. From 1941 two new sovereignties were set up: the *Reichskommissariat* of Outland (comprising White Russia, Estonia, Latvia and Lithuania) and the *Reichskommissariat* of Ukraine. Plans were also drawn up for Muscovy and the Caucasus, which would have accounted for Russia up to the Urals. The Third Reich therefore became the centre of a vast continental empire, which also included administrative responsibilities for occupied territories in the west such as Norway, Denmark, the Low Countries and Atlantic France. These brought further complexities to the state administration which compounded the earlier trend of proliferating agencies, duplication of functions and competing jurisdictions.

After 1942 three administrative processes occurred simultaneously. The first was a narrowing of the number of key personnel in overall charge of the regime and responsible directly to the Führer. These included Goebbels, Bormann, Frank, Speer and, above all, Himmler. According to Frei, 'the composition of the top leadership of the regime during the second half of the war symbolized the advancing decay of rational and orderly structures of government and decision-making'.[11] This inevitably meant that responsibilities were spread thinly and into the gaps flooded a host of smaller officials, or 'little Hitlers', who competed for prominence or claimed special rights to interpret the Führer's will. This second process had already been apparent before 1939 (see Chapter 3, Analysis 2) but the unique pressures imposed on the leadership by the demands of war made the situation worse between 1939 and 1942, and catastrophic between 1942 and 1945. Indeed, 'While the Führer became engrossed in the details of the conduct of the war, the power of the many – mutually competing – chancelleries and special commissars grew'.[12]

The third – and most vital – factor was the ever-increasing importance of Himmler and the SS. This was a process already under way from 1934 (see Chapter 5, Analysis 1) but was enormously enhanced by the demands and opportunities of war. It is significant that a massive step was taken on 27 September 1939, the same day as the fall of Warsaw. This was the establishment of the RSHA as the overall coordinating agency of the SS, which was placed under the control of

Heydrich, the most ruthless of operatives. Indeed, it is arguable that from then onwards the SS came to assume many of the functions of the state itself. By 1944 it was running the army through the *Waffen SS*, the extermination programme through the RSHA, and the eastern occupied territories. It was also in charge of the Reich's racial policy. and had assumed virtual control over the industrial sector. By 1945, it has been argued, the Nazi regime had become the SS state.

All these processes involved the subversion of the law through the tightening of regulations on civilian population. This, of course, was apparent before 1939, with the removal of constitutional constraints on action against individuals or groups. But the process was accelerated with outbreak of war in September 1939. Heydrich issued secret instructions for 'internal protection of the State during the war' and greatly expanded the role of the Gestapo. This was followed by further instructions on 'economic' offences and action against *Feindhörer* (listeners to enemy broadcasts). Special courts, introduced in 1938, were by 1942 being increasingly bypassed by the SS–Gestapo authorities, who took summary action against dissidents of all kinds ranging from deportation to concentration camps to summary and cautionary executions of, for example, members of the Edelweiss Pirates. Towards the end of the war open judicial processes were confined to those cases which were to set an example and were tried in the People's Court (*Volksgerichtshof*) under Roland Freisler. Examples included the trial of Hans and Sophie Scholl and of the conspirators of the 1944 Stauffenberg Plot; in the latter case, 200 death sentences were imposed, although Stauffenberg himself and the others most actively involved were executed beforehand by the SS.

The radicalisation of the economy did not occur immediately. Germany went into war in 1939 on the back of the Four Year Plan which had been introduced in 1936 – when, it could be argued, the real change in direction had occurred. By 1943, however, the sheer scale of Germany's military requirements – with wars in the east and south and one looming in the west – required the additional mobilisation of resources. This involved the deliberate switch to 'total war', announced by Goebbels at the Berlin Sportpalast in February. In this he demanded, and received, support for a war 'more total and more radical than we can even imagine it today'.[13] The extent of this radicalisation has, however, been the subject of two debates. The first, covered in Chapter 7 Analysis 2, concerns the nature of the connection between 'total war' and *Blitzkrieg*. One view is that *Blitzkrieg* was in part an economic strategy, based on the intention to wage war with a limited mobilisation of resources until the conquests had yielded their riches. In this case, 'total war' was a change of direction. The alternative is to see 'total war' as the more complete implementation of *Blitzkrieg*, necessitated by the stalling campaigns in Russia. Both see radicalisation as an essential ingredient – in one case as a turning point, in the other as a gathering of momentum. A more recent controversy concerns the *results* of 'total war' (see Chapter 7, Analysis 2). Under Speer's direction as Armaments Minister, Germany's war production increased steadily, reaching a peak during the course of 1944 despite the damage inflicted by Allied bombing. Yet it remains unclear whether radicalisation meant a sudden boost in production by Speer (the original view) or whether the efforts of Speer were the culmination of earlier preparations that were at last showing their true worth; again it seems to be a choice between 'turning' or 'accelerating'. As for the difference made, it is likely that the war was prolonged by up to a year through a combination of increased production and the uncompromising attitude of Germany's leadership. But there is little doubt that no amount of successful economic management or increase in Germany's mobilisation of resources would have been sufficient to avoid eventual defeat at the hands of a vastly more powerful coalition.

Meanwhile, the *Volksgemeinschaft* was being radicalised in two ways – in terms of the social security system (*Sozialwerk des Deutschen Volkes*) being built up for people who were classed as members and the increasingly drastic measures of 'purification' being taken against those who were not. According to Ley, the leader of the DAF, it was the will of the Führer that 'victory should bring every German a better life'.[14] The emphasis on care for the elderly, health, wage regulation, professional training and house-building was more comprehensive than anything proposed in peacetime Germany and bore some striking similarities to the Beveridge Report, the forerunner of the British welfare state. Except, of course, that a substantial part of the population in Germany was excluded from its provisions. War also radicalised policies towards the 'hereditarily diseased', who were now subjected to a 'euthanasia' programme (see Chapter 8, Analysis 1). The campaign against 'habitual criminals' and 'asocials' was also intensified as hundreds of thousands were sent to concentration camps. Public opinion was diverted from opposition to these measures by the constant exhortations for greater contribution to the war effort. The one source of criticism was the Catholic Church, which brought about the temporary suspension of the 'euthanasia' programme in 1941. Yet this had unintended side-effects in the future. The regime opted for gas chambers as a more effective means of removing 'race enemies' and, at the same time, distancing the process from those sections of the population who might be disturbed by the sheer scale of what was proposed at Wannsee in January 1942.

This brings us to the most extreme example of radicalisation under the impact of war: the transformation of anti-Semitism into the Holocaust. Before 1939 the conditions experienced by Jews in Germany had steadily deteriorated, especially after *Kristallnacht* in November 1938. But it was from 1941 that mass killings were carried out in occupied territories in the East, initially by *Einsatzgruppen*, then through a deliberately industrialised genocide in extermination camps. This, of course entirely transcended anything carried out in the 1930s. But whether or not it represented a 'change' of policy is the subject of the most active debate of all (see Chapter 8, Analysis 2). On the one hand war was a genuine radicalising agent; as Bessel argues, it 'liberated Nazism from the constraints which hitherto had inhibited the fulfilment of the terrible logic of its racist ideology. It allowed Nazi ideology to be made real'.[15] The invasion of Russia in 1941 had brought Nazism into direct contact with the 'ideological' and 'race' enemy, thereby providing a unique opportunity to implement the genocide it had always envisaged. The alternative argument is that war changed the direction that anti-Semitism had hitherto been taking – from exclusion to elimination. The will to do this was certainly there – but the impetus came from the actual conditions of warfare in eastern Europe and the perceived need to clear the way for total conquest against an increasingly elusive enemy. Either way, the impact of the Holocaust was huge. The administration was adapted at all levels to plan the details war crimes on an horrific scale, while the military and SS diverted resources to implement them. From a strategic angle, this helped distort the whole purpose of the war – changing the priority from victory over the Allies to extermination of European Jewry. It created an irresistible momentum which destabilised military campaigns on the eastern front and provided an opportunity for the Soviet counter-attack from 1943.

The war also had a profound effect on official Nazi policy towards Christianity. Initially Hitler had attached some importance to eliciting and maintaining the support of both Protestants and Catholics. After 1939, however, this contact was rapidly eroded by three key developments. The first was the sustained attack launched on Christianity in response to criticism of various aspects of the regime at war – especially the government's policy of 'euthanasia' in 1941. The second was the growing emphasis by the Nazi leadership on the perceived 'Judaisation' of Christianity; in 1941, for example, Bormann openly stated that 'The concepts of National Socialism and Christianity are irreconcilable' and that 'Our National Socialist ideology is far loftier than the concepts of Christianity, which in their essential points have been taken over by Jewry'.[16] And, third, Hitler's own leadership was increasingly sacralised to fill the gap left by the withdrawal of any collaboration between the regime and the churches. All this involved a close connection with the switch from conventional war to a race war in the east, involving, as it did, the antithesis of any possible Christian ethic. Hitler therefore took the logical final step: according to Burleigh, he came to see himself 'as the last chance for mankind before the onset of cosmic desolation, should the race war he envisaged have the wrong outcome'.[17]

Was this an acceleration of pre-war trends or a change of direction? During the 1930s the Nazis had remained ambivalent about Christianity, largely through the necessity of retaining public support through, for example, the 1933 Concordat with the Catholic Church. Yet it could be argued that the Nazis were already moving away from this by undermining the terms of the Concordat, nazifying the Protestant churches and imposing Nazi organisations such as the Cross and Eagle League. After the outbreak of war the regime was simply abandoning any pretext to uphold Christianity as it came out into the open with the beliefs long held but previously constrained. In any case, the opinion of the population now mattered less in view of the larger problems posed by the war. Hitler could now pour scorn on what he saw as the Christian doctrine of 'the infinite significance of the human soul'; instead, all that really mattered was the individual's 'continued existence in the visible immortality of the nation'.[18] The impact of this radicalisation was limited. No lasting damage was inflicted on German Christianity itself. At the same time, there was no mass swing of popular opinion against the Führer's leadership. It is true that some Christian leaders joined the resistance movements, but the vast majority of Germans kept their own religious counsel while remaining politically loyal to the Führer. Perhaps the real significance of the changes was what it revealed of the mentality of the Nazi leadership itself. The racial objective was elevated to the highest possible level – becoming a pseudo-religious quest in itself, even though its pursuit was threatening the military defeat of the regime.

This transformation was reflected by the way in which the war radicalised the attitude of the Führer to the peoples under his control. After the conquest of Poland in 1939 and the invasion of Russia in 1941, the poisoned passages in *Mein Kampf* were no longer mere invective. They became the basis of a policy of subjugation and extermination, enforced by the SS, the *Wehrmacht* and the many new levels of administration. In October 1941, for example, the Commander of the Sixth Army, von Reichenau made it clear to officers and troops that: 'The fundamental aim of the campaign against the Jewish–Bolshevik system is the complete smashing of the power of and the eradication of Asiatic influence in the European cultural realm.'[19] Both the conquest and the occupation of the eastern territories were characterised by the utmost brutality on a scale which could only have been imagined before 1939. Then, as the balance of the war turned from 1943 this fanaticism was directed inwards – against his own German *Volk*. When total victory was no longer achievable the only alternative was self-destruction. Unable to escape from the pull of his own ideology, he turned the concept of 'the survival of the fittest' in upon itself: if the German *Volk* failed to achieve domination then they deserved no less than annihilation. The paradox was that the *Volk* were still tied to their Führer even after the Führer had consigned them to oblivion.

Questions

1. 'Nazism can be properly understood only in the context of war.' Do you agree?
2. Which is the more appropriate term to describe the radicalisation of the Nazi regime in wartime: 'change' or 'acceleration'?

SOURCES

1: WHAT TYPE OF WAR?

Source 1.1: From Hitler's memorandum of 9 October 1939, to the commanders-in-chief of the army and navy, arguing for a rapid offensive against the west

The first threat to Germany lies in the fact that if the war lasts a long time, in certain circumstances other States may be drawn into the opposing front either on grounds of economic necessity or through the development of particular interests.

The second danger lies in the fact that through a long drawn-out war States which might be basically favourable to joining Germany, in view of the experience of the last war, may take the very length of the war as a warning and therefore avoid intervening on our behalf.

The third danger involved in a lengthy war lies in the difficulty of feeding our population and securing the means of fighting the war in view of the limited basis for food supplies and raw materials. The morale of the population will at the very least be adversely affected.

Source 1.2: From Hitler's military directive for the invasion of Russia

The German *Wehrmacht* must be prepared to crush Soviet Russia in a quick campaign (Operation Barbarossa) even before the conclusion of the war against England.

For this purpose the army will have to employ all available units …

For the Luftwaffe it will be a matter of releasing such strong forces for the eastern campaign in support of the army that a quick completion of the ground operation can be counted on …

The main effort of the navy will remain unequivocally directed against England, even during the eastern campaign …

The mass of the Russian army in western Russia is to be destroyed in daring operations, by driving forward deep armoured wedges; and the retreat of units capable of combat into the vastness of Russian territory is to be prevented …

In the course of these operations the Russian Baltic Sea Fleet will quickly lose its bases and thus will no longer be able to fight.

Effective intervention by the Russian Air Force is to be prevented by powerful blows at the very beginning of the operation.

Source 1.3: From a record of a meeting between Hitler and the Japanese ambassador, Oshima, 3 January 1942

All of us and Japan as well were engaged in a joint life and death struggle and so it was vital that we share our military experience.

… Hitler then emphasized that it was probably the first time in history that two such powerful military powers, which were so far apart from one another, stood together in battle. Provided their military operations were coordinated, this offered the possibility of creating leverage in the conduct of the war which must have enormous effects on the enemy, since they would be thereby compelled continually to shift their centres of gravity and in this way would hopelessly fritter away their forces.

… The Führer is of the opinion that England can be destroyed. He is not yet sure how the USA can be defeated … England was the main enemy. We would certainly not be defeated by Russia.

Source 1.4: From the diary of the Italian Foreign Minister, Ciano, recording Hitler's meeting with Mussolini, 29 April 1942

America is a big bluff. This slogan is repeated by everyone, big and little, in the conference rooms and in the antechambers. In my opinion, the thought of what the Americans can and will do disturbs them all, and the Germans shut their eyes to it. But this does not keep the more intelligent and the more honest from thinking about what America can do, and they feel shivers running down their spines.

Hitler talks, talks, talks, talks, talks. Mussolini suffers – he, who is in the habit of talking himself, and who, instead, has to remain practically silent.

Source 1.5: From an account of Hitler's discussion with Mussolini, 22 April 1944

The Führer would never under any circumstances capitulate …

The Führer had spent a lot of time reading history recently and had noted that most coalitions hardly lasted for five years. The fact that our allies had remained loyal to us, despite the long period of war, was only because Fascism ruled in Italy … Our enemies' coalition was unnatural. It involved two different worlds … In addition there was the conflict between England and America. America was quietly and without making a fuss about it plundering England … If one read the English and American press, one could see that tension was growing …

The most important thing was to hold on stubbornly at all events, since the front of our opponents must break down one day.

Questions

1. To what extent are the basic principles of Source 1.1 applied to the detailed directives in Source 1.2?
2. Comment on the reliability and usefulness of Source 1.4 as a record of Hitler's attitude towards the management of the war.
3. Compare the argument used by Hitler in Source 1.3 with that in Source 1.5. How would you explain the difference in emphasis?
4. 'Hitler showed a consistent misunderstanding of Germany's capacity to wage successful war.' Comment on this view in the light of Sources 1.1 to 1.5 and your own knowledge.

GLOSSARY

Anschluss: A term used to denote the union between Germany and Austria. Although specifically forbidden by the Treaty of Versailles (1919), this was carried out by Hitler in 1938.

Autarky: A system or policy of economic self-sufficiency in a country or state, where tariffs and other trade barriers are erected so that international trade is hindered or prevented altogether.

Bund Deutscher Mädel (BDM): League of German Maidens was that part of the Hitler Youth organisation catering for girls between the ages of fourteen and eighteen.

Deutsche Arbeitsfront (DAF): German Labour Front.

Deutsche Demokratische Partei (DDP): The Democratic Party was the left wing part of the liberal movement (see also DVP) which was a member of the original coalition from 1919 and a consistent supporter of the Weimar Republic. It weakened rapidly after 1930 and was banned in June 1933.

Deutsche Volkspartei (DVP): The People's Party was the more right wing of the two liberal parties. Its heyday was under the leadership of Stresemann. It declined rapidly after his death in 1929 and was ended in June 1933.

Deutsche-Nationale Volkspartei (DNVP): The National Party was on the conservative right of the political spectrum. It was largely antagonistic to the Weimar Republic and favoured a more authoritarian regime. It collaborated closely with Hitler after 1929 but dissolved itself in 1933.

Deutscher Frauenorden (DFO): German Women's Order.

Deutsches Jungvolk (DJ): The German Young People were that part of the Hitler Youth movement catering for boys between ten and fourteen.

Deutsches Nachrichtenbüro (DNB): The German News Agency.

Einsatzgruppen: Special task forces within the SS, largely responsible for the shooting of civilians in territories occupied by Germany.

Führer: 'Leader' – the title adopted by Hitler after the death of Hindenburg to fuse the offices of President and Chancellor.

Führerprinzip: The 'leadership principle' or emphasis on the absolute ideological and political authority of the Führer.

Gau: A regional division of the NSDAP.

Gauleiter: Leader of the Gau, responsible to Hitler.

Geheime Staatspolizei (Gestapo): Secret State Police. It was set up by Goering in Prussia in 1933 and was later drawn into the SS.

Gleichschaltung: 'Coordination', a term used to denote the nazification of German institutions from 1933 onwards.

Hitler Jugend (HJ): The term 'Hitler Youth' has two meanings. It was used to denote the whole youth movement, but was also a specific part of that movement, intended for boys between fourteen and eighteen.

Jungmädelbund (JM): The Young Maidens were that part of the Hitler Youth which catered for girls to the age of fourteen.

Kommunistische Partei Deutschlands (KPD): The Communist Party was formed by the merger of two splinter groups which broke away from the SPD as a result of conflicting views over the First World War. One was the Spartacus League and the other the Independent Socialists (USPD).

Kraft durch Freude (KdF): Strength through Joy. This was a subdivision of the DAF, responsible for the use of leisure.

Land (plural *Länder*): A state or province within the German Reich.

Landtag: A parliament within a *Land*.

Lebensraum: The term 'living space' meant the acquisition of land and colonies for German settlement, largely in eastern Europe.

Machtergreifung: 'Seizure of power' by the Nazis in 1933.

Mittelstand: Middle class.

Nationalpolitische Erziehungsanstalten (Napolas): Academies for the education of future government officials and military personnel.

Nationalsozialistische Lehrerbund (NSLB): Nazi Teachers' League.

Nationalsozialistische Partei Deutschlands (NSDAP): The National Socialist German Workers' Party (usually abbreviated to Nazi) was the renamed version of the original DAP, set up in 1918.

Ordensburgen: Castles of Order.

Reich: Empire. The First Reich was the Holy Roman Empire, ended in 1806; the Second Reich was ruled by the Kaisers between 1871 and 1918; the Third Reich was Nazi Germany (1933–45).

Reichsarbeitsdienst (RAD): Reich Labour Service.

Reichsführer SS: The overall commander of the SS, a position occupied by Himmler.

Reichskulturkammer: Reich Chamber of Culture, set up under Goebbels in 1933.

Reichsrat: The second chamber of the German parliament, consisting of representatives appointed by the *Land* governments. It was abolished in 1933.

Reichssicherheitshauptamt (RSHA): Reich Security Head Office, established in 1939 and completing the merger of the SS and Gestapo.

Reichstag: The main chamber of the German parliament, consisting of representatives elected by the people. The last Reichstag election was held in March 1933.

Reichsstatthälter: Reich governors installed after 1933, comprising the most senior *Gauleiters*.

Schönheit der Arbeit (SDA): Beauty of Labour, one of the subdivisions of the DAF, responsible for working conditions and regulations.

Schutzstaffeln (SS): Security squads. Formed in 1925 as an elite within the SA, it expanded rapidly under Himmler's leadership from

1929. As a result of the Night of the Long Knives (1934), it developed control over the whole police and security system, including the Gestapo.

Sicherheitsdienst (SD): Security service within the SS – responsible largely for the collection of intelligence.

Sonderweg: A (controversial) term used by some historians to describe Germany's 'special route' to modernity and Nazism.

Sopade: The Social Democratic Party in Exile was a movement to oppose the Nazi regime from abroad.

Sozialdemokratische Partei Deutschlands (SPD): This was one of the two parties which survived from the Second Reich, although without its radical left wing, which formed the KPD instead. An important part of several of the coalition governments during the Weimar Republic, the SPD was eventually banned in July 1933.

Sturmabteilung (SA): Stormtroopers, founded in 1921 and purged in the Night of the Long Knives (1934).

Völkisch: Literally 'concerning the people', but applied in a nationalist and racist sense.

Volksgemeinschaft: 'National Community' or 'People's Community' which, in the Nazi sense, transcended class barriers, being based instead on racial identity.

Waffen SS: Military units of the SS, which served in the *Wehrmacht*.

Wehrmacht: The reorganised German army, which replaced the earlier *Reichswehr*.

Zentrum (Z): The Centre Party represented religious interests in the Weimar Republic – mainly, although not exclusively, Catholic. It dissolved itself in 1933.

NOTES

1 THE RISE OF NAZISM

1 Extracts from the *Party Programme* of 1920.
2 Quoted from *Mein Kampf* in G. Layton, *Germany: The Third Reich 1933–45* (London, 1992), p. 20.
3 Quoted in M. Housden, *Hitler: Study of a Revolutionary?* (London, 2000), p. 36.
4 I. Kershaw: *Hilter* (London 1991), p. 7.
5 A. Bullock, *Hitler and Stalin: Parallel Lives* (London, 1991), p. 152.
6 A.J.P. Taylor, *The Course of German History* (London, 1945), p. 213.
7 W.L. Shirer, *The Rise and Fall of the Third Reich* (London, 1960), p. 129.
8 Ibid., p. 148.
9 Quoted in A. Dorpalen, *German History in Marxist Perspective: The East German Approach* (London, 1985), p. 393.
10 M. Broszat, *Hitler and the Collapse of the Weimar Republic* (Oxford, 1987), p. 37.
11 Ibid.
12 H. Trevor-Roper's introduction, 'The Mind of Adolf Hitler', in N. Cameron and R.H. Stevens (trans.), *Hitler's Table Talk* (London, 1953).
13 H. Trevor-Roper, *The Last Days of Hitler* (London, 1968), p. 54.
14 A. Bullock, *Hitler and Stalin: Parallel Lives* (London 1991), p. 152.
15 See S.M. Lipset, *Political Man: The Social Base of Politics* (New York, 1960).

16 See T. Childers and J. Caplan (eds), *Reevaluating the Third Reich* (New York, 1993).
17 P.D. Stachura, 'The Nazis, the Bourgeoisie and the Workers during the *Kampfzeit*', in P.D. Stachura (ed.), *The Nazi* Machtergreifung (London, 1983), p. 28.
18 D. Mühlberger, 'Conclusion to Hitler's Followers', in C. Leitz (ed.), *The Third Reich: The Essential Readings* (Oxford: Blackwell, 1983; 1999 edn), p. 20.
19 T. Kirk, *Nazi Germany* (Basingstoke: Palgrave Macmillan, 2007), p. 20.
20 J. Hiden, *Republican and Fascist Germany* (Harlow, 1996), p. 172.
21 D.J. Peukert, *Inside Nazi Germany: Conformity, Opposition and Racism in Everyday Life* (trans.) (London: Penguin, 1989), p. 87.
22 P.D. Stachura, 'Who were the Nazis?', *European Studies Review*, *1*, 1981.
23 C. Fischer, *The Rise of the Nazis* (Manchester, 1995), p. 108.
24 Ibid., p. 111.
25 See M. Stibbe, *Women in the Third Reich* (London: Arnold, 2003); H. Boak, 'The Female Nazi Voter', in A. McElligott and T. Kirk (eds), *Working Towards the Führer* (Manchester, 2003); J. Stephenson, 'National Socialism and Women before 1933', in P.D. Stachura (ed.), *The Nazi* Machtergreifung (London, 1983).
26 M. Stibbe, op. cit., p. 27.
27 Ibid.
28 Ibid.
29 T. Kirk, op. cit., p. 27.

Source 1.1 J. Remak (ed.), *The Nazi Years* (Englewood Cliffs, NJ: Prentice-Hall, 1969), pp. 28–9.
Source 1.2 J. Remak (ed.), *The Nazi Years,* p. 32.
Source 1.3 Hitler, *Mein Kampf* (1925).
Source 1.4 Otto Strasser, *Hitler and I* (London, 1940).
Source 1.5 C. Fischer, *The Rise of the Nazis* (Manchester, 1995), pp. 138–9.
Source 1.6 Otto Strasser, *Hitler and I* (London, 1940), p. 114.
Source 2.1 P.D. Stachura, 'The Nazis, the Bourgeoisie and the Workers during the *Kampfzeit*', in P.D. Stachura (ed.), *The Nazi* Machtergreifung (London, 1983), p. 28.
Source 2.2 D. Mühlberger, 'Conclusion to Hitler's Followers', in C. Leitz (ed.), *The Third Reich: The Essential Readings* (Oxford: Blackwell, 1983; 1999 edn), p. 20.
Source 2.3 T. Kirk, *Nazi Germany* (Basingstoke: Palgrave Macmillan, 2007), pp. 23–4.
Source 2.4 C. Fischer, *The Rise of the Nazis* (Manchester, 1995), p. 111.

2 THE ACHIEVEMENT AND CONSOLIDATION OF POWER 1933–4

1 K.D. Bracher, 'Stages of Totalitarian "Integration" (*Gleichschaltung*): The Consolidation of National Socialist Rule in 1933 and 1934', in H. Holborn (ed.), *Republic to Reich: The Making of the Nazi Revolution* (New York, 1972), pp. 112–13.
2 Ibid., p. 113.
3 Ibid., p. 114.
4 A. Tyrell, 'Towards Dictatorship: Germany 1930 to 1934', in C. Leitz (ed.), *The Third Reich: The Essential Readings* (Oxford: Blackwell, 1983; 1999 edn), p. 29.
5 Ibid., p. 33.
6 H.W. Koch, '1933: The Legality of Hitler's Assumption of Power', in H.W. Koch (ed.), *Aspects of the Third Reich* (London: Macmillan, 1985), p. 41.
7 Ibid., p. 51.
8 A. Tyrell, op. cit., p. 27.
9 Quoted in H.W. Koch, op. cit., p. 45.
10 Quoted in K. Hildebrand, *The Third Reich* (trans.) (London: George Allen & Unwin, 1984), p. 3.
11 J. Remak (ed.), *The Nazi Years* (Englewood Cliffs, NJ: Prentice-Hall, 1969), p. 52.
12 See K. Hildebrand, op. cit., especially 'Concluding Remarks'.
13 D. Schoenbaum, *Hitler's Social Revolution* (New York, 1980), p. 240.

Source 1.1 L.L. Snyder, *The Weimar Republic* (Princeton, NJ: Anvil Books, 1966) Reading no. 18.
Source 1.2 J. Remak (ed.), *The Nazi Years,* pp. 52–3.
Source 1.3 J. Remak (ed.), *The Nazi Years,* p. 54.
Source 1.4 J. Noakes and G. Pridham (eds), *Nazism 1919–1945: A Documentary Reader* (Exeter: University of Exeter Press, 1983–8), vol. 1, p. 185.
Source 1.5 J. Laver, *Nazi Germany 1933–1945* (London: Hodder & Stoughton, 1991), p. 12.
Source 1.6 Quoted in J.L. Snell (ed.), *The Outbreak of the Second World War* (Boston, 1962); extract from the Nuremberg Judgement.
Source 2.1 K.D. Bracher, 'Stages of Totalitarian "Integration" (*Gleichschaltung*): The Consolidation of National Socialist Rule in 1933 and 1934', in H. Holborn (ed.), *Republic to Reich: The Making of the Nazi Revolution* (New York, 1972), p. 116.
Source 2.2 H.W. Koch, '1933: The Legality of Hitler's Assumption of Power', in H.W. Koch (ed.), *Aspects of the Third Reich* (London: Macmillan, 1985), p. 54.

Source 2.3 C. Leitz (ed.), *The Third Reich: The Essential Readings* (Oxford: Blackwell, 1983; 1999 edn), p. 27.

Source 2.4 H.W. Koch, '1933: The Legality of Hitler's Assumption of Power', in H.W. Koch (ed.), *Aspects of the Third Reich* (London: Macmillan, 1985), p. 57.

Source 2.5 K.D. Bracher, *The German Dictatorship* (trans.) (London: Penguin, 1973), p. 244.

3 THE NAZI DICTATORSHIP

1 K.D. Bracher, *The German Dictatorship: The Origins, Structure and Consequences of National Socialism* (trans.) (London, Penguin, 1973), p. 286.
2 Quoted in ibid., p. 285.
3 Quoted in J. Remak (ed.), *The Nazi Years: A Documentary History* (Englewood Cliffs, NJ: Prentice-Hall, 1969), p. 63.
4 J. Noakes and G. Pridham (eds), *Nazism 1919–1945: A Documentary Reader* (Exeter: University of Exeter Press, 1983–8), vol. 2, p. 490.
5 Quoted in I. Kershaw, *The Nazi Dictatorship: Problems and Perspective of Interpretation* (London: Arnold, 4th edn, 2000), p. 74.
6 See K.D. Bracher, *The German Dictatorship* (trans.) (London, Penguin, 1973).
7 K. Hildebrand, *The Third Reich* (trans.) (London: George Allen & Unwin, 1984), p. 7.
8 See M. Broszat, *Hitler and the Collapse of the Weimar Republic* (Oxford, 1987).
9 H. Mommsen, 'National Socialism – Continuity and Change', in W. Laqueur (ed.), *Fascism: A Reader's Guide* (Aldershot: Scolar Press, 1991), p. 196.
10 H. Mommsen, *From Weimar to Auschwitz* (trans. P. O'Connor) (Princeton NJ, 1991), pp. 178–9.
11 J. Noakes and G. Pridham (eds), *Nazism*, vol. 2, p. 207.

Source 1.1 J. Noakes and G. Pridham (eds), *Nazism*, vol. 2, p. 252.

Source 1.2 J. Noakes and G. Pridham (eds), *Nazism*, vol. 2, p. 207.

Source 1.3 J. Laver, *Nazi Germany 1933–1945* (London: Hodder & Stoughton, 1991), p. 16.

Source 1.4 K.D. Bracher, *The German Dictatorship* (trans.) (London: Penguin, 1973), p. 297.

Source 1.5 H. Mommsen, 'National Socialism – Continuity and Change', in W. Laqueur (ed.), *Fascism: A Reader's Guide* (Aldershot: Scolar Press, 1991), p. 196.

Source 1.6 I. Kershaw, '"Working towards the Führer": Reflections of the Nature of the Hitler Dictatorship', in I. Kershaw and M. Lewin (eds), *Stalinism and Nazism: Dictatorships in Comparison* (Cambridge: CUP, 1997), pp. 104–5.

4 INDOCTRINATION AND PROPAGANDA

1 Quoted in J. Noakes and G. Pridham (eds), *Nazism 1919–1945: A Documentary Reader* (Exeter: University of Exeter Press, 1983–8), vol. 2, p. 381.
2 Quoted in G. Layton, *Germany: The Third Reich 1933–45* (London, 1992), p. 95.
3 Quoted in L. Pine, *Hitler's 'National Community'* (London, 2007), ch 3.
4 Ibid.
5 J. Hiden and J. Farquharson, *Explaining Hitler's Germany: Historians and the Third Reich* (London, 1983), p. 55.
6 See R. Grunberger, *A Social History of the Third Reich* (London, 1971), ch. 19.
7 L. Pine, *Hitler's 'National Community'* (London, 2007), ch. 3.
8 T. Kirk, *The Longman Companion to Nazi Germany* (London, 1995), p. 107.
9 L. Pine, op. cit., ch. 3.
10 G. Rempel, *Hitler's Children: The Hitler Youth and the SS* (Chapel Hill, NC, 1989), p. 10.
11 Based on figures provided in T. Kirk, *The Longman Companion to Nazi Germany* (London, 1995), p. 110.
12 Quoted in M. Burleigh and W. Wippermann, *The Racial State: Germany 1933–1945* (Cambridge, 1991), p. 206.
13 T.L. Jarman, *The Rise and Fall of Nazi Germany* (New York: Signet Books, 1961), p. 183.
14 See M. Burleigh and W. Wippermann, op. cit., ch. 7.
15 See R. Bessel (ed.), *Life in the Third Reich* (Oxford, 1987), pp. 25–40.
16 See D.J.K. Peukert, *Inside Nazi Germany: Conformity, Opposition and Racism in Everyday Life* (trans.) (London: Penguin, 1989), ch. 8.
17 Ibid., p. 153.
18 M. Burleigh and W. Wippermann, op. cit., p. 220.
19 See G. Rempel, *Hitler's Children: The Hitler Youth and the SS* (Chapel Hill, NC, 1989).
20 Ibid., p. 256.
21 Ibid., p. 258.
22 Quoted in L. Pine, *Hitler's 'National Community'* (London, 2007), ch. 12.

23 Figures from ibid., ch. 13.
24 Quoted in ibid., ch. 13.
25 Quoted in ibid., ch. 12.
26 Quoted in J. Remak (ed.), *The Nazi Years: A Documentary History* (Englewood Cliffs, NJ: Prentice-Hall, 1969), p. 85.
27 Quoted in ibid., p. 86.
28 Quoted in ibid., pp. 66–7.
29 A.E. Steinweiss, 'The Nazi Purge of Artistic and Cultural Life', in R. Gellately and N. Stoltzfus (eds), *Social Outsiders in Nazi Germany* (Princeton, NJ, 2001), p. 111.

Source 1.1 J. Noakes and G. Pridham (eds), *Nazism,* vol. 2, p. 381.
Source 1.2 J. Noakes and G. Pridham (eds), *Nazism,* vol. 2, p. 382.
Source 1.3 J. Noakes and G. Pridham (eds), *Nazism,* vol. 2, p. 386.
Source 1.4 J. Noakes and G. Pridham (eds), *Nazism,* vol. 2, p. 394.
Source 1.5 Louis P. Lochner (ed.), *The Goebbels Diaries 1942–3* (Washington, DC, 1948), pp. 177–80.
Source 1.6 T. Jones, *Lloyd George* (Cambridge, MA, 1951).
Source 2.1 Quoted in M. Burleigh and W. Wippermann, *The Racial State: Germany 1933–1945* (Cambridge, 1991), pp. 206–7.
Source 2.2 T.L. Jarman, *The Rise and Fall of Nazi Germany* (New York: Signet Books, 1961), pp. 182–3.
Source 2.3 D.J.K. Peukert, *Inside Nazi Germany: Conformity, Opposition and Racism in Everyday Life* (trans.) (London: Penguin, 1989), p. 153.
Source 2.4 M. Burleigh and W. Wippermann, *The Racial State: Germany 1933–1945* (Cambridge, 1991), pp. 217–20.
Source 2.5 G. Rempel, *Hitler's Children: The Hitler Youth and the SS* (Chapel Hill, NC 1989), pp. 2–3, 256–8.

5 THE SS AND GESTAPO

1 J. Noakes and G. Pridham (eds), *Nazism 1919–1945: A Documentary Reader* (Exeter: University of Exeter Press, 1983–8), vol. 2, p. 490.
2 See G. Rempel, *Hitler's Children: The Hitler Youth and the SS* (Chapel Hill, NC, 1989), p. 6.
3 J. Noakes and G. Pridham (eds), op. cit., vol. 2, p. 497.
4 K.D. Bracher, *The German Dictatorship* (trans.) (London: Penguin, 1973), p. 296.
5 G.C. Browder, *Hitler's Enforcers: The Gestapo and the SS Security Service in the Nazi Revolution* (Oxford, 1996), p. 5.
6 K.D. Bracher, op. cit., p. 527.
7 H. Höhne, *The Order of the Death's Head* (London, 1967), p. 12.
8 G.C. Browder, op. cit., p. 6.
9 Quoted in J. Noakes and G. Pridham (eds), op. cit., vol. 2, pp. 495–6.

10 Quoted in ibid., p. 500.
11 E.J. Passant, *A Short History of Germany 1815–1945* (Cambridge, 1962), p. 196.
12 E. Crankshaw, *Gestapo: Instrument of Tyranny* (London: Putnam, 1956), p. 13.
13 K. Mallmann and G. Paul, 'Omniscient, Omnipotent, Omnipresent? Gestapo, Society and Resistance', in D.F. Crew (ed.), *Nazism and German Society 1933–1945* (London, 1994), p. 169.
14 Ibid., pp. 169–70.
15 W.S. Allen, *The Nazi Seizure of Power. The Experience of a Single German Town 1922–1945* (London, 1989), pp. 188–9.
16 *Völkischer Beobachter*, 17 February 1941.
17 R. Gellately, 'Surveillance and Disobedience: Aspects of the Political Policing of Nazi Germany', in C. Leitz (ed.), *The Third Reich: The Essential Readings* (Oxford: Blackwell, 1983; 1999 edn), p. 184.
18 K. Mallmann and G. Paul, op. cit., p. 167.
19 Browder, op. cit., p. 231.
20 K. Mallmann and G. Paul, op. cit., p. 178.
21 Ibid., p. 174
22 R. Gellately, op. cit., p. 187.
23 Ibid.
24 Ibid.
25 Quoted in R. Gellately, op. cit., p. 199.
26 See R. Gellately, op. cit.
27 K. Mallmann and G. Paul, op. cit., pp. 180–1.
28 E.A. Johnson, *Nazi Terror: Gestapo, Jews and Ordinary Citizens* (New York, 1999), p. 483.
29 R.J. Evans, *The Third Reich in Power 1933–1939* (Allen Lane/Penguin, 2005), p. 114.
30 Ibid., p. 115.
31 Ibid.
32 M. Burleigh, *The Third Reich. A New History* (London: Macmillan, 2000), p. 183.
33 E. Jäckel, quoted in M. Housden, *Resistance and Conformity in the Third Reich* (London: Routledge, 1997), p. 13.

Source 1.1 D. Orlow, *The History of the Nazi Party*, Vol. 2 (Newton Abbot: David and Charles, 1971).
Source 1.2 J. Noakes and G. Pridham (eds), *Nazism*, vol. 2, p. 500.
Source 1.3 J. Noakes and G. Pridham (eds), *Nazism*, vol. 2, pp. 495–6.
Source 1.4 J. Noakes and G. Pridham (eds), *Nazism*, vol. 2, p. 500.
Source 1.5 J. Noakes and G. Pridham (eds), *Nazism*, vol. 2, p. 514.
Source 1.6 J. Laver, *Nazi Germany 1933–1945* (London: Hodder & Stoughton, 1991), pp. 73–4.

Source 2.1 E. Crankshaw, *Gestapo: Instrument of Tyranny* (London: Putnam, 1956), p. 112.

Source 2.2 R. Gellately, *The Gestapo and German Society: Enforcing Racial Policy 1933–1945* (Oxford 1990), p. 212.

Source 2.3 K. Mallmann and G. Paul, 'Omniscient, Omnipotent, Omnipresent? Gestapo, Society and Resistance', in D. Crew (ed.), *Nazism and German Society 1933–1945* (London 1994), pp. 166–7.

Source 2.4 M. Burleigh, *The Third Reich: A New History* (London: Macmillan, 2000), p. 183.

Source 2.5 R.J. Evans, *The Third Reich in Power 1933–1939* (Allen Lane/Penguin, 2005), pp. 114–17.

6 SUPPORT, OPPOSITION AND RESISTANCE

1 I. Kershaw, 'Hitler and the Germans', in R. Bessel (ed.), *Life in the Third Reich* (Oxford, 1987), p. 49.

2 This was the view of a report by the Social Democratic Party in Exile (*Sopade*) quoted in D.J.K. Peukert, *Inside Nazi Germany: Conformity, Opposition and Racism in Everyday Life* (trans.) (London: Penguin, 1989), p. 71.

3 Quoted in ibid., p. 74.

4 D. Welch, 'Adolf Hitler in Nazi propaganda', in A. McElligott and T. Kirk (eds), *Working Towards the Führer* (Manchester, 2003), p. 107.

5 R.J. Overy, 'Germany, "Domestic Crisis" and War in 1939', in C. Leitz (ed.), *The Third Reich: The Essential Readings* (Oxford: Blackwell, 1983; 1999 edn), p. 120.

6 Quoted in D.F. Crew (ed.), *Nazism and German Society, 1933–1945* (London, 1994), pp. 4–5.

7 Ibid., p. 6.

8 D.J.K. Peukert, *Inside Nazi Germany*, p. 69.

9 T. Mason, 'Women in Germany 1925–1940: Family, Welfare and Work, Part 1', *History Workshop Journal*, 1, 1976, p. 75.

10 S. Haffner, *The Meaning of Hitler* (London, 1979), p. 250.

11 See L. Pine, *Nazi Family Policy, 1933–1945* (Oxford, 1997), p. 24.

12 See R. Grunberger, *A Social History of the Third Reich* (London, 1971).

13 Sir J. Wheeler-Bennett, *The Nemesis of Power: The German Army in Politics 1918–1945* (London, 1953), part III, ch. 2.

14 O. Bartov, 'The Missing Years: German Workers, German Soldiers', in D.F. Crew (ed.), *Nazism and German Society 1933–1945*, p. 46.

15 G.C. Boehnert, 'The Third Reich and the Problem of "Social Revolution": German Officers and the SS', in V.R. Berghahn and

M. Kitchen (eds), *Germany in the Age of Total War* (London, 1981), p. 213.

16 Quoted in J. Noakes and G. Pridham (eds), *Documents on Nazism* (London: Jonathan Cape, 1974), p. 369.

17 P. Steinbach, 'The Conservative Resistance', in D.C. Large (ed.), *Contending with Hitler: Varieties of German Resistance in the Third Reich* (Cambridge: CUP, 1991), p. 90.

18 See K. Mallmann and G. Paul, 'Omniscient, Omnipotent, Omnipresent? Gestapo, Society and Resistance', in D.F. Crew (ed.), *Nazism and German Society,* pp. 180–9.

19 See D.J. Goldhagen, *Hitler's Willing Executioners: Ordinary Germans and the Holocaust* (London: Little Brown & Co., 1996), especially ch. 15.

20 I. Kershaw, *The Nazi Dictatorship: Problems and Perspective of Interpretation* (London: Arnold, 4th edn, 2000), p. 185.

21 M. Stibbe, *Women in the Third Reich* (London: Arnold, 2003), pp. 132–3.

22 I. Kershaw, *Popular Opinion and Political Dissent in the Third Reich* (Oxford, 1983), pp. 2–4.

23 I. Kershaw, *Popular Opinion*, p. 373.

24 Quoted in I. Kershaw, *Popular Opinion*, p. 126.

25 See D.J.K. Peukert, 'Youth in the Third Reich', in R. Bessel (ed.), *Life in the Third Reich* (Oxford, 1987).

26 Quoted in H.A. Winkler, *Germany: The Long Road West. Volume 2: 1933–1990* (trans.) (Oxford, 2007).

27 See ibid. pp. 93–4.

28 M. Broszat, *Alternatives to Hitler: German Resistance Under the Third Reich* (trans.) (Princeton, NJ, 2003), p. 251.

Source 1.1 Hitler, *Mein Kampf* (1925).

Source 1.2 J. Dülffer, *Nazi Germany 1933–1945: Faith and Annihilation* (trans.) (London: Arnold, 1996), p. 90.

Source 1.3 D.J.K. Peukert, *Inside Nazi Germany: Conformity, Opposition and Racism in Everyday Life* (trans.) (London: Penguin, 1989), p. 74.

Source 1.4 D.J.K. Peukert, *Inside Nazi Germany,* p. 195.

Source 1.5 D.J.K. Peukert, *Inside Nazi Germany,* p. 109.

Source 2.1 Quoted in J. Remak (ed.), *The Nazi Years: A Documentary History* (Englewood Cliffs, NJ: Prentice-Hall, 1969), p. 93.

Source 2.2 M. Housden, *Resistance and Conformity in the Third Reich* (Routledge, London, 1997), p. 51.

Source 2.3 M. Housden, *Resistance and Conformity in the Third Reich*, p. 52.

Source 2.4 J. Laver, *Nazi Germany 1933–1945* (London: Hodder & Stoughton, 1991), p. 79.

Source 2.5 M. Housden, *Resistance and Conformity in the Third Reich*, pp. 57–8.

Source 2.6 Quoted in J. Remak (ed.), *The Nazi Years: A Documentary History* (Englewood Cliffs, NJ: Prentice-Hall, 1969), p. 93.

Source 2.7 M. Housden, *Resistance and Conformity in the Third Reich*, p. 61.

Source 3.1 Quoted in I. Kershaw, *The Nazi Dictatorship: Problems and Perspective of Interpretation* (London: Arnold, 4th edn, 2000), p. 185.

Source 3.2 M. Stibbe, *Women in the Third Reich* (London: Arnold, 2003), p. 133.

Source 3.3 M. Broszat, 'A Social and Historical Typology of the German Opposition to Hitler', in D.C. Large (ed.), *Contending with Hitler: Varieties of German Resistance in the Third Reich* (Cambridge: CUP, 1991), pp. 27–9.

Source 3.4 J. Fest, *Plotting Hitler's Death: The German Resistance to Hitler 1933–1945* (trans.) (London: Weidenfeld and Nicholson, 1996), pp. 28–31.

7 THE NAZI ECONOMY

1 H. James, 'Innovation and Conservatism in Economic Recovery: The Alleged "Nazi Recovery" of the 1930s', in T. Childers and J. Caplan (eds), *Reevaluating the Third Reich* (New York, 1993), p. 115.
2 N. Frei, *National Socialist Rule in Germany: The Führer State 1933–1945* (trans.) (Oxford, 1993), p. 71.
3 J. Noakes and G. Pridham (eds), *Nazism 1919–1945: A Documentary Reader* (Exeter: University of Exeter Press, 1983–8), vol. 2, p. 287.
4 M. Kitchen, *Nazi Germany at War* (London: Longman, 1995), p. 41.
5 R.J. Overy, '"Domestic Crisis" and War in 1939', in C. Leitz (ed.), *The Third Reich: The Essential Readings* (Oxford: Blackwell, 1983; 1999 edn), p. 115.
6 P. Hayes, 'Polycracy and Policy in the Third Reich: The Case of the Economy', in T. Childers and J. Caplan (eds), *Reevaluating the Third Reich* (New York, 1993), p. 201.
7 See A. Tooze, *The Wages of Destruction: The Making and Breaking of the Nazi Economy* (London, 2006); also H. James, 'Review of A. Tooze, "The Wages of Destruction"', *Central European History*, 40(2), 2007, p. 368.
8 C.W. Guillebaud, *Economic Recovery in Germany* (London: Macmillan, 1939), p. 218.
9 T.L. Jarman, *The Rise and Fall of Nazi Germany* (New York: Signet Books, 1961), p. 179.
10 C. Buccheim, 'The Nazi Boom: An Economic Cul-de-Sac', in H. Mommsen (ed.), *The Third Reich Between Vision and Reality: New*

Perspectives on German History 1918–1945 (Oxford: Berg, 2001), p. 79.

11 Ibid., p. 82.

12 R.J. Overy, '"Domestic Crisis" and War in 1939', in C. Leitz (ed.), op. cit., p. 108.

13 P. Hayes, op. cit., p. 195.

14 B.H. Klein, 'Germany's Economic Preparations for War', in H.W. Koch (ed.), *Aspects of the Third Reich* (London: Macmillan, 1985), p. 366.

15 Ibid., p. 360.

16 Ibid., p. 363.

17 See A. Tooze, *The Wages of Destruction: The Making and Breaking of the Nazi Economy* (London, 2006).

18 H. James, 'Review of A. Tooze, "The Wages of Destruction"', p. 368.

19 See A. Tooze, op. cit., pp. 10–11.

20 Hitler, *Mein Kampf* (1925), quoted in J. Laver, *Nazi Germany 1933–1945* (London: Hodder & Stoughton, 1991), p. 82.

21 See A. Tooze, op. cit., pp. 8–9.

22 Quoted in J. Remak (ed.), *The Nazi Years: A Documentary History* (Englewood Cliffs, NJ: Prentice-Hall, 1969), pp. 32–3.

23 B.H. Klein, 'Germany's Economic Preparations for War', in H.W. Koch (ed.), *Aspects of the Third Reich* (London: Macmillan, 1985), p. 362.

24 Extract in R.G.L. Waite (ed.), *Hitler and Nazi Germany* (New York, 1965).

25 J. Hiden and J. Farquharson, *Explaining Hitler's Germany: Historians and the Third Reich* (London, 1983), p. 151.

26 B.H. Klein, op. cit., p. 367.

27 Ibid., p. 368.

28 V.R. Berghahn, *Modern Germany: Society, Economy and Politics in the Twentieth Century* (Cambridge: CUP, 1987), p. 149.

29 Quoted in J, Noakes and G. Pridham (eds), *Nazism*, vol. 3, p. 684.

30 Quoted in G. Layton, *Germany: The Third Reich 1933–45* (London, 1992), p. 77.

31 Ibid.

32 C.W. Guillebaud, *The Economic Recovery of Germany from 1933 to the Incorporation of Austria in March 1938* (London, 1939).

33 V.R. Berghahn, *Modern Germany*, table 18, p. 284.

34 Statistics in this paragraph from R. Grunberger, *A Social History of the Third Reich* (London, 1971), ch. 14.

35 V.R. Berghahn, *Modern Germany*, table 25, p. 290.

36 R. Grunberger, *A Social History of the Third Reich* (London, 1971), ch. 14.

37 V.R. Berghahn, *Modern Germany*, table 10, p. 279.

38 R. Grunberger, op. cit., ch. 14.

Source 1.1 J. Noakes and G. Pridham (eds), *Nazism*, vol. 2, pp. 281–7.
Source 1.2 H. Schacht, *Account Settled* (London: Weidenfeld and Nicholson, 1949), pp. 98–9.
Source 1.3 K. Hildebrand, *The Third Reich* (trans.) (London: George Allen & Unwin, 1984), p. 43.
Source 1.4 J. Noakes and G. Pridham (eds), *Nazism*, vol. 2, pp. 292–3.
Source 2.1 C. Buchheim, 'The Nazi Boom: An Economic Cul-de-Sac', in H. Mommsen (ed.), *The Third Reich Between Vision and Reality: New Perspectives on German History 1918–1945* (Oxford: Berg, 2001), pp. 79–87.
Source 2.2 P. Hayes, 'Polycracy and Policy in the Third Reich: The Case of the Economy', in T. Childers and J. Caplan (eds), *Reevaluating the Third Reich* (New York, 1993), p. 201.
Source 2.3 R.J. Overy, '"Domestic Crisis" and War in 1939', in C. Leitz (ed.), *The Third Reich: The Essential Readings* (Oxford: Blackwell, 1983; 1999 edn), pp. 118–19.
Source 2.4 M. Kitchen, *Nazi Germany at War* (London: Longman, 1995), pp. 41–3.

8 OUTSIDE THE *VOLKSGEMEINSCHAFT*

1 Quoted in J. Remak (ed.), *The Nazi Years: A Documentary History* (Englewood Cliffs, NJ: Prentice-Hall, 1969), p. 4.
2 Quoted in M. Burleigh and W. Wippermann, *The Racial State: Germany 1933–1945* (Cambridge, 1991), p. 31.
3 Hitler, *Mein Kampf* (1925).
4 Ibid.
5 Quoted in M. Burleigh and W. Wippermann, op. cit., p. 142.
6 Hitler, *Zweites Buch* (1928).
7 D.J.K. Peukert, *Inside Nazi German: Conformity, Opposition and Racism in Everyday Life* (trans.) (London: Penguin, 1989), p. 208. See also T.W. Mason, *Social Policy in the Third Reich: The Working Class and the 'National Community'* (Oxford, 1993), pp. 279–80.
8 D.J.K. Peukert, op. cit., p. 209.
9 Quoted in M. Burleigh and W. Wippermann, op. cit., p. 173.
10 G. Grau, 'Persecution, "Re-education" or "Eradication" of Male Homosexuals between 1933 and 1945', in G. Grau (ed.), *Hidden Holocaust? Gay and Lesbian Persecution in Germany 1933–45* (Chicago, 2008), p. 3.
11 Quoted in M. Burleigh and W. Wippermann, op. cit., p. 128.
12 Quoted in J. Remak (ed.), op. cit., p. 5.
13 Hitler, *Mein Kampf* (1925).

14 Quoted in M. Burleigh and W. Wippermann, op. cit., p. 44.
15 J. Dülffer, *Nazi Germany 1933–1945: Faith and Annihilation* (trans.) (London: Arnold, 1996), p. 179.
16 D.J. Goldhagen, *Hitler's Willing Executioners: Ordinary Germans and the Holocaust* (London: Little Brown & Co., 1996), p. 162.
17 See R. Hilberg, *The Destruction of the European Jews* (Chicago, 1961).
18 Quoted in D. Cesarini (ed.), *The Final Solution: Origins and Implementation* (London, 1994), p. 8.
19 See M. Kitchen, *Nazi Germany at War* (London: Longman, 1995), p. 200.
20 J. Dülffer, op. cit., p. 179.
21 D.J. Goldhagen, op. cit., p. 162.
22 G.D. Rosenfeld, 'The Controversy that isn't: The Debate over Daniel J. Goldhagen's "Hitler's Willing Executioners" in Comparative Perspective', *Contemporary European History*, 8(2), 1999, p. 262.
23 See J. Connelly, 'Poles and Jews in the Second World War', *Contemporary European History*, 11, 2002, pp. 641–58.
24 Quoted in D. Cesarini, *Becoming Eichmann: Rethinking the Life, Crimes and Trial of a 'Desk Murderer'* (Cambridge, MA, 2006).
25 D.J. Goldhagen, op. cit., 'Conclusion'.
26 Quoted in H. Höhne, *The Order of the Death's Head* (trans.) (London, 1967), p. 352.
27 Ibid., p. 353.
28 Götz Aly, *'Final Solution': Nazi Population Policy and the Murder of the European Jews* (trans.) (London, 2003), p. 1.
29 Claudia Koonz, *The Nazi Conscience* (Cambridge, MA, 2003), 'Prologue'.
30 Ibid.
31 Quoted in E.B. Westermann, 'Shaping the Police Soldier as an Instrument for Annihilation', in A.E. Steinweis and D.E. Rogers (eds), *The Impact of Nazism: New Perspectives on the Third Reich and its Legacy* (Lincoln: University of Nebraska Press, 2003), p. 143.
32 M. Housden, *Hans Frank: Lebensraum and the Holocaust* (London, 2005), pp. 192–193.
33 Quoted in H. Höhne, op cit.; p. 352.

Source 1.1 J. Remak (ed.), *The Nazi Years*, p. 145.
Source 1.2 J. Noakes and G. Pridham (eds), *Nazism*, vol. 3, p. 1049.
Source 1.3 J. Remak (ed.), *The Nazi Years*, p. 156.
Source 1.4 J. Noakes and G. Pridham (eds), *Nazism*, vol. 3, pp. 1067–8.
Source 1.5 J. Noakes and G. Pridham (eds), *Nazism*, vol. 3, p. 1199.
Source 1.6 J. Noakes and G. Pridham (eds), *Nazism*, vol. 3, p. 1204.
Source 1.7 Quoted in H. Höhne, op. cit., p. 352.
Source 2.1 G. Fleming, *Hitler and the Final Solution* (University of California Press, 1984).

Source 2.2 D.J. Goldhagen, *Hitler's Willing Executioners: Ordinary Germans and the Holocaust* (London: Little Brown & Co., 1996), p. 162.

Source 2.3 H. Mommsen, in D. Cesarini (ed.), *The Final Solution: Origins and Implementation* (London, 1994), p. 7.

Source 2.4 H. Mommsen, 'The Realization of the Unthinkable', in G. Hirschfield (ed.), *The Policies of Genocide* (Unwin Hyman, HarperCollins, 1986), pp. 35–6.

Source 3.1 D.J. Goldhagen, *Hitler's Willing Executioners*, 'Conclusion'.

Source 3.2 C.R. Browning, *The Origins of the Final Solution: The Evolution of Nazi Jewish Policy, September 1939 – March 1942* (London: Heinemann, 2004), 'Conclusion'.

9 FOREIGN POLICY

1 J. Noakes and G. Pridham (eds), *Nazism 1919–1945: A Documentary Reader* (Exeter: University of Exeter Press, 1983–8), vol. 3, pp. 616–17.

2 H.R. Trevor-Roper, 'Hitler's War Aims', in H.W. Koch (ed.), *Aspects of the Third Reich* (London: Macmillan, 1985), p. 240.

3 E. Jäckel, *Hitler in History* (Hanover, 1984), ch. 2.

4 A.J.P. Taylor, *The Origins of the Second World War* (Hamish Hamilton, 1961; Penguin edn, 1964), ch. 7.

5 H.R. Trevor-Roper, 'Hitler's War Aims', in H.W. Koch (ed.), *Aspects of the Third Reich* (London: Macmillan, 1985), p. 235.

6 See F. Fischer, *Germany's Aims in the First World War* (trans.) (London, 1967).

7 I. Kershaw, *The Nazi Dictatorship: Problems and Perspective of Interpretation* (London: Arnold, 4th edn, 2000), p. 149.

8 Quoted in ibid., p. 141.

9 See extract in R.G.L. Waite (ed.), *Hitler and Nazi Germany* (New York, 1965).

10 I. Kershaw, lecture at Aston University, 1997.

11 Quoted in J.L. Snell (ed.), *The Outbreak of the Second World War* (Boston, MA, 1962), extract from the Nuremberg Judgement.

12 H. Trevor-Roper, 'A.J.P. Taylor, Hitler and the War', *Encounter*, 1961, p. xvii.

13 J. Spielvogel, *Hitler and Nazi Germany: A History* (Englewood Cliffs, NJ, 1988), p. 209.

14 Extracts from A.J.P. Taylor, op. cit., ch. 7.

15 See M. Burleigh and W. Wippermann, *The Racial State: Germany 1933–1945* (Cambridge, 1991).

16 See Chapter 8, Notes 16–32.

17 Quoted in Telford Taylor, *Munich: The Price of Peace* (London, 1979), p. 978.
18 Ibid., p. 375.
19 Quoted in P. Finney (ed.), *The Origins of the Second World War* (London, 1997), p. 37.
20 R. Stackelberg, *Hitler's Germany: Origins, Interpretations, Legacies* (London: Routledge, 1999), pp. 171–2.
21 Quoted in P. Finney (ed.), *The Origins of the Second World War* (London, 1997), p. 39.
22 G.L. Weinberg, *The Foreign Policy of Hitler's Germany: Diplomatic Revolution in Europe 1933–36* (Chicago, 1970), p. 362.
23 Ibid., p. 261.
Source 1.1 Quoted in J. Laver, *Nazi Germany 1933–1945* (London: Hodder & Stoughton, 1991), p. 82.
Source 1.2 J. Noakes and G. Pridham (eds), *Nazism,* vol. 3, pp. 616–17.
Source 1.3 Documents on German Foreign Policy, Series D, Vol. I, pp. 29ff.
Source 1.4 Documents on German Foreign Policy, Series D, Vol. I, pp. 55ff.
Source 2.1 H.R. Trevor-Roper, 'Hitler's War Aims', in H.W. Koch (ed.), *Aspects of the Third Reich* (London: Macmillan, 1985), p. 235.
Source 2.2 A.J.P. Taylor, *The Origins of the Second World War* (Hamish Hamilton, 1961; Penguin edn, 1964), 'Foreword: Second Thoughts', ch. 7 and ch. 11.
Source 2.3 D. Kaiser, 'Hitler and the Coming of the War', in G. Martel (ed.), *Modern Germany Reconsidered 1870–1945* (London: Routledge, 1992), pp. 178 and 193.
Source 2.4 P. Bell, 'Hitler's War? The Origins of the Second World War in Europe', in P. Hayes (ed.), *Themes in Modern European History 1890–1945* (Routledge, 1992), p. 227.

10 GERMANY AT WAR

1 Quoted in J. Noakes and G. Pridham (eds), *Documents on Nazism* (London: Jonathan Cape, 1974), p. 665.
2 E. Jäckel, *Hitler in History* (Hanover and London, 1984), ch. 2.
3 Quoted in K. Hildebrand, *The Third Reich* (trans.) (London: George Allen & Unwin, 1984), p. 51.
4 B. Bonwetsch, 'Stalin, the Red Army, and the "Great Patriotic War"', in I. Kershaw and M. Lewin (eds), *Stalinism and Nazism: Dictatorships in Comparison* (Cambridge: CUP, 1997), p. 186.

5 A. Hillgruber, 'England's Place in Hitler's Plans for World Dominion', *Journal of Contemporary History*, 9, 1974.
6 K. Hildebrand, op. cit., p. 75.
7 Quoted in R. Bessel, *Nazism and War* (London, 2004), p. 126.
8 Quoted in ibid., p. 161.
9 Quoted in N. Frei, *National Socialist Rule in Germany: The Führer State 1933–1945* (trans.) (Oxford, 1993), p. 146.
10 I.L. Horowitz, foreword in I. Ehrenburg and V. Grossman, *The Complete Black Book of Russian Jewry* (New Brunswick, NJ, 2000), p. vii.
11 N. Frei, op. cit, p. 137.
12 Ibid., p. 137.
13 Quoted in J. Noakes and G. Pridham (eds), *Nazism 1919–1945: A Documentary Reader* (Exeter: University of Exeter Press, 1983–8), vol. 3, p. 665.
14 Quoted in N. Frei, op. cit., p. 117.
15 R. Bessel, op. cit., pp. 88–9.
16 Quoted in R. Grunberger, *A Social History of the Third Reich* (London, 1971), ch. 29.
17 M. Burleigh, *The Third Reich: A New History* (London: Macmillan, 2000), p. 254.
18 Quoted in M. Burleigh, op. cit., p. 256.
19 Quoted in R. Bessel, op. cit., p. 109.

Source 1.1 J. Noakes and G. Pridham (eds), *Nazism*, vol. 3, p. 761.
Source 1.2 Documents on German Foreign Policy, Series D, Vol. XI, p. 52.
Source 1.3 J. Noakes and G. Pridham (eds), *Nazism*, vol. 3, pp. 836–7.
Source 1.4 J. Noakes and G. Pridham (eds), *Nazism*, vol. 3, p. 838.
Source 1.5 J. Noakes and G. Pridham (eds), *Nazism*, vol. 3, pp. 867–8.

SELECT BIBLIOGRAPHY

A vast number of books has been published on Nazi Germany. This list is therefore particularly selective, concentrating mainly on the works that have been especially helpful in the preparation of the Second Edition of this volume.

An invaluable introductory reference book to the Nazi period is T. Kirk, *The Longman Companion to Nazi Germany* (London, 1995).

The main primary sources are: Hitler, *Mein Kampf* (1925); Hitler, *Zweites Buch* (1928); and *Hitler's Table Talk* (1953). By far the most valuable and extensive selection of primary sources is contained in J. Noakes and G. Pridham, *Nazism 1919–1945: A Documentary Reader* (3 volumes, Exeter, 1983–8). Other collections can be found in: L. Snyder, *The Weimar Republic* (Princeton, NJ, 1966); D.G. Williamson, *The Third Reich* (Harlow, 1982); J. Remak (ed.), *The Nazi Years: A Documentary History* (Englewood Cliffs, NJ: Prentice-Hall, 1969); and G. Layton, *Germany: The Third Reich 1933–45* (London, 1992).

The best known of the long-established major works on Hitler are: A. Bullock, *Hitler: A Study in Tyranny* (London, 1952); W.L. Shirer, *The Rise and Fall of the Third Reich* (London, 1960); J. Fest, *Hitler* (London, 1974); and N. Stone, *Hitler* (London, 1980). More recent publications include: I. Kershaw, *Hitler 1889–1936: Hubris* (London, 1998); I. Kershaw, *Hitler 1936–1945: Nemesis* (London, 2000); R.J. Evans, *The Coining of the Third Reich* (London, 2003); R.J. Evans, *The Third Reich in Power 1933–1939* (London, 2005); and M. Burleigh, *The Third Reich: A New History* (London, 2000).

The Weimar period and Hitler's rise to power are the focus of: A.J. Nicholls, *Weimar and the Rise of Hitler* (London, 1968); J. Hiden,

Republican and Fascist Germany (Harlow, 1996); C. Fischer, *The Rise of the Nazis* (Manchester, 1995); M. Broszat, *Hitler and the Collapse of the Weimar Republic* (Oxford, 1987); and W.S. Allen, *The Nazi Seizure of Power. The Experience of a Single German Town 1922–1945* (London, 1989).

Especially recommended as overall interpretations of the Nazi era are: M. Broszat, *The Hitler State* (London, 1981); K.D. Bracher, *The German Dictatorship* (trans.) (London, 1973); E. Jäckel, *Hitler in History* (Hanover and London, 1984); A. Hillgruber, *Germany and the Two World Wars* (Cambridge, MA, 1981); K. Hildebrand, *The Third Reich* (London, 1984); J. Hiden and J. Farquharson, *Explaining Hitler's Germany: Historians and the Third Reich* (London, 1983); I. Kershaw, *The Nazi Dictatorship: Problems and Perspective of Interpretation* (London, 1985; 4th edn, 2000); and J. Lukacs, *The Hitler of History* (New York, 1998).

Other books recommended for the Nazi period as a whole are: M. Housden, *Hitler: Study of a Revolutionary?* (London, 2000); D. Welch, *Hitler* (London, 1998); T. Kirk, *Nazi Germany* (Basingstoke, 2007); J. Spielvogel, *Hitler and Nazi Germany: A History* (Englewood Cliffs, NJ 1988); R. Stackelberg, *Hitler's Germany: Origins, Interpretations, Legacies* (London, 1999); H. Mommsen, *From Weimar to Auschwitz* (trans. P. O'Connor) (Princeton, NJ, 1991); H.A. Winkler, *Germany: The Long Road West. Volume 2: 1933–1990* (trans.) (Oxford, 2007); N. Frei, *National Socialist Rule in Germany: The Führer State 1933–1945* (trans.) (Oxford, 1993); and D.G. Williamson, *The Third Reich* (Harlow, 1982); and A. Dorpalen, *German History in Marxist Perspective: The East German Approach* (London, 1985).

Comparisons with the Soviet system are provided by: A. Bullock, *Hitler and Stalin: Parallel Lives* (London, 1991); and I. Kershaw and M. Lewin (eds), *Stalinism and Nazism: Dictatorships in Comparison* (Cambridge, 1997). A comprehensive treatment of Nazi ideology is to be found in: W. Laqueur (ed.), *Fascism: A Reader's Guide* (Aldershot, 1991); and N. Gregor (ed.), *Nazism* (Oxford, 2003).

Internal developments within Nazi Germany are covered in: D.J.K. Peukert, *Inside Nazi Germany: Conformity, Opposition and Racism in Everyday Life* (trans.) (London, 1989); R. Bessel (ed.), *Life in the Third Reich* (Oxford, 1987); V.R. Berghahn, *Modern Germany: Society, Economy and Politics in the Twentieth Century* (Cambridge, 1987); H. Höhne, *The Order of the Death's Head* (London, 1967); E. Crankshaw, *Gestapo: Instrument of Tyranny* (London, 1956); E.A. Johnson, *Nazi Terror: Gestapo, Jews and Ordinary Citizens* (New York, 1999); G.C. Browder, *Hitler's Enforcers: The Gestapo and the SS Security Service in the Nazi Revolution* (Oxford, 1996); R. Grunberger, *A Social History of the Third Reich* (London, 1971); D. Schoenbaum, *Hitler's Social Revolution* (New York, 1980); L. Pine, *Hitler's 'National Community'* (London, 2007); L. Pine, *Nazi Family Policy, 1933–1945* (Oxford, 1997); D.F. Crew (ed.), *Nazism and German Society 1933–1945* (London, 1994); M. Stibbe, *Women in the Third Reich* (London, 2003); G. Rempel, *Hitler's Children: The Hitler Youth and the SS* (Chapel Hill, NC, 1989); T.W. Mason, *Social Policy in the Third Reich: The Working Class and the 'National Community'* (Oxford, 1993); C.W. Guillebaud, *The Economic Recovery of Germany from 1933 to the Incorporation of Austria in March 1938* (London, 1939); H.A. Turner, *German Big Business and the Rise of Hitler* (Oxford, 1985); and A. Tooze, *The Wages of Destruction: The Making and Breaking of the Nazi Economy* (London, 2006).

Support and opposition are dealt with in: R. Gellately, *Backing Hitler: Consent and Coercion in Nazi Germany* (Oxford, 2001); D.C. Large (ed.), *Contending with Hitler: Varieties of German Resistance in the Third Reich* (Cambridge, 1991); I. Kershaw, *Popular Opinion and Political Dissent in the Third Reich* (Oxford, 1983); M. Broszat, *Alternatives to Hitler: German Resistance Under the Third Reich* (trans.) (Princeton, NJ, 2003); and J. Fest, *Plotting Hitler's Death: The German Resistance to Hitler 1933–1945* (trans.) (London, 1996).

Race and the persecution of minorities are the themes of: M. Burleigh and W. Wippermann, *The Racial State: Germany 1933–1945* (Cambridge, 1991); R. Gellately and N. Stoltzfus (eds), *Social Outsiders in Nazi Germany* (Princeton, NJ, 2001); G. Grau (ed.), *Hidden Holocaust? Gay and Lesbian Persecution in Germany 1933–45* (Chicago, 2008). The Holocaust is covered extensively in: C.R. Browning, *The Origins of the Final Solution: The Evolution of Nazi Jewish Policy, September 1939 – March 1942* (London, 2004); D.J. Goldhagen, *Hitler's Willing Executioners: Ordinary Germans and the Holocaust* (London, 1996); G. Eley (ed.), *The 'Goldhagen Effect'* (Ann Arbor, MI, 2000); O. Bartov, *Germany's War and the Holocaust* (Ithaca, NY, 2003); M. Housden, *Hans Frank: Lebensraum and the Holocaust* (London, 2005); R. Hilberg, *The Destruction of the European Jews* (Chicago, 1961); D. Cesarini (ed.), *The Final Solution: Origins and Implementation* (London, 1994); D. Cesarini, *Becoming Eichmann: Rethinking the Life, Crimes and Trial of a 'Desk Murderer'* (Cambridge, MA, 2006); Götz Aly, *'Final Solution': Nazi Population Policy and the Murder of the European Jews* (trans.) (London, 2003); Claudia Koonz, *The Nazi Conscience* (Cambridge, MA, 2003); and G. Hirschfield (ed.), *The Policies of Genocide* (London, 1986).

Foreign policy and war are covered in: F. Fischer, *Germany's Aims in the First World War* (trans.) (London, 1967); G.L. Weinberg, *The Foreign Policy of Hitler's Germany: Diplomatic Revolution in Europe 1933–36* (Chicago, 1970); K. Hildebrand, *The Foreign Policy of the Third Reich* (trans.) (London, 1973); J.L. Snell (ed.), *The Outbreak of the Second World War* (Boston, MA, 1962); P.M.H. Bell, *The Origins of the Second World War in Europe* (London 1986; 1997 edn); P. Finney (ed.), *The Origins of the Second World War* (London, 1997); V.R. Berghahn and M. Kitchen (eds), *Germany in the Age of Total War* (London, 1981); M. Kitchen, *Nazi Germany at War* (London, 1995); and R. Bessel, *Nazism and War* (London, 2004)

Finally, there is a range of invaluable collections of symposia, historical debates and historiographical surveys on all aspects of the Nazi period. Particularly useful are: R.G.L. Waite (ed.), *Hitler and Nazi Germany* (New York, 1965); H. Holborn (ed.), *Republic to Reich: The Making of the Nazi Revolution* (New York, 1972); P.D. Stachura (ed.), *The Nazi* Machtergreifung (London, 1983); H. Mommsen (ed.), *The Third Reich Between Vision and Reality: New Perspectives on German History 1918–1945* (London, 2001); H.W. Koch (ed.), *Aspects of the Third Reich* (London, 1985); G. Martel (ed.), *Modern Germany Reconsidered* (London, 1992); T. Childers and J. Caplan (eds), *Reevaluating the Third Reich* (New York, 1993); R. Stackelberg, *Hitler's Germany: Origins, Interpretations, Legacies* (London, 1999); C. Leitz (ed.), *The Third Reich: The Essential Readings* (Oxford, 1983; 1999 edn); A.E. Steinweis and D.E. Rogers (eds), *The Impact of Nazism: New Perspectives on the Third Reich and its Legacy* (Lincoln, NE, 2003); and A. McElligott and T. Kirk (eds), *Working towards the Führer* (Manchester, 2003).

INDEX